Belligerent Muse

Belligerent

CIVIL WAR AMERICA *Gary W. Gallagher,*
Peter S. Carmichael, Caroline E. Janney,
and Aaron Sheehan-Dean, editors

This landmark series interprets
broadly the history and culture of
the Civil War era through the long
nineteenth century and beyond.
Drawing on diverse approaches
and methods, the series publishes
historical works that explore all
aspects of the war, biographies of
leading commanders, and tactical
and campaign studies, along with
select editions of primary sources.
Together, these books shed new
light on an era that remains
central to our understanding of
American and world history.

Muse

FIVE NORTHERN WRITERS *and How They Shaped Our Understanding of* THE CIVIL WAR

Stephen Cushman

FOREWORD BY *Gary W. Gallagher*

The University of North Carolina Press   Chapel Hill

Library of Congress Cataloging-in-Publication Data
Cushman, Stephen, 1956–
Belligerent muse : five northern writers and how they shaped our understanding of the Civil War / Stephen Cushman ; foreword by Gary W. Gallagher.
    pages cm. — (Civil War America)
Includes bibliographical references and index.
ISBN 978-1-4696-1877-7 (cloth : alk. paper)
ISBN 978-1-4696-3339-8 (pbk. : alk. paper)
ISBN 978-1-4696-1878-4 (ebook)
1. United States—History—Civil War, 1861–1865—Historiography.
2. Lincoln, Abraham, 1809–1865—Influence. 3. Whitman, Walt, 1819–1892—Influence. 4. Sherman, William T. (William Tecumseh), 1820–1891—Influence. 5. Bierce, Ambrose, 1842–1914?—Influence. 6. Chamberlain, Joshua Lawrence, 1828–1914—Influence. I. Title.
E468.5.c94 2014
973.7072—dc23
2014013884

Portions of this work have appeared previously, in somewhat different form, as "Ambrose Bierce, Chickamauga, and Ways to Write History," in *Gateway to the Confederacy: New Perspectives on the Chickamauga and Chattanooga Campaigns, 1862–1863*, ed. Evan Jones and Wiley Sword (Baton Rouge: Louisiana State University Press), copyright © 2014 by Louisiana State University Press and reprinted with permission of Louisiana State University Press; "Lincoln's Gettysburg Address and Second Inaugural Address," in *The Cambridge Companion to Abraham Lincoln*, ed. Shirley Samuels (New York: Cambridge University Press, 2012); "Walt Whitman's Real Wars," in *Wars within a War: Controversy and Conflict over the American Civil War*, ed. Joan Waugh and Gary W. Gallagher (Chapel Hill: University of North Carolina Press, 2009); and "When Lincoln Met Emerson," *Journal of the Civil War Era* 3, no. 2 (June 2013).

For those who learn and those who teach

Contents

Foreword

I always have admired William Tecumseh Sherman's *Memoirs*. Second only to his friend U. S. Grant among Union military heroes, Sherman lacked an effective filter between his brain and either his mouth or his pen—which renders him both fascinating and eminently quotable. I have quoted the *Memoirs* in various things I have written and frequently urged others to explore their pages. If asked a year ago whether I had a good command of the text, I would have answered in the affirmative. Then I read Stephen Cushman's essay that appears here, an exercise that yielded great enjoyment but also left me chastened. The analysis breathed such new life into the *Memoirs*, and into Sherman himself, that I wondered how I could have missed so much.

All of the chapters in *Belligerent Muse* inspired similar reactions. Amid the welter of books on diverse aspects of the Civil War published over the past two decades or so, there is nothing quite like this work. Cushman places himself in the tradition of Edmund Wilson's *Patriotic Gore: Studies in the Literature of the American Civil War* (1962), George M. Fredrickson's *The Inner Civil War: Northern Intellectuals and the Crisis of the Union* (1965), and Daniel Aaron's *The Unwritten War: American Writers and the Civil War* (1973), which is accurate in some ways but a bit deceptive in others. Most obviously, Cushman takes more seriously, and knows far more about, the military side of the conflict than any of those three authors. That is important for one who writes about William Tecumseh Sherman, Ambrose Bierce, and Joshua Lawrence Chamberlain—as well as about Abraham

Lincoln and Walt Whitman in the midst of overwhelming military events. Cushman combines in unusual fashion—perhaps unique, I would say—poetic and literary credentials of the first order and serious engagement with the historical literature of the war, though I suspect he would make only modest claims about his mastery of the latter.

Belligerent Muse ties the insights and contributions of military historians to literary sensibilities in ways no one other than Cushman, at least as far as I know, has attempted. It draws on the sometimes abstract and theoretical work of academic departments of English (without descending into the often incomprehensible jargon of that world) while also embracing the pragmatic and empirical work of professional military historians and the writings of "amateur" historians, many of them talented but best known to those who attend Civil War Round Table meetings and other nonacademic study groups and conferences. To a degree not present in other works I have encountered that deal with literary figures and the war, this study acknowledges the importance of understanding military organizations and events on the battlefield if one intends a productive analysis of writings that touch on martial dimensions of the war.

I will return briefly to Sherman to say that I find many parts of his *Memoirs* very evocative. None exceeds his description of how, as his veterans began the March to the Sea on November 16, 1864, he paused on a piece of high ground to take in the scene: "Behind us lay Atlanta, smouldering and in ruins, the black smoke rising high in air, and hanging like a pall over the ruined city." The moment quickly passed: "Then we turned our horses' heads to the east; Atlanta was soon lost behind the screen of trees, and became a thing of the past. Around it clings many a thought of desperate battle, of hope and fear, that now seem like the memory of a dream; and I have never seen the place since. The day was extremely beautiful, clear sunlight, with bracing air, and an unusual feeling of exhilaration seemed to pervade all minds—a feeling of something to come, vague and undefined, still full of venture and intense interest."

Above all, Cushman reminds us that historical sources may also be literary works—sometimes very self-consciously both when they come from pens such as Sherman's and deal with material so dramatic as commencing the campaign from Atlanta to Savannah. *Belligerent Muse* reveals the rich possibilities of work that transcends the narrow conception of "specialties" so common in the academic world. Historians and literary scholars alike, as well as lay readers drawn to the blood-soaked moment of truth for the American nation, will discover fresh and revealing material in the pages that follow. Joining Cushman as he traverses the war's landscape in the company of the president of the United States, a poet and sometime hospital volunteer, a general in the regular army, and two volunteer military officers yields, to borrow directly from Sherman, an experience "full of venture and intense interest."

GARY W. GALLAGHER

Acknowledgments

I have incurred many happy obligations during the writing of this book, some of them to anonymous readers who will feel, I trust, the real gratitude behind this blanket thanks. Those who assisted with archival work will find themselves thanked in various notes to the following chapters. Among the editorial benefactors I name here with special pleasure are William Blair, Evan Jones, Shirley Samuels, Wiley Sword, and Joan Waugh, who scrupulously oversaw the publications in which earlier versions of some of these chapters first appeared. Stephen Arata was an encouraging friend to each of the chapters in its earliest form. To Lindsay Turner I am very grateful for timely help with assembling and polishing the final version of the manuscript. Alice Fahs gave the entire manuscript the close and comprehensive attention of an ideal reader. My largest obligation is to Gary Gallagher, whose intellectual generosity is as capacious as his knowledge of the American Civil War.

Belligerent Muse

Introduction

War destroys. Destruction is its business. "War" descends from Old High German and means confusion or strife; one of its Old English cousins is "worst." War is the worst, our worst, the worst confusion and strife humans know and have known for as long as there have been humans. On its way to doing its worst, war wrecks and ruins, wastes and ravages, devastates and desolates. It does its worst to bodies, minds, spirits, lives, families, communities, towns, cities, farms, factories, economies, social systems, ecosystems, regions, nations, continents.

But in the process of doing its worst, war can also make and create. We use the phrase "war of words" to refer to forms of confusion and strife that are purely verbal, but the phrase also points to one of the major products of war: words themselves. Wars produce words and, where literacy operates, writing. Anyone who types "United States" and "Civil War" into the guided search boxes of the Library of Congress online catalog (with quotation marks around each term) will probably receive a message reading, "Your search retrieved more records than can be displayed. Only the first 10,000 will be shown." If we assume for the purposes of illustration that these are all individual pieces of writing, as opposed to duplicates, or photographs, or other materials (if they are not, enough replacements will be found in the second 10,000), and you read one a day, it would take more than twenty-seven years to get through them all.

After those twenty-seven years, however, you would only have scratched the surface of writing generated by the American Civil

War. Imagine that one-third of the people numbered in the U.S. census of 1860, or roughly 10 million of them, wrote one hundred words apiece, a little more than the first paragraph of this book, during the four years of war. They would have produced a billion words. If each of those people wrote one hundred words—perhaps the equivalent of a very short letter or diary entry—every day for a thousand days, about two-thirds of those the war took up, the total would be a trillion words. Then add the writing of people who wrote much more than one hundred thousand words (roughly the equivalent of four hundred typed, double-spaced pages), perhaps government or military officials, newspaper reporters, writers for the illustrated weeklies; add the writing of people living outside the wartime United States, particularly in Europe, which paid close attention to, and had much to say about, our confusion and strife; and finally add the writing of people alive after the war—memoirists, biographers, historians, novelists—including all those still writing today.

War destroys, but it also inspires, stimulates, and creates. It is, in this way, a muse, a belligerent muse, and a powerful one at that. We have estimates of the number of war deaths and war wounds and war losses of many kinds, but estimates of the number of words and pieces of writing the American Civil War brought forth and continues to bring forth, if they could be come by, would rapidly approach the vast and overwhelming scale of the astronomical. How do we begin to sort and map and classify all the writing the Civil War muse has given us? A first distinction might be to separate public writing from private writing, to imagine a spectrum running from words written for large readerships to words written for the individual writer only. Along this spectrum we would encounter words written originally for only the individual writer but then subsequently discovered by others and made available to a large readership. Many diaries fall into this category. Contemplating this spectrum for even a few moments, we can see quickly that at the private end it leads to attics and trunks and desks and drawers containing writing we do not yet know and are unlikely ever to know or possess entirely, no matter how many new finds are made public, either in print or on line.

A second way to sort or map or classify might be to focus on the identities of individual authors. What is a particular author's race or class or gender? This kind of approach makes sense because it can yield various groupings and cross-sections that enable us to subdivide the overwhelming whole and begin to make it comprehensible, or apparently so. In an effort to enhance comprehensiveness, or the appearance of it, one might sample Civil War writings by selecting examples from a range of authorial identities, aiming to represent as many as possible.

Then there is another approach, one that does not preclude representative selection according to authorial identity but complements it. That approach, the one taken by this book, is concerned with developing a way of reading whatever examples might be selected from the vast and overwhelming body of material available. This approach blends an interest in the history of the American Civil War with an interest in the verbal patterns, shapes, conventions, and strategies of written narratives about it.

The argument of this book, implicit throughout and explicit here, is that although writings by various authors provide keys to a historical understanding of the American Civil War, that understanding should not treat those writings simply as transparent windows opening onto the past, particularly when they come from the pens and pencils of people self-conscious about their powers as writers, quite likely, but not exclusively, writing publicly for large readerships. The writings of such people are here represented by five of the most significant and best-known narrators of the Civil War: Abraham Lincoln, Walt Whitman, William Tecumseh Sherman, Ambrose Bierce, and Joshua Lawrence Chamberlain. In considering their writings as literary expressions as well as engagements with momentous events of the war, the following chapters undertake to show that those windows on the past will always be stained glass, sometimes only faintly tinted, sometimes richly colored.

That said, I do not belong to the class of readers who insist, with breathtaking skepticism, that there really is no such thing as an event apart from the stained-glass writing about it. Any wartime family receiving a telegram beginning, "The Secretary of War desires me to express his deep regret," as my own mother's did, cannot sustain such skepticism for long. True, complete transparency in any writing is an impossible ideal; one need only attempt the translation of the sparest, most literal report from one language into another to discover how quickly language colors references to wordless events and actions. To be born into a language is to be subject to its ways of shaping the world. One's objectivity, when presented in that language, necessarily will be shaped accordingly.

But it is also true that if some readers overestimate the aesthetic determinants of writing that aspires to transparency, other readers underestimate them, and it is to this latter group of readers that this book is addressed. "Aesthetic" comes from a Greek verb meaning "to perceive," so aesthetic determinants are, in part, the inescapable features and limitations of writers' and readers' perceptions. Originally aesthetic appreciation of an object implied detachment from the utilitarian or instrumental value of that object. In *Walden* (1854), for example, Henry David Thoreau was careful to distinguish between his (presumably higher) aesthetic appreciation of the farms around Concord, Massachusetts—because of the walks they afforded him or the vistas or the sunsets—and the simpler appreciations of the farmer on whose land he trespassed, a farmer presumably much more interested in crop rotation and market prices. But aesthetic appreciation can, and here will, invoke another kind of historical sensibility, one that parallels the sensibility of the Civil War specialist, whether one professionally trained at a university, one in the venerable nonacademic tradition of Bruce Catton and Douglas Southall Freeman, or one who reads privately for sheer interest alone.

The kind of historically informed aesthetic sensibility I have in mind treats historical documents from the Civil War not only as histories of events but as instances of the history of writing, as historical configurations of rhetorical strategies, rhythmic patterns, quotations, allusions, echoes, and revisions. In other words, this book is about how a piece of writing about the Civil War is an interweaving of two sets of histories: on the one hand, war history, and on the other, linguistic, rhetorical, and literary history. It is not simply a matter of reading a piece of writing in historical context, with "historical" designating the overlapping accumulations of political, social, economic, and military events; it is a matter of reading a piece of writing with as full an awareness of all its histories, including the history of its writing, as possible.

Three precursors have formed tributaries flowing into any discussion of Civil War writings: Edmund Wilson's *Patriotic Gore: Studies in the Literature of the American Civil War* (1962), George M. Fredrickson's *The Inner Civil War: Northern Intellectuals and the Crisis of the Union* (1965), and Daniel Aaron's *The Unwritten War: American Writers and the Civil War* (1973). The works of this triumvirate—Wilson and Aaron approached Civil War writings from perspectives primarily literary, Fredrickson from one informed by a professional historian's interest in racial perspectives and race relations—continue to exert their power, as Randall Fuller, in a recent contribution to the expanding field, *From Battlefields Rising: How the Civil War Transformed American Literature* (2011), likewise has testified. From the work of Wilson, Fredrickson, and Aaron a partial genealogy of this book begins to emerge.

The genealogy is only partial because it does not include the writings and insights of Civil War historians, both professional and amateur. Debts to the former will appear in notes to the chapters that follow; debts to the latter have accumulated during years of walking over battlefields with these so-called amateurs, many of whom carry with them extensively detailed knowledge—"amateur," after all, means lover—and during afternoons and evenings spent talking to Civil War roundtables and nonacademic study groups, the many members of which have had much to teach. Whether professional or amateur, many people who have devoted hours and years to the study of the Civil War read from perspectives that are bracingly empirical and pragmatic, often supplying much-needed correctives to the overly abstract and theoretical approaches that can arise in the academic world. It is not that the abstract and theoretical are necessarily wrongheaded, no matter how tempting they are for nonacademics to caricature; it is that without the complementarities of the pragmatic and empirical, they can obscure the intractable specificities of the American Civil War without necessarily offering compensating illuminations.

The chapters of this book aim to demonstrate what can happen when discussions of historical detail, generally absent from treatments of Civil War writings as "literature," complement discussions of verbal artistry, generally absent from works of history and historiography. The approach taken here, the approach of treating Civil War writings, especially writings that fall under the heading of military history, as both historical documents and aesthetic productions, is transferable to writings other than those by five white male northerners, who, despite their similarities in some respects, present a wide range in others: a president, a hospital visitor and poet, and three officers in the United States Army, two of them volunteers with very different backgrounds and one a West Point graduate from the regular army.

Of the five narrators considered here, Lincoln, Whitman, and Bierce have received extensive and sustained attention as writers. The two-part chapter on Lincoln begins in 1862 with a kind of prologue, a detailed look at a moment in the overlapping of literary history with the history of wartime politics, when Ralph Waldo Emerson visited the president at the White House. It then shifts to an examination of Lincoln's two most famous speeches, attempting to balance new thoughts about their verbal artistry with attention to their military historical background.

Next the discussion moves to 1875 with a chapter on Whitman's *Memoranda During the War*, published that year. Much has been and continues to be written about Whitman's Civil War years, although the body of writing about him remains dwarfed by that about Lincoln. Among other aims, this chapter seeks to reveal what one can learn about Whitman and his narrative endeavor when his writing about the war—for example, the battle of Chancellorsville—confronts the details of the historical record.

The chapter on Sherman, the longest in the book and its center in more ways than one, also connects to 1875, the year of the publication of the first edition of *Memoirs of William T. Sherman*. Unlike the first two chapters, which hope to contribute to considerable bodies of existing work, the one on Sherman aims to begin to address a want of writing about Sherman as a writer. A significant exception in this regard is Wilson's discussion of Sherman in *Patriotic Gore*, but anyone reading Wilson's chapter will discover quickly that his violent antipathy toward "Attila Sherman" has twisted his approach in dramatic ways. The last ten pages of Wilson's chapter, for example, focus entirely, and digressively, on the sad and debilitating effects of Sherman's influence on his son, Father Thomas Sherman. This conclusion reveals much about the volatility of Sherman in Wilson's imagination but little about Sherman as a writer. Here the discussion of Sherman's *Memoirs* draws frequent comparisons with *Personal Memoirs of U. S. Grant* (1885–86), which has generated much more commentary.

The chapter on Ambrose Bierce continues with the 1880s, the same decade that brought forth the second edition of Sherman's *Memoirs*, as well as Bierce's turn to writing about his Civil War experiences. Bierce's Civil War writings have attracted much attention, though less than Whitman's, but, as with Whitman's, they have not been held up to the exacting scrutiny of the military historical record, despite Bierce's hectoring insistence on the importance of that record and, in particular, on his firm ideas of the right way to go about the business of constructing it. Finally, the chapter on Joshua Lawrence Chamberlain, about whose Civil War writings little has been written by people other than biographers and military historians, takes a look at his repeated attempts, from 1865 to his death in 1915, to narrate the ending of his war at Appomattox Court House.

In the case of each of the five writers, the war muse produced exceptional results and made him a canonical figure. Two of the five, Sherman and Chamberlain, enjoyed the privileges of higher education, but the other three did not. Their effectiveness as writers that we still read in a century of rapidly changing writing practices and reading habits testifies, surely, to their individual capabilities; yet it also testifies to the nature of literacy at an extraordinary moment in our past. The Civil War erupted into the midst of that literacy, into writing practices and reading habits increasingly remote from our own. If we are to grasp as fully as possible the many textures of that time, we must grasp as fully as possible the many textures of the medium in which we mostly know it.

....

CHAPTER ONE

When Lincoln Met Emerson, and the Two Addresses

In the history of the United States the convergence of Civil War writing with verbal artistry remains particularly notable in the case of Abraham Lincoln. In part this distinction has to do with the fact that Lincoln's written English—with its distinct blendings of the elegantly lyrical and the pungently vernacular; the rhetoric of the courtroom and the rhetoric of the pulpit; the slap of short, simple sentences and the extended caresses of syntactically parallel units, so often parceled into groups of three—is simply more sonorous, memorable, and meaningful than the written English not only of his presidential successors or their professional speechwriters, but of most people who write in English. Many commentators have already done important work in appraising Lincoln's verbal artfulness, among them Douglas L. Wilson, whose 2006 book, *Lincoln's Sword: The Presidency and the Power of Words*, won the Lincoln Prize.[1] But before turning to the language of Lincoln's two most famous addresses, in the second part of this chapter, my aim is to meditate first on the convergence of statecraft with the world of letters, and especially on one aspect of Lincoln's awareness of that world, from another angle, that of his meeting with Ralph Waldo Emerson in Washington, D.C., on Saturday, February 1, and Sunday, February 2, 1862. By looking closely at this particular meeting and its implications, we can deepen our understanding of the mind that produced such powerful public utterances in response to military exigencies.

Emerson had been invited to lecture at the Smithsonian Institution, where he delivered an address entitled "American Civilization" on January 31, only a few hundred yards from the site of wartime hospitals standing between the Smithsonian and the Capitol. Focusing on slavery and the war, while calling for immediate emancipation, "American Civilization" spoke to the "existing administration" with "the utmost candor": "The end of all political struggle is to establish morality as the basis of all legislation. . . . Morality is the object of government." Emerson's biographers disagree about whether or not Lincoln heard the Sage of Concord the night before they met.[2] Lincoln's biographers make almost no mention of either the lecture or the meeting.[3] Newspaper coverage of the lecture included nothing about the president's going to hear it.[4] Whether or not Lincoln attended the lecture, the best pictures we have of his meetings with Emerson come from the latter's journal, which he started keeping the first month of the new year in a copybook, on the cover of which he wrote in ink "1862" above the word "WAR."[5]

The pictures that emerge from Emerson's journal give us richly textured glimpses of the president, whose weekend included mulling over the conviction and sentence of Nathaniel P. Gordon, hanged in New York three weeks later for slave trading and the first person in the United States to be executed for this crime. It also included skipping church to read Charles Sumner's speech on the *Trent* affair, the international aftermath of which continued in the form of communications with Lord Lyons, the British minister in Washington, and messages on the same topic from France and Spain, all of which were mentioned or discussed with Secretary of State William Seward, Emerson's guide for the day, in Emerson's presence.[6]

The pictures from the journal contain precious candid shots of Lincoln as well: Seward telling Emerson that Lincoln had told him not to tell Emerson a "smutty" story, although the secretary of state apparently ignored the president's instructions and delivered an anecdote involving the punch line, "I can't say I have carnal knowledge of him," an anecdote the reserved Emerson described as an "extraordinary exordium";[7] Lincoln overseeing the Sabbath barbering of his sons, which the father called "whiskeying their hair," as he watched Tad and Willie, noted by Emerson as "his two little sons,—boys of 7 & 8 years perhaps," though in reality Tad was almost nine at the time and Willie, who would die eighteen days later, eleven; Lincoln listening to the Episcopalian Seward tell him about the Reverend Smith Pyne's sermon, which the lapsed-Unitarian Emerson judged to be an instance of a "hopeless blind antiquity of life & thought," though Lincoln, whom Seward had chided for not going to church that day, told his secretary of state that "he intended to show his respect for him some time by going to hear him" at St. John's, just across Lafayette Park from the White House.[8]

Although perhaps lacking the spontaneity of some of his other more casual observations of Lincoln, Emerson's initial study of the president at their first meeting in the White House also deserves attention: "The President impressed me more favorably than I had hoped. A frank, sincere, well-meaning man, with a lawyer's habit of mind, good clear statement of his fact, correct enough, not vulgar, as described; but with a sort of boyish cheerfulness, or that kind of sincerity & jolly good meaning that our class meetings on Commencement Days show, in telling our old stories over. When he made his remark, he looks up at you with great satisfaction, & shows all his white teeth, & laughs."[9] In moments such as this one, narrative brakes and shifts into neutral, so that detailed description can take over for as long as necessary to introduce us to someone new, as in the case of a new character in certain kinds of prose fiction. Unlike, say, in a police description, which notes the common-denominator basics of height, weight, the color of eyes and hair, there is no pretension to complete objectivity here. In such moments the describer's, here Emerson's, own assumptions, biases, and moralizings are everywhere implicit and occasionally explicit. From this portrait of Lincoln we gather that Emerson, the educated, cultured, fastidious New Englander, had not expected much from the rough westerner, especially since, like many members of his intellectual class and geographical section, he had supported Seward for the presidential nomination in 1860. We also hear the man of poetry, philosophy, inspiration, and imagination sizing up "a lawyer's habit of mind," not unfavorably but perhaps with a whiff of condescension, a condescension also informing the remark about "boyish cheerfulness" and the extended comparison of Lincoln's "jolly" demeanor to the storytelling, backslapping tone of college reunions.

A little over three years later Emerson described Lincoln once again, this time when delivering "Remarks at the Funeral Services Held in Concord, April 19, 1865," and the description then polished these initial impressions, with the help of the elegiac past tense, into a eulogistic glow:

> A plain man of the people, an extraordinary fortune attended him. He offered no shining qualities at the first encounter; he did not offend by superiority. He had a face and manner which disarmed suspicion, which inspired confidence, which confirmed good will. He was a man without vices. He had a strong sense of duty, which it was very easy for him to obey. Then, he had what farmers call a long head; was excellent in working out the sum for himself; in arguing his case and convincing you fairly and firmly. Then, it turned out that he was a great worker; had prodigious faculty of performance; worked easily. . . . Then, he had a vast good nature, which made him tolerant and accessible to all; fair-minded, leaning to the claim of the petitioner; affable, and not sensible to the affliction which the innumerable visits paid to him when President would have brought to any one else.[10]

Among those innumerable visits was Emerson's own in February 1862, and as part of the general idealizing of this postmortem portrait the onetime presidential visitor retrospectively projected onto his subject an inexhaustible goodwill at odds with the account of at least one other visitor to the White House, Walt Whitman, who upon seeing Lincoln the evening of his second inauguration described him as "drest all in black, with white kid gloves, and a claw-hammer coat, receiving, as in duty bound, shaking hands, looking very disconsolate, as if he would give anything to be somewhere else."[11]

Having shown us how the laughing president appeared to him in February 1862—less than a year after, as "the new pilot" recalled in Emerson's 1865 eulogy, Lincoln had been "hurried to the helm in a tornado"[12]—the visitor from New England then let his host speak: "When I was introduced to him, he said, 'O Mr Emerson, I once heard you say in a lecture, that a Kentuckian seems to say by his air & manners, '*Here am I; if you don't like me, the worse for you.*'"[13] Here the journal captured a fascinating and complex moment, Emerson's own botched quotation marks reflecting the twists and turns of quoting Lincoln quoting Emerson back to Emerson. In greeting Emerson by repeating this remembered sentence, Lincoln immediately identified himself with Kentucky, which he left with his family for Indiana when he was only four, as he also identified himself with it the previous year, during February 1861, as he made his way east for his inauguration as president. As Harold Holzer has shown, Lincoln had cut and pasted from a draft of his inaugural address several paragraphs he hoped to deliver to "an audience of my native state," along with the declaration, "Gentlemen, I too am a Kentuckian." But for security reasons, "Kentucky remained off limits," and the cut-and-pasted speech went undelivered there.[14] Meanwhile, the passage from Emerson's journal would seem to support those who argue that Lincoln did not attend Emerson's Smithsonian lecture the night before, since, first, it would be a rare lecturer who would fail to notice, and note in his journal, the president of the United States in his audience and, second, Lincoln's greeting would make no sense if he had just heard Emerson lecture a few hours before.

In the remainder of my discussion I want to follow out various lines of thought radiating from this small moment, lines that may help us reconsider Lincoln's connection to the world of letters. To begin with, we might ask whether Lincoln ever really went to hear Emerson lecture, or was he simply performing as a smooth and savvy politician, replaying for Emerson a stray line he remembered having heard or read somewhere, perhaps even a line someone else had prepped him with a few minutes earlier? But to begin this way is to surrender to an anachronistic cynicism, one derived from too many films and television shows about smiling politicians turning on a dime to glad-hand, as well-met friends, people they would know nothing about if not for their loyal entourages of prompting aides. Even if we risk appearing naive and gullible, we stand a much better chance of discovering something useful if instead we follow Douglas Wilson, in remarks he delivered on accepting the Lincoln Prize, and consider questions such as these: "So Lincoln had been in the audience for one of Emerson's famous lectures, but when? where? and which lecture? And what, if anything, did Lincoln make of what Emerson had to say?"[15]

Wilson responded to his own questions by claiming that "there is a fairly straightforward answer" to the first two of them, the when and the where. This straightforward answer begins with F. A. Moore, editor of the (Springfield) *Illinois Daily Journal*, whom Emerson described as "a young New Hampshire editor, who overestimated the strength of both of us" and urged the touring lecturer to add Springfield to his itinerary after he finished with his commitments in St. Louis early in January 1853. Emerson obliged by traveling to Springfield, where he wrote to his wife, "Here I am in the deep mud of the prairie," and where he delivered three lectures on the successive nights of January 10, 11, and 12. Thanks to the *Illinois Daily Journal*, we know the names of the lectures as "The Anglo-Saxon," "Power," and "Culture," respectively, but at this point the straightforwardness begins to break down, for although the diary of future U.S. senator Orville Hickman Browning tells us that he himself was in Emerson's audience at the Illinois State House each of the three successive nights, Browning does not state positively that he took his friend Lincoln with him to any or all of the lectures. Instead of noting this desirable information, Browning gives us these three brief summaries instead:

[Monday, January 10, 1853]
At night I attended in the hall of the house, and heard a lecture from Ralph Waldo Emmerson [*sic*] on the Anglo Saxon. His language was chaste, strong and vigorous— much of his thought just—his voice good—his delivery

clear, distinct and deliberate—his action [meaning his physical gestures?] nothing. He limned a good picture of an Englishman, and gave us some hard raps for our apishness of English fashions & manners.

[Tuesday, January 11, 1853]
Heard Emmerson's lecture in the House of Rep: upon power. He is chaste & fascinating, and whilst I cannot approve all his philosophy, I still listen with delight to his discourses. They contain much that is good, and are worth hearing. After the lecture I attended a supper in the Senate Chamber given by the ladies of the first Presbyterian Church and spent a pleasant evening. The weather is still very cloudy & disagreeable—the mud making the streets almost impassable.

[Wednesday, January 12, 1853]
Went to Ridgelys to supper, and attended Miss Julia to the State House to hear Emmersons third lecture on culture
    No improvement in the weather[16]

When Lincoln met Emerson in Washington in February 1862 and claimed to have heard him lecture once, was he referring to one or more of the three lectures in Springfield in January 1853? Among those who have thought about the question at all, the consensus seems to be that despite the silence of Browning's diary, yes, these are the where and the when of Lincoln's hearing Emerson. The assumptions behind this consensus apparently are that an Emerson lecture would have been too large an attraction for Lincoln to pass up in 1853 and that wherever Browning went in Springfield, there went Lincoln.[17] But even if Lincoln was not in the audience, Emersonianism had come to Springfield, however briefly, and between the people he knew and the newspapers he read it seems reasonable to assume that Lincoln would have absorbed something of what Emerson had to say there.

What did Emerson have to say in Springfield in January 1853, as he earned $110 for the three-lecture series?[18] If we consider briefly each of his three lectures in turn, we can begin to recreate something of the intellectual ambience surrounding Lincoln at this particular moment. To begin with the Monday lecture, "The Anglo-Saxon," full disclosure requires an admission that Orville Browning seems to have missed the point, since he came away from it with the mistaken impression that Emerson meant to chastise his American audience for aping English manners. To be sure, Emerson carried out such chastisement elsewhere, as in his celebrated address of 1837, "The American Scholar," delivered at Harvard. But the closest he came in "The Anglo-Saxon" to dealing out what Browning calls a "hard rap" for chronic North American Anglo-mimicry would be something like this:

> The English are stiff to their own ways. . . . It is the remark
> of our people employing English workmen, that they
> show great reluctance to deviate from their own methods,
> or proper work; whilst an American will turn his hand
> to anything. The very existence of our manufactures is
> a proof of aptitude: The stone cutters become sculptors.
> The house painters take to landscape portraits. We can
> make everything but music and poetry. But also he has
> chambers opened in his mind which the English have not.
> He is intellectual and speculative, an abstractionist. He has
> solitude of mind and fruitful dreams.[19]

One can argue about whether or not this excerpt limns a good portrait of the English, but although it does contain some implicit criticism of Americans, as people who cannot make music or poetry (this latter charge would soon drop with the advent of Whitman), one cannot argue persuasively that it concerns itself with American imitation of the English. If anything, the passage, like much of the lecture, concerns itself with basic differences between Anglo-Saxon Americans and their English ancestors.

But Browning's apparent misunderstanding or oversimplification was not his fault and is part of the point. Like many of

Emerson's best-known essays, such as *Nature* or "Self-Reliance," "The Anglo-Saxon" made few concessions either to cohesiveness, in its movement from sentence to sentence, or to coherence, in its larger focus on one or two main ideas. Appropriately enough for someone who elsewhere dismissed consistency as foolish, Emerson built a distinctive style of isolated, solitary sentences, which at their best continue to resonate in aphoristic autonomy and at their worst maintain an antisocial alienation from the sentences around them. Likewise, in moving from paragraph to paragraph, "The Anglo-Saxon" had little or no patience with orderly exposition.

In the case of "The Anglo-Saxon," some of the resistance to cohesiveness and coherence may have reflected Emerson's ambivalence toward his subject. Whereas Browning took Emerson to be campaigning for an end of American aping of Englishness, in fact Emerson was interested in three groups, not two: English Anglo-Saxons, Anglo-Saxons of the eastern United States, and Anglo-Saxons of the western United States. Whether or not Browning heard what Emerson was really saying, the latter was particularly interested in examining the strengths and the weaknesses of westerners, whom he first encountered on their home ground during a lecture tour in May and June 1850. "The condition of the Western states is today what was the condition of all the states fifty or a hundred years ago. It is the country of poor men."[20] In other words, in trying to explicate the North American Anglo-Saxon, Emerson the easterner, standing before an audience from the muddy prairie, had somehow to account for a western variant of the Anglo-Saxon, a variant in relation to whom he stood much as he thought of the English as standing in relation to him. One wonders how the Springfield audience received a paragraph such as this one, for example: "Go to the states on the Mississippi. Your western romance fades into reality of some grimness. Everything wears a raw and ordinary aspect. You find much coarseness in manners; much meanness in politics; much swagger, and vaporing, and low filibusterism; the men have not shed their canine teeth. Well, don't be disgusted; 'tis the work of this river,—this Mississippi River,— that warps the men, warps the nations, and dinges them all with its own mud."[21] It would be one thing to have made such remarks in Portland, Maine, or Philadelphia or Brooklyn or Concord, but to make them before a roomful of people who could not help but feel implicated by images of unshed canine teeth and dingy mud was something else altogether. If anything, Emerson often sounded as though he would not object to prescribing a good stiff dose of English gentility as an antidote to some of the western coarseness and meanness.

If Lincoln was in the audience, sitting beside Browning, who was also born in Kentucky, what did he think of such remarks? More pointedly, since we know he had a memory for what Emerson said about people from Kentucky, whom Emerson had first observed during the earlier lecture tour of 1850, what would Lincoln have made of the two references to Kentuckians in "The Anglo-Saxon"? The first came about one-quarter of the way through the lecture, as Emerson contrasted the "slow, sure finish" of the English with what he called "the irresistibility of the American":

> The man's irresistibility is like nature's. Like nature, he has
> no conscience. His motto, like her's [sic], is, Our country
> right or wrong. He builds shingle palaces, shingle cities,
> picnic universities; extemporizes a state in California;
> in an altered mood, I suppose, he will build stone cities
> with equal celerity. Tall, restless Kentucky strength: good
> stock;—but, though an admirable fruit, you shall not find
> one good sound, well-developed apple on the tree. Nature
> herself was in a hurry with these racers, and never finished
> one.[22]

Not one good sound, well-developed apple to be found on the whole Kentucky tree? Avid reader of German idealist philosophy and founding father of American transcendentalism, Emerson showed throughout his writing life a sweet tooth for abstraction and generalization, but this particular sweeping dismissal smacked of an embarrassing condescension, not to mention a sectional prejudice, that could easily sting or infuriate anyone from Kentucky.

Emerson's second reference to Lincoln's home state, though bordering on caricature, stung somewhat less and came in a paragraph near the end of the lecture, one that contrasts the English and the Americans: "Climate draws the teeth, emaciates the body, spends the constitution, unbuilds and recomposes the bulky Briton into the loose-jointed, spare, swaggering Kentuckian. The Englishman, well-made, and even fatted by his climate of clouded sunshine, walks and sits erect, and his chair rests squarely on its legs. The American lolls and leans, tips his chair, adds rockers to it to keep it tipped, but is capable of equal energy in action and the mental powers are not impaired."[23] The statement "the mental powers are not impaired" perhaps fell short of exalting loose-jointed, spare, swaggering Kentuckians, but at least Kentuckians who fit that description could have left Emerson's lecture that Monday evening without feeling that the Massachusetts Buddha had explicitly denied them their mental powers.

If Lincoln attended either or both of Emerson's next two lectures, he would have heard no references to Kentucky, but he would have heard a reference to Illinois in the Tuesday lecture, "Power," a reference encoded in the nickname "Sucker" for a citizen of that state and enfolded in one of Emerson's long, complex sentences:

> As long as our people quote English standards they will
> miss the sovereignty of power; but let these rough riders—
> legislators in shirt-sleeves, Hoosier, Sucker, Wolverine,
> Badger, or whatever hard head Arkansas, Oregon or Utah
> sends, half orator, half assassin, to represent its wrath and
> cupidity at Washington,—let these drive as they may, and
> the disposition of territories and public lands, the necessity
> of balancing and keeping at bay the snarling majorities
> of German, Irish and of native millions, will bestow
> promptness, address and reason, at last, on our buffalo-
> hunter, and authority and majesty of manners.[24]

Happily for his adopted state, Lincoln came along to give it a new nickname, saving it from ending up as the Sucker State, but once again one wonders how he would have heard Emerson's sentence, if indeed he did. The opening warning against "English standards" corresponded more clearly than anything in the Monday lecture to Orville Browning's diary note about hard raps for aping Englishness; yet even though Emerson followed this long sentence with a punchy short one, "The instinct of the people is right," his glib nod to democracy did not offset his extraordinary image of the United States Congress as some kind of finishing school for half-savage western wild men, one of whom can go to Washington, as Lincoln did after his election to the House of Representatives in 1846, and, in the process of xenophobically "keeping at bay snarling" immigrants and natives, develop his reason, along with, so important for the well-bred Emerson, his manners.

Even if he felt jabbed by this characterization, Lincoln could have heard in "Power" plenty of Emersonian aphorisms to savor and brood over during his own subsequent rise to political power: "There are men who by their sympathetic attractions carry nations with them and lead the activity of the human race"; "Life is a search after power"; "All power is of one kind, a sharing of the nature of the world"; "There is always room for a man of force, and he makes room for many"; "Power educates the potentate"; "Politics is a deleterious profession, like some poisonous handicrafts"; and "These Hoosiers and Suckers are really better than the snivelling opposition."[25]

In his Lincoln Prize remarks, Douglas Wilson singled out Emerson's second lecture to linger over "with the possibility of Lincoln's presence in mind," suggesting quite reasonably that the subject of "Power" would "presumably have appealed most to Lincoln," as it would have also to Emerson's German admirer, Friedrich Nietzsche. Quoting parts of a paragraph beginning, "All successful men have agreed in one thing,—they were *causationists*,"[26] Wilson went on to point out that like the Emerson of 1853 and the Emerson of the essay "Fate," Lincoln also exerted himself to try to reconcile the seeming inconsistencies of causality and individual will or, in Emerson's terms, of fate and freedom. I will return to this important point shortly, but for now let us briefly consider the third lecture,

"Culture," which Lincoln may have heard on Wednesday, or heard about afterward, and which, though perhaps not as obviously relevant to him as "Power," still has features he might have pondered.

Positioned fourth in *The Conduct of Life* (1860), when the lecture appeared in book form, "Culture" followed "Fate," "Power," and "Wealth," and its second sentence declared its relation to the previous two essays: "Whilst all the world is in pursuit of power, and of wealth as a means of power, culture corrects the theory of success." Like many, if not most, of Emerson's other essays, "Culture" did not bow to the confines of a crisp organizational scheme, flowing instead from topic to topic, the boundaries of which are not always clear. But his basic principle that public culture corrects or balances the excesses of personal success was clear enough, and Emerson's first extended meditation took up the subject of egotism, with which his own detractors often charged him: "The pest of society is egotists." The meditation on egotism then wound through another seven pages or so and culminated in the sentence, "The antidotes against this organic egotism are the range and variety of attractions, as gained by acquaintance with the world, with men of merit, with classes of society, with travel, with eminent persons, and with the high resources of philosophy, art and religion; books, travel, society, solitude."[27]

Although Lincoln found himself charged with many things at various points in his career—awkwardness, uncouthness, opportunism, infidelism, and despotism among them—as an egotist he ranked far below such apparent colossi as Emerson and Whitman; however, his subsequent services as chief executive and commander-in-chief consisted, at many moments, of confronting and managing the virulent egotism of other people, both civilian and military, and Emerson's remarks, if he ever knew and recollected them, may have resonated more deeply for Lincoln years after the Springfield lectures. More immediately relevant to him in January 1853, in the course of Emerson's loose musings on education, books, traveling, cities, and solitude, could have been the sudden formulation, "We look that a great man should be a good reader, or in proportion to the spontaneous power should be the assimilating power."[28]

In our popular mythology of Lincoln we have imagined the log-cabin president as a voracious reader, who supplemented a year's worth of intermittent education in a log schoolhouse with long evenings spent poring over books by candlelight, books such as Mason Locke Weems's life of Washington, which went through numerous editions in the early part of the nineteenth century. In his 1868 painting *Boyhood of Lincoln*, Eastman Johnson represented this image of Lincoln as a youth sitting on a four-legged stool with a book open before his face, which wears an expression of rapt attention, as the boy leans his upper body backward toward a huge fireplace in order to catch its illumination on his page. But, in fact, how good a reader was Lincoln? How much culture did he actually absorb through the careful reading of books? The testimony of Lincoln's law partner, William Herndon, which came in the form of a letter dated February 16, 1870, quoted by one of Lincoln's early biographers, Ward H. Lamon, might make us wonder: "I used to loan him Theodore Parker's works: I loaned him Emerson sometimes, and other writers; and he would sometimes read, and sometimes would not, as I suppose,—nay, know."[29] Another biographer, Carl Sandburg, listed several books borrowed from the Library of Congress by the Lincoln household during 1861, among them titles by Plutarch, Shakespeare, Emerson, Longfellow, and Stowe, in addition to four volumes of Jefferson's works, eight volumes on the United States Constitution, and Henry Halleck's *Elements of Military Art and Science.* Sandburg then commented that these "were titles of books in which Lincoln was interested, though he could not have had time to read them."[30]

Such evidence, slim though it is, would seem to render Lincoln's credentials as a good reader somewhat shaky, but Emerson's description of great men as good readers left the largely autodidact Lincoln an important loophole: "or in proportion to the spontaneous power should be the assimilating power." What does it matter that I do not read every page of, say, Emerson, if I have the power to assimilate by other means the important things that Emerson says? That Lincoln had prodigious powers of assimilation, whether in legal, political, or military matters, has been abundantly documented. Looking ahead to the 1862 meeting between Lincoln and Emerson, we can see how the fruits of the former's assimilative powers would show themselves in his opening reference to the latter's words about someone from Kentucky. Although Lincoln could not have known it in 1853, Emerson prophesied, toward the end of "Culture," the huge importance of Lincoln's assimilative powers, among the other distinguishing characteristics of his personality, during the war years ahead: "When the state is unquiet, personal qualities are more than ever decisive."[31]

At this point it would seem convenient to sum up the argument so far by saying that, whether or not Lincoln heard Emerson lecture in Springfield in January 1853, he assimilated much of what Emerson said there, either by reading reports of the lectures, if not the lectures themselves when two of them appeared in *The Conduct of Life*, or by listening to people around him talk about them. In turn, following the lead of Douglas Wilson, one could argue that what Lincoln assimilated from Emerson, anywhere from 1853 on, was Emerson's thinking about the operations in our lives of what he called "fate," which for him meant not a supernaturally preordained outcome but the limiting influences exerted by various forces, causes, and circumstances on the freedoms of an individual—forces, causes, and circumstances involving the social, historical, economic, racial, geographic, psychological, and genetic aspects of our lives. If two consecutive sentences can stand for the shift in Emerson's thinking from the essays of the late 1830s and early 1840s, on the one hand, to the essays of the late 1840s and early 1850s, on the other, a good nomination for such sentences would be these two terse ones from "Fate": "Once we thought positive power was all. Now we learn that negative power, or circumstance, is half."[32] In the beginning of Emerson's career, he celebrated the individual powers and freedoms of self-reliance. Later in that career he came to admit that those individual freedoms and powers operate in antagonistic relation to powers outside or beyond the individual.

What caused the change in Emerson? Some might say he finally grew up and matured. Others might point to circumstances in his personal life, circumstances such as the death of his beloved son Waldo in 1842, the year after the publication of his *Essays, First Series*. Still others might direct us to the intellectual history of the 1840s, one Emerson shared with Lincoln every bit as much as he shared the biographical bereavement of fathers who lose sons. One event in that intellectual history that proved important to both men was the 1844 publication of Robert Chambers's *Vestiges of the Natural History of Creation*.[33] From the testimony of William Herndon, we know this is one book that Lincoln actually read from cover to cover:

> A gentleman in Springfield gave him a book called, I believe, "Vestiges of Creation," which interested him so much that he read it through. The volume was published in Edinburgh, and undertook to demonstrate the doctrine of development or evolution. The treatise interested him greatly, and he was deeply impressed with the notion of the so-called "universal law"—evolution: he did not greatly extend his researches, but by continued thinking in a single channel seemed to grow to a warm advocate of the new doctrine. Beyond what I have stated he made no further investigation into the realm of philosophy.[34]

With more time and space, one could discuss at length various aspects of Chambers's book that might have impressed Lincoln deeply. Especially suggestive, for example, is Chambers's penultimate chapter, "Purpose and General Condition of the Animated Creation," which contains a paragraph on war that poses the question, "But what is it that produces war?," and answers the question in language inviting comparison with Lincoln's Second Inaugural Address: "War, then, huge evil though it be, is, after all, but the exceptive case, a casual misdirection of properties and powers essentially good. God has given us the tendencies for a benevolent purpose. He has only not laid down any absolute obstruction to our misuse of them."[35]

Like Darwin before him in the account of the voyage of the *Beagle*, published in 1839, and contrary to many people's understanding, or misunderstanding, of early theorists of evolution, the Scotsman Chambers was no atheist, though neither was he an early proponent of what we might now think of as the theory, or theology, of intelligent design. Chambers saw nothing necessarily incompatible between his scientific research and his belief in God, and whatever Lincoln may have thought of Chambers's last sentence—"Thus we give, as is meet, a respectful reception to what is revealed through the medium of nature, at the same time that we fully reserve our reverence for all that we have been accustomed to hold sacred, not one tittle of which it may ultimately be found necessary to alter"[36]—Emerson would have recognized a kindred spirit behind a book culminating in such a statement. In fact, Emerson not only read Chambers's book; he made a point of visiting Chambers in 1848 during his second trip to Europe.[37]

What Herndon describes as the universal law of evolution, which Lincoln learned from Chambers, was certainly part of the bundle of circumstances, causes, and forces lumped by Emerson under the broad, catchall heading "fate." Knowing what we know of what was to come between 1853 and 1865, we may well find deeply attractive the multiple possibilities for reading Lincoln's version of fate in the context of Emerson's version of fate, or for reading both within wider contexts of contemporary discussions of fate, whether that sense of fate manifested itself in emerging narratives of evolution or in some other form. Through its Latin etymology the word "fate" carries the meaning of something spoken (*fatum* is the past participle of *fari*, to speak), and for both Emerson and Lincoln, two of our most important writers, the understanding of fate could not separate itself from memorable speaking about fate, as in the case of one of Lincoln's greatest sentences, the four-word masterpiece of understatement that closed the second paragraph of the Second Inaugural Address and with its sublimely indeterminate opening anticipated the style Ernest Hemingway would later make famous: "And the war came."

All discussions of Lincoln's version of fate are fated to end with his assassination, and it is hard to resist the cathartic ecstasies of Aristotelian tragedy when contemplating the grand convergence of Lincoln's words with his personal fate on Good Friday in April 1865. Linking Emerson, the leading public intellectual in the United States during Lincoln's life, to Lincoln's own understanding of power and limitation, of freedom and fate, offers to solemnize and exalt the situations of both men.[38] But there are at least two problems with this kind of reading, and I want to focus on them now, in order to return to the moment when Lincoln met Emerson in the White House in February 1862.

The first problem is one of method. Since Emerson was famous, some might say notorious, for shuffling through his papers at many points during a lecture, as he patched together different parts of his manuscripts and improvised from them spontaneously, what right do we have to assume that the version of a lecture delivered in, say, Springfield, Illinois, in January 1853 is the same as the version recently published in a scholarly edition of Emerson's lectures? As his editors themselves note, "Not only were the lectures constantly being written under deadline, they were rewritten throughout Emerson's career as well, for multiple deliveries, for wholesale revision and incorporation into other lectures, and as practice for what would become book chapters."[39] Not everyone found Emerson an electric lecturer, but demand for his performances was large enough for him to deliver approximately fifteen hundred lectures during his career, so any one lecture could have been heard in numerous forms.[40] In other words, even if we had solid evidence documenting that Lincoln was in the audience for, say, "Power" on Tuesday, January 11, 1853—and Browning's detail about the supper hosted afterward by the Presbyterian church ladies suggested a small-scale intimacy that would have made it possible for Lincoln to meet Emerson that evening, if indeed he had been there—we still would not know what Emerson actually said in Springfield, let alone what Lincoln actually heard after a long day at work.

The second problem returns us to the White House in February 1862 and to what Lincoln actually said to Emerson: "'O Mr Emerson, I once heard you say in a lecture, that a Kentuckian seems to say by his air & manners, 'Here am I; if you don't like me, the *worse for you.*" In this moment Lincoln the assimilator showed admirable powers of recall, or perhaps Emerson did in recalling Lincoln recalling him, since the actual sentence in the final version we now have is impressively similar: "The frank Kentuckian has a way of thinking concerning his reception by his friend that makes him whole: Here I am. If you do not appreciate me, the worse for you."[41] The problem is not with Lincoln's recall; the problem is that what he recalled appears nowhere in any of the three lectures delivered in Springfield in January 1853, or at least nowhere in their final published versions. In tracking down the provenance of Lincoln's quotation of Emerson, one gets no help from the most recent (1982) edition of Emerson's journals, which did not annotate Lincoln's quotation. Instead, one must return to the original appearance of an excerpt from Emerson's journal entitled "Washington in Wartime," published in the *Atlantic Monthly* in July 1904, to discover there a note by Edward Waldo Emerson, who identified the lecture quoted by Lincoln as "Manners and Customs of New England," a lecture "given by Mr. Emerson in New York in February, 1843," or ten years before the Springfield lectures and seven years before he actually went to Kentucky for the first time to encounter the people who, as of 1843, could only have served him as idealized abstractions or personifications of certain qualities.[42]

This helpful note answers one question, but in doing so it raises several others. For one thing, Lincoln was in Springfield and nowhere near New York at any point in February 1843.[43] Could Lincoln have heard the lecture somewhere else Emerson delivered it between January 1843 and April 1844, when he was giving the series that included it: Philadelphia, Brooklyn, Concord, Woonsocket, Providence, Newburyport, Salem, Billerica? Not according to the records we have, which tell us Lincoln was in Illinois during this entire time. Could Lincoln have heard Emerson some other time, such as, for example, during his service in Congress, which began in December 1847? Unlikely, since Emerson sailed on his second trip to England on October 5, 1847, not returning until July 27, 1848, and not resuming his lecturing until November 22 of that year. Lincoln returned to Washington, late for his second session in Congress, on December 7, 1848, and stayed there until March 20, 1849, when he began traveling back to Springfield. William Charvat's chronological list of Emerson's lectures shows nothing in Washington during this time.[44] Could Lincoln have heard Emerson still somewhere else, perhaps during Emerson's 1850 trip west, which included lectures in Cincinnati and a sightseeing trip to Mammoth Cave in Kentucky in June?[45] Lincoln did not leave Illinois during this period. Perhaps when Lincoln traveled to Cincinnati in September 1855? Emerson's only lecture that month was in Boston. How about when Lincoln returned to Ohio in September 1859? Emerson gave no lectures that month.

If Lincoln told Emerson the truth in telling him that he had once heard him make the remark about Kentuckians, then since he would have missed the lecture series that included the remark in its original setting, what seems most likely is that we have here an example of Emerson's infamous paper-shuffling at the lectern. Even lecturers who appear to be more organized than Emerson will occasionally or often ad-lib, slipping in something improvised or recycled from another context. If Lincoln was in the audience in Springfield in January 1853, did he hear Emerson's 1843 remark about Kentuckians slipped in beside the 1853 remarks about Kentuckians in "The Anglo-Saxon" or beside those about Suckers in "Power"?

At this point the existing historical record can no longer help us, and unless someone turns up a new document, we have nothing to go on but conjecture. What is not conjecture, however, is the nature of the Emersonian statement that Lincoln chose to remember. The Emerson that Lincoln quoted back to Emerson was not the later Emerson of "Fate," who has come to realize that positive power must go halves with negative power; he was entirely the earlier Emerson of "Self-Reliance," who in celebrating his own power and freedom and autonomy could declaim, "Few and mean as my gifts may be, I actually am, and do not need for my own assurance or the assurance of my fellows any secondary testimony."[46] In other words, whatever may have happened or occurred to Lincoln after reading Robert Chambers's *Vestiges of the Natural History of Creation* or after serving in Congress or after winning the presidency or after watching the outbreak of war, the version of Emerson he carried with him, and had ready on the tip of his tongue, was the Emerson of self-assured self-reliance.

In remembering and showing he remembered this particular declaration of Emersonian independence, even during, or especially during, the tornado of his wartime presidency, was Lincoln implicitly paying homage to the master? Was he saying that Emersonian self-reliance meant much to him, especially during the trials of his presidency? If not, was he simply flattering Emerson? Or was there something ironic, something tongue-in-cheek about Lincoln's greeting, as if he were saying, with some implicit self-deprecation, so much for all that self-assured self-reliance; look where it has landed us now? And if there was something ironic or tongue-in-cheek or sly about what Lincoln said when he met Emerson, was some of the irony also at Emerson's expense, as though the westerner were nudging the easterner to remind the latter of all the condescending remarks he had made about Kentucky and Kentuckians, a reminder implicitly responding to all the things Emerson might have stood for in Lincoln's mind: the northeastern social establishment; radical Republicanism agitating for emancipation before the United States armies had earned Lincoln any political clout abroad; and the rarefied world of letters, as opposed to the gritty world of statecraft? Whatever the answer, in quoting the visiting Emerson back to Emerson, apparently Lincoln did not mind reminding his guest that here he was, president of the United States, and if Emerson did not like it, the worse for him.

THE GETTYSBURG ADDRESS
AND THE SECOND INAUGURAL

Twenty-one months after his meeting with Emerson, Lincoln drafted and delivered his address at Gettysburg, followed sixteen months later by the address at his second inauguration. Among the political scriptures of the United States, these two addresses, each an object of voluminous commentary and interpretation, stand preeminent. Even the Declaration of Independence, for all

the stirring reverberations of its memorable opening and closing, included an extended middle section, an inventory of specific
grievances against King George III, that still sounds rhetorically
closer to legal documentation than to anything in Lincoln's two
addresses. The fact that few can reproduce this section of the declaration from memory partly reflects its generic difference from
Lincoln's two famous speeches, not just its greater length. The declaration announced and justified the breaking of an existing contract in order to form a new one, and so, whatever the beauties and
powers of its language, it belonged to the genre of the legal contract, whereas Lincoln's two speeches did not. Instead, they mixed
and blended various genres, among them dedication, exhortation,
historical narration, political argument, psalm, and prayer. In the
United States the two addresses are so often memorized, so often
recited, and so often quoted in other speeches that many citizens
take their generic mixings for granted.

But the stature and fame of the two addresses are not confined
to the United States. Not quite fourscore and seven years after Lincoln delivered them, for example, South African writer Alan Paton
wove the two addresses and their author into his great novel of broken families and unequal races, *Cry, the Beloved Country* (1948).
Reading the two addresses in the library of his son, recently murdered by a misguided Zulu boy who had moved to the city of Jo-
hannesburg and fallen into bad company there, a bereaved white
father slowly begins to understand his murdered son's zealous efforts to heal the rift between races in South Africa, as Paton also
used the references to Lincoln's addresses to advance and deepen
a larger vision of justice, compassion, and forgiveness, both public
and private. In this novel, as in many nonliterary contexts, such as
Steven Spielberg's film *Lincoln* (2012), the Great Emancipator's
two greatest speeches function as icons of an egalitarian racial vision and of an enlightened social reconciliation, the Gettysburg
Address often construed as endorsing "a new birth of freedom" for
an enslaved race in a true democracy and the Second Inaugural
Address usually read as urging magnanimity and charity toward
former enemies, once the work of correcting racial imbalance

has gotten under way. But these abbreviated descriptions of the two addresses, though in wide circulation around the globe and though to some extent valid, fall seriously short of acknowledging their many complexities, both historical and rhetorical.

Lincoln's Gettysburg Address has become so identified with the political aspirations and self-descriptions of the United States that in 1972 the Library of Congress published a collection of translations of the address into twenty-nine languages. Roy Basler, who gathered the translations, introduced them this way: "Such a booklet might serve foreign visitors to the several Lincoln shrines with an opportunity to come to grips with Lincoln's expression of the essence of American democracy rendered beautifully into their mother tongues."[47] Although foreign tourists to Lincoln shrines no doubt benefit from the availability of Lincoln's speech in their native languages, the singling out of Lincoln's speech as the superlative encapsulation of "the essence" of democracy in the United States risks exalting it beyond our individual and collective powers to see and hear it, or the Second Inaugural Address, as a verbal arrangement by a resolutely pragmatic man working strenuously to accomplish specific goals at a particular moment of national convulsion.

In the case of the Gettysburg Address, those who intone with reverence its superbly crafted periods do not have to deny their reverence in order to bear in mind that by the time Lincoln delivered his address on the afternoon of Thursday, November 19, 1863, the victory at Gettysburg of the Army of the Potomac over the Army of Northern Virginia four months earlier had lost some of its luster, since, from Lincoln's point of view, Union general George Gordon Meade had squandered a precious opportunity to defeat the Confederate army of Robert E. Lee, allowing it to escape southward over the Potomac River. After a frustrating and inconclusive series of subsequent engagements in Virginia, Meade, under pressure from Lincoln, was about to launch the ill-fated Mine Run Campaign (November 27 to December 2, 1863). Meanwhile, in the west a decisive Confederate victory at the battle of Chickamauga, fought two months earlier in northwestern Georgia, had led to the penning-up of United States forces in Chattanooga, Tennessee, and Ulysses S. Grant had not yet given Lincoln the crucial victories around that city that would convince the president to promote Grant and bring him east to face Lee in 1864, although those victories were only days away. In other words, when Lincoln delivered what many around the world now regard as the quintessential hymn to democracy in the United States, that democracy, precariously unstable, easily could have turned out a failed experiment, a quixotic delusion not worth hymning. Thirteen months after the battle of Gettysburg, and nine months after the address there, Lincoln penned a private memorandum in which he anticipated losing the 1864 presidential election to Democratic rival George McClellan. If he had lost the election to McClellan and McClellan had concluded a peace with the Confederate States of America that recognized the independence of the latter, as he promised to do, it is questionable whether the Gettysburg Address would be read or remembered, whatever its intrinsic literary or stylistic merits.

The high honor in which many hold those literary or stylistic merits is, to some extent then, an honor conferred retrospectively in light of later historical unfoldings, among them Union victory over the two major armies of the Confederacy in April 1865; the assassination of Lincoln the same month; the outpouring of Civil War memoirs and other writings in the last two decades of the nineteenth century, as many veterans' organizations began to hold local and national reunions; the development and dedication of the first national military park at Chickamauga; and the growing trend toward reconciliation, at least in public, of the white populations of North and South. If part of the rhetorical majesty of the Gettysburg Address comes from what now feels like its visionary prophetic force, that visionary prophetic force originated in November 1863, with Lee's defiant Army of Northern Virginia dug in behind the Rapidan River in central Virginia, as a more limited exhortation in the optative mood, an exhortation on behalf of something uncertain and desired, not something inevitable and accomplished. It is important to acknowledge that in itself the Gettysburg Address made nothing happen. It did not, for example, inoculate citizens of the northern states against the extreme war-weariness of the summer of 1864, which, as Lincoln well knew, could have cost him reelection if it had not been for William Tecumseh Sherman's capture of Atlanta in September of that year, a capture that inspired northern soldiers to vote overwhelmingly for Lincoln and reflected a strategic shift to total war, subsequently prosecuted by Sherman during his famous March to the Sea, which ended at Savannah in December 1864, after his army had deliberately and systematically reduced the abilities of Georgia's civilians to support the Confederate war effort.

To acknowledge that the Gettysburg Address does not consist of magically efficacious words, which by themselves accomplished northern war aims and preserved the Union or by themselves adequately performed public rituals of mourning and consolation—with the unparalleled casualties of 1864 still to come (in one four-week period, from May 5 to June 3, Grant lost nearly 50,000 soldiers, killed, wounded, captured, or missing), no 1863 utterance could have been adequate—in no way diminishes the distinct qualities of the address. If anything, such an acknowledgment clears the way for our realistic appraisal of the deliberate verbal means by which Lincoln achieved the distinct qualities that subsequent historical events and developments made so attractive to national retrospection and self-description.

These verbal means would not impress us so deeply in the present if a large shift in popular sensibility, taste, and expectation had not taken place since the Civil War, a shift both reflected in and furthered by changing norms in education. At Gettysburg, on November 19, 1863, Edward Everett's two-hour peroration fulfilled the expectations of educated taste and sensibility, whereas Lincoln's short speech did not attempt to. But for many reasons Everett's speech is unthinkable now, and Lincoln's, modest as it may have sounded in 1863 by comparison, now brims and resonates with sonorities that far exceed our expectations for speeches made by presidents.[48]

Consider the famous first sentence, as it appears in the Second Draft or Hay text, which recent scholarship identifies as the one

Lincoln probably read: "Four score and seven years ago our fathers brought forth, upon this continent, a new nation, conceived in Liberty, and dedicated to the proposition that all men are created equal."[49] Sheer repetition of this nearly sacred sentence has made it almost impossible for us to imagine it any other way, but a comparison with translations into Romance and Germanic languages in Basler's collection, most of which open with some version of "eighty-seven years ago" (though the Italian speaks in terms of *lustri*, or five-year periods, and the German of "thirteen years" more until "it will be a century"), vividly confirms Lincoln's artistry. If he had begun, "In 1776 our ancestors established a new government based on certain assumptions about individual freedom and on the principle that everyone has the same rights," he would have said much the same thing, but he would have forfeited two crucial features of the opening. The first is an echo of Psalm 90, verse 10, in the King James version: "The days of our years are threescore years and ten; and if by reason of strength they be fourscore years, yet is their strength labour and sorrow; for it is soon cut off, and we fly away." The Hebrew original does not include a literal equivalent of "fourscore," meaning four groups of twenty; this particular locution is a flourish of the King James translators, and it is a word Lincoln's audience would connect, either consciously or unconsciously, with this well-known biblical verse, a *memento mori* acknowledging the brevity of human life in a way wholly appropriate for a speech at a new rural cemetery, although the echo carries with it some hard irony, too, since none of the soldiers interred at Gettysburg had managed to live seventy or eighty years.

The second sacrifice, which points beyond the first sentence to the entire address, as well as to the Second Inaugural, would have been sonority. The opening sentence bundles "Four," "score," "our," "fathers," "forth," "are" with varying degrees of rhyme, assonance, consonance, and alliteration, as it does "score," "continent," "dedicated," "created," and "equal." Since the literary modernism of the second and third decades of the twentieth century, fewer readers of English necessarily associate rhyme, or its subdivisions, with verse, let alone prose, but in fact the antecedents of

Lincoln's rhyming prose include ancient Latin and Arabic precursors, although he would not have known it.[50] What he would have known, or felt, is what the writers of ancient rhyming prose knew and felt, that there are gradations and shadings on the spectrum leading from prose to verse, and certain occasions call for prose that is closer to verse. That Lincoln could also write prose wholly free of verse qualities should be immediately apparent to anyone reading through the Emancipation Proclamation. When he had to write like a lawyer and subordinate the resonating sonorities of language to more precise specifications, he certainly could do so. As the historian Richard Hofstadter commented wryly, "The Emancipation Proclamation of January 1, 1863 had all the moral grandeur of a bill of lading."[51]

Some may object at this point that to treat one of the preeminent scriptures of the United States as an aesthetic performance, without dwelling on the content of the speech, is as blasphemous as reading the Bible as literature. What about Lincoln's ignoring the Constitution, which is what legally "brought forth" the new nation and which did not dedicate the new nation to the proposition that all men are created equal, as the original version of Article 1, Section 2, which based representation and taxation on "the whole Number of free Persons" and "three-fifths of all other persons," makes perfectly clear? What about his not mentioning the South? What about his associating the war effort with bringing about "a new birth of freedom," thereby identifying emancipation as a primary war aim, although he never explicitly mentions slavery? What about the last sentence with its famous triad, "of the people, by the people, for the people" (Second Draft), which echoes, according to one dictionary of quotations, similar formulations by John Wycliffe, Daniel Webster, William Lloyd Garrison, and Theodore Parker, thereby linking Lincoln's speech with antecedents in the Protestant Reformation, antebellum Whig Unionism, abolitionism, and transcendentalism?[52]

To focus on Lincoln's verbal artistry is not to discount or dismiss any of these questions or the significance of any of the issues they raise; it is to point out that, significant as these issues were and still are, many, many people wrote and spoke about them in writings and speeches we no longer know or read. It cannot be the issues alone that keep us reading and reciting the Gettysburg Address or the Second Inaugural, and to admit this conclusion enables us to raise another question, one that begins in verbal artistry but rapidly ramifies in several directions: What is the political or social function of eloquence? Take, for example, the famous triad in the last sentence of the Gettysburg Address. Yes, its antecedents may associate Lincoln's utterance with Protestantism, Unionism, abolitionism, and transcendentalism, with all of which he had affinities of varying complexity. But in addition to these considerations we must also recognize that Lincoln simply loved and used verbal triads throughout his writings and speeches, and the verbal triad, as a schematic rhetorical archetype, especially effective as a device for closure, descended to Lincoln with the accumulated resonances and authority of the Bible ("the power, the kingdom, and the glory"), the classical world (Caesar's *veni, vidi, vici*), Shakespeare (the Second Apparition's "Be bloody, bold, and resolute," speaking to Macbeth), and earlier statesmen (Jefferson's "we mutually pledge to each other our lives, our Fortunes, and our sacred Honor").

Many readers may want, quite understandably, to connect the verbal form of the Gettysburg Address with the content of the speech, but there is something naive about the insistence that, for example, Lincoln's careful auditory connections between and among words, phrases, clauses, and sentences—another of his favorite rhetorical devices is syntactic parallelism, which, like rhyme, is a scheme of verbal repetition—somehow reflect or represent or imitate or enact the binding together of the wounded and disintegrating Union. Lincoln's favorite verbal patterns also appear in writings composed before the Civil War, when binding together a wounded and disintegrating Union would have been neither his chief concern nor his chief responsibility. In his early "Address Before the Young Men's Lyceum of Springfield, Illinois," delivered January 27, 1838, a quarter of a century before the Gettysburg Address, verbal triads abound, along with anaphora (repetition of an initial word or phrase in successive clauses or sentences), as in these two consecutive sentences from the penultimate paragraph: "Reason, cold, calculating, unimpassioned reason, must furnish all the materials for our future support and defence. Let those materials be moulded into *general intelligence, sound morality* and, in particular, *a reverence for the constitution and laws*; and, that we improved to the last; that we remained free to the last; that we revered his name to the last; that, during his long sleep, we permitted no hostile foot to pass over or desecrate his resting place; shall be that which to learn the last trump shall awaken our WASHINGTON."[53] What these two sentences demonstrate is that by the time he was approaching his twenty-ninth birthday, Lincoln had already developed his ability to organize his words into sonorous, eloquent patterns he could apply to many different subjects.

Since words are units of both sound and meaning, their sounds can never be wholly separated from their meanings, and vice versa. But the sounds of words can produce meanings beyond the sum of their dictionary definitions. Take the notorious example of Edgar Allan Poe's "The Philosophy of Composition," published in 1846, the same year Lincoln ran successfully for election to the United States House of Representatives. In that essay, which purports to explain the genesis of his poem "The Raven" and which many suspect of some degree of parody, Poe accounts for his refrain, the raven's "Nevermore," this way: "That such a close, to have force, must be sonorous and susceptible of protracted emphasis, admitted no doubt: and these considerations inevitably led me to the long *o* as the most sonorous vowel, in connection with *r* as the most producible consonant." With his faith in the forceful, protracted sonorities of the *o-r* pairing, Poe anticipated the first sentence of the Gettysburg Address, and subsequent theorists of expressiveness in sound-patterning can illuminate why the history of childhood language acquisition might cause us to hear the *o-r* pairing as sonorous or beautiful or as integral to a feeling of aesthetic or emotional intensity.[54]

For this brief discussion what matters more than the linguistic specifics of how or why Lincoln's combinations of particular sounds produce impressions of aesthetic or emotional intensity is *that* they produce impressions of intensity. Furthermore, especially in the case of the Gettysburg Address, one could argue that whatever its other aims—to honor the soldiers killed at Gettysburg; to express sympathy for and solidarity with those bereaved by the battle and the war; to dedicate a new cemetery, with all the connotative changes Lincoln rings on the word "dedicate" (committing to a proposition, opening a new cemetery, sanctifying its ground, devoting oneself to a cause); to identify Union war aims with the Declaration of Independence, rather than the Constitution—another aim was to produce feelings of emotional intensity.

Why did Lincoln want to intensify emotion in his immediate audience and his subsequent readership? In the Gettysburg Address intensity grows toward the end, as the various levels of repetition pile up, and it grows still more with the final shift in verb tenses away from the past and present to the future perfect ("shall not have died in vain") and the future ("shall not perish from the earth"). Not coincidentally, the growing intensity and the shift toward the future correspond to a loss of specificity in Lincoln's remarks. The Gettysburg Address consists of ten sentences. Each of the first nine refers to something concrete or specific: the Declaration of Independence, the Civil War, the Gettysburg battlefield, the dedication of the cemetery, the appropriateness of the dedication, the larger sense of dedication, the dead soldiers, the nature of memory (this remarkable sentence, with its fluid stream of nonspirant continuants, *w, r, l, m, n, ng*, in the phrase "The world will little note, nor long remember," includes the only other future-tense verbs), the need for northerners to dedicate themselves to carrying on the war. But the tenth sentence, the longest by far, and made even longer by the insertion of "under God" in some of the versions,[55] soars off into what James Joyce's Stephen Dedalus calls "vague words for a vague emotion," thrilling and intoxicating as that emotion may be. At this point the address becomes pure exhortation, pure pep talk for the northern citizens who will be called on to pay more taxes; make do, perhaps forever, without men who have entered military service; submit to the draft instituted a few months before; submit to rigorous military training and discipline; suffer wounds, physical or mental; or lose their lives to violence or, more often, to disease.

In his final soaring sentence Lincoln mentioned none of these specifics. What he did mention is that his listeners must "highly resolve"—the hazy, straining, unnecessary adverb "highly" vying for distinction as the weakest moment in the address—not to let their soldiers' deaths amount to sheer waste by preparing themselves for a new birth of freedom. In trying to stir and unify the people he governed by focusing them on a vision of newness, Lincoln is not alone. As Kenneth Burke has shown in his classic discussion of the rhetoric of Hitler's *Mein Kampf*, the promise of newness also played a significant part in the Führer's attempts to unify. Many will reject this pairing immediately as unthinkable and unacceptable, and there are vast differences between Lincoln and Hitler, neo-Confederate extremist views to the contrary notwithstanding.[56] One crucial difference is that Lincoln adamantly refused the strategy of scapegoating, whereas Hitler based his politics on it. But as Burke points out, one of the ways that Hitler appealed to Germans struggling in the crippling aftermath of World War I was by offering them a vision of "symbolic rebirth": "They can again get the feel of *moving forward*, towards a *goal*" (italics in original).[57] Different as their political methods and visions were, the sixteenth president of the United States and the first and only Führer of the German Third Reich both found themselves trying to lead at moments of acute national crisis that included severe losses in the recent past, increasing hardships in the present, and debilitating uncertainties about the future. Given their respective inabilities to restore past losses, ease present hardships, and guarantee future improvements, both leaders attempted to place the difficulties of past and present in the uplifting context of impending transformation that would compensate for those difficulties.

For Lincoln the source of language about rebirth was the Bible, specifically the gospel according to John and the first letter of Peter (see John 1:12–13, 3:3–7; 1 Peter 1:3). In his Second

Inaugural Address, Lincoln's use of the New Testament included direct quotation, but in the Gettysburg Address New Testament sources hovered implicit in the background, providing imagery and with it augmented scriptural resonance. Again, it is no coincidence that this resonance became more prominent at the close of the speech, as Lincoln turned to futurity, to an abstract vision of some new development still to come, in the absence of certainty in the present. With another year and a half of the war to go, and close to 100,000 casualties in major battles still ahead, Lincoln could give the people who heard and read him little more than sonorous eloquence, the function of which was to generate emotional intensity and focus them on a description of the future abstract enough to encompass the stern and mournful specificities of lost lives, wounded bodies, and expended treasure. Noted by the Associated Press reporter for the *New York Tribune*, the "long-continued applause" that followed Lincoln's speech suggests that, at least at Gettysburg in November 1863, he succeeded.[58]

Sonorous eloquence—with triads, parallelism, and various shadings of rhyme—played an important part in the magnificent closure of the Second Inaugural Address as well, though the verb tense rooted Lincoln's imperative "let us" firmly in the present, as it projected onto the impending challenge of Reconstruction a vision described in the epistle of James, in the language of the King James Version, as pure religion: "Pure religion and undefiled before God and the Father is this, To visit the fatherless and widows in their affliction" (James 1:27). Appropriately enough, the reelected commander-in-chief closed this address, delivered not quite sixteen months after the one at Gettysburg, with a command. In turn, this command repeated the rhetorical form of Lincoln's version of Matthew 7:1, echoed earlier in the address but tellingly shifted from the second-person plural form of the King James original ("Judge not, that ye be not judged") to the first-person plural, in which Lincoln included himself: "But let us judge not that we be not judged."

In the sixteen months since the Gettysburg Address enough had changed to allow Lincoln to speak in a different mode and tone. With the capture by Union forces of Fort Fisher on January 15,

1865, a capture that meant the Confederacy could no longer use its last blockade-running port, Wilmington, North Carolina, and with Sherman's army about to cross into North Carolina and move toward connection with Grant in Virginia, Lincoln had good reason to comment at the close of his first paragraph, "The progress of our arms . . . is, I trust, reasonably satisfactory and encouraging to all." Rightly judicious in venturing "no prediction" for the future—a month later the relatively quick cessation of hostilities depended in part on Lee's wise discouragement of continuing guerrilla war after Appomattox, not solely on the progress of United States arms—Lincoln availed himself of both the improving military picture and his own newly secured political standing to focus much of the Second Inaugural on describing the recent past in a particular way. In doing so, he was not simply exercising the victor's privilege to write the history; he was laying the ground for his vision of Reconstruction.

Built of four paragraphs, the fourth of which is the most famous and most often quoted, the Second Inaugural, in its second and long third paragraphs, did what the Gettysburg Address did not do: it named the South, it named slavery, and it narrated the past, not the distant, storied past of 1776 and the Declaration of Independence, but the immediate past of 1854, the Kansas-Nebraska Act, and what followed as a result. What was both shrewd and tricky about Lincoln's account was that he ended up having it both ways, on the one hand, calling the country to rise above sectional partisanship as it moved toward Reconstruction, on the other, assigning a little more of the blame to the South. One does not have to be a Confederate sympathizer to wonder who was included in Lincoln's "us."

To appreciate the nature of Lincoln's narration, we can compare it productively with the point of view of two outsiders deeply interested by the American Civil War. Writing in November 1861 for *Die Presse*, one of the leading newspapers in Vienna, Karl Marx and Friedrich Engels summarized the war this way for their Austrian readership: "The present struggle between the South and North is, therefore, nothing but a struggle between two social systems, between the system of slavery and the system of free labor. The struggle has broken out because the two systems can no longer live peacefully side by side on the North American continent. It can only be ended by the victory of one system or the other."[59] Not all students of the Civil War will find this unidealized representation of the conflict palatable. It says nothing, for example, about democracy, the Constitution, or a theory of states' rights. But it does serve as an instructive contrast with Lincoln's representation of the same war in his Second Inaugural Address.

In his short second paragraph Lincoln adopted something of the detachment of Marx and Engels, describing the moment of "impending civil war" in March 1861 also by contrasting North and South, though Lincoln contrasted them not as competing social systems but as opposites with respect to the Union, one side committed to continuing the Union—Lincoln's word was "saving"—the other to ending the Union—his not quite neutral word was "destroying." Placing the genesis of the war solely in the context of Union, Lincoln appeared to refrain from assigning responsibility for the outbreak of belligerence, acknowledging a basic likeness between North and South: "Both parties deprecated war." The series of parallel constructions, in which he laid out the opposition between North and South, culminated in the four-word marvel of concision and understatement, which contrasted with the paragraph-long sentence at the end of the address and recalled the shortest verse in the King James Bible, "Jesus wept" (John 11:35): "And the war came." Known to students of rhetoric as parataxis, this use of the conjunction "and," reminiscent of the opening verses of Genesis, left unspecified the logical relationship of Lincoln's short sentence to what preceded it. It withheld the causal connection, as, for example, "So the war came" would not, and in withholding that connection appeared to set aside a discussion of causality altogether.

But it did so only for a moment. Leading into the long third paragraph, this short sentence functioned as the hinge on which Lincoln swung his narrative, now moving to join Marx and Engels in explicitly identifying slavery as cause—"All knew that this interest was, somehow, the cause of the war"—while diverging from them by framing his narrative according to a pattern of apostasy and retribution straight out of the Hebrew Bible, which despite the echo of Matthew 7:1 and a quotation of Matthew 18:7, drove both vision and rhetoric, as the quotation from Psalm 19, which closed the paragraph, confirmed ("the judgments of the Lord are true, and righteous altogether"): slavery was the offence, and the war was the compensation God exacted for it.

Two stylistic features of Lincoln's biblical account of the war and its causes are particularly noteworthy and revealing. The first appears in the first clause of the sentence containing the echo of Matthew 7:1: "It may seem strange that any men should dare to ask a just God's assistance in wringing their bread from the sweat of other men's faces; but let us judge not that we be not judged." Despite his appearances earlier as detached and somewhat objective, here the lawyer in Lincoln slyly worked his audience by means of the rhetorical figure known as paralipsis, a Greek word meaning "passing by omission." (Another shrewd lawyer, Stephen A. Douglas, had turned the same verse from Matthew against Lincoln five and a half years earlier, in their sixth debate, at Quincy, Illinois, on October 13, 1858.[60]) In paralipsis, according to the *Oxford English Dictionary*, "the speaker emphasizes something by affecting to pass it by without notice." In this case, what he affected to pass but actually emphasized was the strangeness—an understated synonym for something like "the indefensible hypocrisy"— of slaveholders who defend slavery while thinking of themselves as entitled by their faith to divine support and favor. The irony here was that in anticipation of Reconstruction, at a moment when he hoped to prevent continued acrimony between the warring sections, Lincoln should have resorted to such a pointed jab at the South, whereas in the Gettysburg Address, which focused on the northern war effort and losses, and in which such a jab would have been more appropriate, he did no such thing. Although he quickly followed his semicolon with an injunction against judging, he had already judged, and the "us" in "let us not judge" clearly stood for those opposed to slaveholding. If Lincoln had truly wished to leave judgment out of the Second Inaugural, or at least the judgment of one section by another, as opposed to the divine judgment to which all must answer, he could and should have left this sentence out altogether.

The second feature appears four sentences later, immediately after the long question beginning "If we shall suppose that American Slavery is one of those offences" and climbing steadily, through various right-branching segmentations, to the high plateau of sermonic fervor. We should not be surprised that Lincoln's prose made pronounced use of rhyme at this moment, but what many who hear the rhyme may not realize is that the prose suddenly took the metrical shape of a four-line hymn stanza: "Fondly do we hope— / fervently do we pray— / that this mighty scourge of war / may speedily pass away." The model here is what a hymnal would identify as short meter, rhyming *xaya*, and Mary Stanley Bunce Dana's 1840 Presbyterian hymn "Oh, Sing to Me of Heaven" typifies any number of such hymns Lincoln and his hearers might have known and sung: "Oh, sing to me of heaven / When I am called to die, / Singing songs of holy ecstasy, / To waft my soul on high."[61] This breaking into song, and not just song but hymn, marked an extraordinary moment in the Second Inaugural and distinguished it from Lincoln's other major speeches, including the Gettysburg Address, which from start to finish may have been pitched closer to the verse end of the prose spectrum than the later speech, but which as a consequence did not have to travel as far to its heights as the Second Inaugural.

Having reached this rhetorical and auditory high ground, the Second Inaugural did not descend again. By the time he concluded, Lincoln had sounded loudly the call to northern magnanimity and forgiveness, which we can only infer and imagine would have been the hallmarks of Reconstruction if he had lived to oversee it. The final vision here was not of democracy but of peace, and, unlike the vision of the Gettysburg Address, it had no place for the words "dead" or "died." With more than six hundred thousand deaths still accumulating a month from the end of the war, Lincoln resorted to periphrastic roundaboutness in the Second Inaugural, referring to the widow and the orphan of "him who shall have borne the battle," as well as to "every drop of blood drawn with the lash . . . paid by another drawn with the sword," a quaint archaism in the context of a war in which swords did a minute fraction of the killing. But nowhere bluntly did he name the dead as dead. Inaugurating a second presidency, in which war would end and rebuilding would begin, called for different language from one used in dedicating a cemetery while that war continued. At Gettysburg Lincoln not only honored the dead; he also used them to strengthen northern resolve with a vision that attempted to put their deaths in a bearable perspective. On the platform in front of the Capitol, with northern resolve having nearly fulfilled its purpose, he needed to quiet the dead in order to quiet the living.

CHAPTER TWO

Walt Whitman's Real Wars

One of Lincoln's fervent admirers was Walt Whitman, who on the fourteenth anniversary of the president's assassination delivered a lecture he repeated nineteen times between 1879 and 1890.[1] Four years before his inaugural Lincoln lecture, Whitman had published an earlier narrative of the assassination in *Memoranda During the War*, which carried on the cover of at least one copy of its privately printed first edition the gold-lettered words "WALT / WHITMAN'S / MEMORANDA / OF THE WAR / Written on the Spot / in 1863-'65" and showed on its title page the publication date "1875-'76." In the first few pages of Whitman's little book appeared this passage: "Future years will never know the seething hell and the black infernal background of countless minor scenes and interiors, (not the few great battles) of the Secession War; and it is best they should not. In the mushy influences of current times the fervid atmosphere and typical events of those years are in danger of being totally forgotten."[2] As his critical jab at the "mushy influences of current times" clearly reveals, Whitman did not write this prophetic passage on the spot during the years 1863–65. Instead, the tone of this mini-jeremiad suggests that he wrote it in the later 1860s, when he was also working on his sweeping indictments of postwar mushiness in *Democratic Vistas*—the first part of which appeared in 1867—or in the early 1870s. He prepared his *Memoranda* for publication (much of the book first appeared in articles published during 1874 in the *New York Weekly Graphic*) at a moment when the title of Mark Twain and Charles Dudley Warner's *The Gilded Age* (published in 1873 but dated 1874) was giving the "current times" an enduring nickname.

Whitman's lament about the ignorance and amnesia of the future combined with his anger at the present to express a passionate commitment to memory, loyalty, patriotism, and nationalism, about which much remains to be said.[3] But for the moment let us complicate our sense of Whitman's commitment, or his expression of that commitment, by looking at a later version of this same passage, no longer in the first few pages of *Memoranda During the War* but shifted to the last pages of the Civil War section of his autobiographical *Specimen Days & Collect*, published in 1882. In this later version the passage read: "Future years will never know the seething hell and the black infernal background of countless minor scenes and interiors, (not the official surface-courteousness of the Generals, not the few great battles) of the Secession war; it is best they should not—the real war will never get in the books. In the mushy influences of current times, too, the fervid atmosphere and typical events of those years are in danger of being totally forgotten."[4] Although even the minor differences between these two passages—the lowercase "war" and the insertion of "too"—invite productive commentary, let us pass to the two large differences, both of which could point to Whitman's experiences in the late 1870s and early 1880s as also a reader rather than solely a writer of Civil War history. The first large difference, the dismissive reference to "the official surface-courteousness of the Generals," could have reflected Whitman's assessment of any number of recently published works, among them writings by generals for the first numbers of the *Century Illustrated Monthly Magazine*, which began publication in 1881, or the letters and reports of generals collected and published by the U.S. War Department in *The War of the Rebellion: A Compilation of the Official Records of the Union and Confederate Armies*, the first volume of which appeared the year before.

But it is over the second large difference, the insertion of the famous clause "the real war will never get in the books," that I would like to linger, since this often-quoted statement, which appears in many treatments of the Civil War that have little or nothing to do with Whitman, and which recently served as the title for an anthology of Civil War writings by well-known American authors, usually passes unexamined by those who quote it. What does Whitman mean by this provocative, peremptory pronouncement? What can such a statement mean, and what has it come to mean to us? What does it tell us about Whitman's sense of the Civil War or the memory of that war? And what does it tell us about his own little Civil War book, *Memoranda During the War*?

At least one of Whitman's readers argues that Whitman's prophecy has proven to be flat-out wrong: "Contrary to Whitman's famous prediction, the 'real war' would eventually 'get into [*sic*] the books' because historians and writers have learned so much in the twentieth century about unearthing and telling the stories of real people." I take this statement, which comes from David Blight's prize-winning *Race and Reunion* (2001),[5] to be basically an accurate one about the development of historiographic methodologies in the twentieth century, although it tends toward tautology (we represent the real war in books by representing real people's representations of the real war), and it takes at face value the slippery term "real." Admittedly, the dictates of pragmatism, whether historical or philosophical, discourage us from subjecting every word we use to intensive analysis, but since this particular word, "real," and the phrase it inhabits, "real war," necessarily push us toward the heart of any discussion of the Civil War and memory, a little more rigor would seem to be in order.

So let us consider various ways of reading and hearing Whitman's statement. The first might go this way: *the real war will never get in the books because there is no such thing as the real war.* In considering the statement this way, we are free to practice whatever brand of epistemological skepticism we hold dearest, whether a post-structuralist version that derives from Jacques Derrida or an American pragmatic version that derives from Ralph Waldo Emerson or an ancient Greek version that returns us to Democritus, Protagoras, Gorgias, Pyrrho, and others. According to one or more of these views, we could not know the real war or could not communicate our knowledge of it in books or could communicate our knowledge of it in books but only in ways that show the knowledge to depend on language that is itself nothing but an endlessly self-referential construction. Although Whitman had a healthy skeptical streak, as we see in the small poem "Are You the New Person Drawn toward Me?" with the ominous final line "Have you no thought O dreamer that it may be all maya, illusion?," his statement is not that of someone who did not believe in something called "the real war"; it is the statement of someone who did and who associated the real war with seething hells and infernal backgrounds, as well as with countless minor scenes and interiors, which by implication he himself has witnessed.[6] Furthermore, if all Whitman meant by his famous statement is that he did not believe that we could know anything to be real, he would perhaps have been saying something profound about human existence but also at some point something rather trivial about the Civil War as a particular instance of human existence.

A second way of reading and hearing Whitman's pronouncement would assume that in fact there is such a thing as the real war, and it would go something like this: *the real war will never get in the books because it is too huge and cannot be contained in any one book and will still exceed all the books we might ever write.* According to this view, which I admit comes closer to my own than the extremely skeptical one, the real war consists of nothing less than every event, thought, feeling, or trace in perception, imagination, memory, writing, photography, painting, drawing, music, monumental sculpture, ceremonial commemoration, reenactment, artifactual materiality, landscape, and the environment leading up to and away from the years 1861 to 1865, and only a limitless, omniscient repository could contain it all. The corollary of this view would be that all books about the war, as well as a good many others not explicitly about it, whether good or bad, earnestly truth-telling or deliberately falsifying, contain some metaphysically charged particle of the real war. Ontologically dazzling as such a notion may be, and welcome as it may be to those of us still deeply engaged in writing books about the war, this way of reading and hearing Whitman's statement, by expanding it to include so much, eventually dilutes and also trivializes it.

A third possible reading, a much more specific and less comprehensive one, takes its cue from the clause to which Whitman attached his statement about the real war, the clause "and it is best they should not," referring to future years never knowing the real war. Read or heard this way, Whitman's statement would seem to refer to the tastes and mores prevailing among writers, publishers, and readers in the United States in the late nineteenth century, as though he were saying the real war was rated X, whether for violence or obscenity or thoughts and emotions too hard to reconcile with loyalty, patriotism, and nationalism, so it is best for the mushy, timid, squeamish future that it stick to books about the war rated G or perhaps PG. If Whitman meant something along these lines, his readers might recognize the analogy between his sense of something hidden and unspeakable about the war, on the one hand, and something hidden and unspeakable about his own sexuality, on the other. For whatever reason or reasons, Whitman would have been making an elaborate show of protecting his vulnerable readers from truths he implied they could not bear at the same time that he unmistakably announced the existence of such truths. This way of reading or hearing Whitman's statement does not exclude either of the two already mentioned, but it does justify David Blight's contradiction of that statement. Since the second half of the nineteenth century, the tastes and mores of writers, publishers, and readers have changed considerably, and especially after the wars of the twentieth century, we are much more grimly aware of seething hells and infernal backgrounds in war than Whitman's readers were, and we are much more likely to write and read books testifying to that awareness.

Whitman's famous statement may have meant and continue to mean all these things and more at different times, both to him and to his readers, but in moving now to the heart of the matter for this discussion, I want to suggest one last possibility, which again does not necessarily exclude any of those already discussed. To hear this possibility we need to imagine momentarily shifting rhetorical emphasis from "the *real* war will never get in the books," where most quotations of the statement seem to place it, to "the real war will never get in the *books*," as opposed, say, to the photographs, in which so many early viewers naively believed the real war could be gotten. In other words, what happens when we begin to listen to Whitman's statement not as one about the Civil War, and its real or unreal versions, but as a writer's statement about books and bookmaking? On one level, this reading once again would seem to trivialize Whitman's statement, since, after all, very little that is real gets in books because books are mostly abstracted representations of reality. When they talk about food, they do not serve food one can really eat. When they talk about rain, they do not cause rain to fall on ground that needs it. When they talk about war, they do not maneuver armies and fight battles and bury the dead and hospitalize the wounded.

On another level, both for Whitman and for all subsequent makers of books about the Civil War, this is precisely the point. Since no book includes real war, how does one go about making a book that most persuasively appears to include real war? What are the rhetorical conventions of sentence- and paragraph-building, argument-arranging, evidence-presenting, and conclusion-drawing that mark one book's verbal abstraction of war as more authentic than another's? To what extent do these conventions vary with specific genres, differentiating the poem from the novel, from the memoir, from the doctoral dissertation in Civil War history, and to what extent do the conventions transcend generic boundaries? In the remainder of this discussion what I am going to be arguing is that in *Memoranda During the War* Walt Whitman carried out various prose experiments in writing Civil War history; that those experiments had as their common aim the production of an illusion or appearance of reality; that, despite several failures, at many moments in *Memoranda* his experiments were and still are powerfully successful; that his statement about the real war not getting in the books was disingenuous when it came to his own, in which he developed, if not pioneered, new verbal conventions for representing real war; and that at least two of the conventions he developed still characterize much Civil War historiography and by extension many of the ways in which the Civil War gets remembered in writing.

The first convention that marked Whitman's attempts at representing real war was neither one he pioneered nor one that characterizes professional Civil War historiography, and that is the convention of prominent first-person narration that tends repeatedly toward self-referentiality and self-description. Consider this parenthetical insertion, which appeared almost a quarter of the way into *Memoranda*:

> (In my visits to the Hospitals I found it was in the simple
> matter of Personal Presence, and emanating ordinary
> cheer and magnetism, that I succeeded and help'd more
> than by medical nursing, or delicacies, or gifts of money, or
> anything else. During the war I possess'd the perfection of
> physical health. My habit, when practicable, was to prepare
> for starting out on one of those daily or nightly tours, of
> from a couple to four or five hours, by fortifying myself with
> previous rest, the bath, clean clothes, a good meal, and as
> cheerful an appearance as possible.) (18; 30)

In subsequently transposing this paragraph to *Specimen Days*, Whitman decided to drop the parentheses and give this casual aside, first inserted after a paragraph describing the wounds and death of Amer Moore, Second U.S. Artillery, the distinction of its own section and title, "My Preparation for Visits" (*PW*, 51–52).

This paragraph, which we can use to label what we might call Whitman's convention of personal presence, belongs to the genre of autobiography, a term that, according to the *Oxford English Dictionary*, the poet Robert Southey coined in 1809. That this term for "the writing of one's own history" should have appeared in English during the heyday of Romanticism, when exaltation of the individual self and its imagination was the order of the day, makes perfect sense and perhaps confirms the worst suspicions of those inclined to roll their eyes at what they think of as Whitman's insufferable Romantic egotism. After all, they might argue, how can we take seriously the history of someone who constantly shifted the focus from the war he wanted to depict to himself and his own personal habits? For that matter, how can we excuse the bad taste of someone who allowed descriptions of his ablutions, sartorial regimen, and diet to intrude on our response to a description of a young man shot in the head and paralyzed from the waist down?

For Whitman, representing the real war and representing himself remained inseparable through *Memoranda During the War*, and their inseparability produced many extraordinary moments, such as the one in a section dated "Aug. 12" (1863) in which he described seeing Lincoln "almost every day" (22; 39) and then gave us this memorable pair of sentences: "They pass'd me once very close, and I saw the President in the face fully, as they were moving slow, and his look, though abstracted, happen'd to be directed steadily in my eye. He bow'd and smiled, but far beneath his smile I noticed well the expression I have alluded to" (24; 41). Of course it was not just Lincoln's gaze that looked into Whitman's eye but the reader's as well, so that a passage about Lincoln ended up being a passage about Lincoln's wordless connection with Whitman, our narrator.

Whitman's insistence on his own personal presence also emerged in second-person addresses to his "Reader dear" (32; 56) and in his experiments with second-person pronouns more generally, of which sections called "An Army Hospital Ward" and "Death of a Wisconsin Officer" offered prime examples. In these sections, which are not, in my opinion, among the most effective in *Memoranda*, though they are not the worst failures either, Whitman cast himself in the role of guide, playing Virgil to our Dante, as he led readers into the other world of the hospitalized wounded: "Let me specialize a visit I made. . . . Let us go into Ward 6. . . . You walk down the central passage. . . . You may hear groans. . . . Look at the fine large frames. . . . Look at the patient and mute manner of our American wounded, as they lie in such a sad collection" (11–12; 18–19; ellipses added). This kind of stagy presentation had affinities with both fiction and nineteenth-century journalism, two other genres Whitman worked in, the latter much more than the former, and it clearly demonstrated an attempt to authenticate his narrative by, first, appearing to take the reader with him into a zone traveled only by authorized personnel and, second, establishing his authority as a guide on whom a subordinate reader depended. In experimenting with this approach, Whitman exploited one of the grammatical distinctions of English, as opposed to French or German, because in English the second-person pronoun "you" does double duty, meaning both "you" and "one," the latter quickly shading toward "I," so that "one walks down the central passage" really means "I walk down the central passage." In these second-person experiments Whitman not so subtly manipulated these multiple possibilities to lead his reader toward his own loyal, patriotic, and nationalist affirmation of the special qualities of "our American wounded."

Before we dismiss the convention of personal presence as, among other things, altogether different from the current procedures of Civil War historiography, we would do well to remember a few points. One is that the classical antecedents of historical writing show how in the beginning autobiography and history often had much in common, as many moments in, for example, Xenophon's *Anabasis* make abundantly clear. Although he talked about himself in the third person, Xenophon's story of the fifteen hundred–mile retreat after the Battle of Cunaxa in 401 B.C. was also in fact the story of Xenophon himself, after he had been chosen to lead the march from Persia. A second point is that although a dissertation committee would be likely to take a dim view of work that included many passages like the one in which Whitman talked about bathing and dressing and eating before he went to the hospitals, it is also true that at least one recent version of Civil War memory, Tony Horwitz's popular *Confederates in the Attic* (1998), depended heavily on the convention of personal presence, using first-person pronouns on nearly every page.

But it is a third point that bears most directly on the discussion at hand. To judge Whitman's experiments with the convention of personal presence harshly is to forget how closely we now identify the personal with the real. Personal details, personal revelations, personal anecdotes: the high value we put on these phenomena, on their power to establish the real texture of a particular narrative, reflects the converging legacies of the Reformation, the

Enlightenment, Romanticism, and, most recently, psychoanalysis. Although extensive talk about oneself would amount to unprofessional behavior in writing about the Civil War now, we have little use, as either scholars or general readers, for narratives of the war in which personal details, about civilians or combatants, are absent. David Blight's contradiction of Whitman confirms this point. During the twentieth century writers of history got much better at telling the real stories of real people, or, to put it another way, the personal stories of people who did not make headlines. Although they did not necessarily need Whitman's example to make this improvement, we can test the power Whitman generated by means of the personal, in ways that anticipate much to come in the twentieth century, by considering a passage from *Memoranda* in which the personal is absent:

> Such, amid the woods, that scene of flitting souls—amid the crack and crash and yelling sounds—the impalpable perfume of the woods—and yet the pungent, stifling smoke—shed with the radiance of the moon, the round, maternal queen, looking from heaven at intervals so placid—the sky so heavenly—the clear-obscure up there, those buoyant upper oceans—a few large placid stars beyond, coming out and then disappearing—the melancholy, draperied night above, around....... [*sic*] And there, upon the roads, the fields, and in those woods, that contest, never one more desperate in any age or land—both parties now in force—masses—no fancy battle, no semi-play, but fierce and savage demons fighting there—courage and scorn of death the rule, exceptions almost none. (15; 25)

This highly wrought paragraph, which consists of nothing but grammatical fragments lacking a main verb to produce a single complete sentence, appeared in a section headed "May 12—A Night Battle, over a week since." Whitman opened this section, which runs more than three pages, by recurring to a by-now familiar theme: "We already talk of Histories of the War, (presently to accumulate)—yes—technical histories of some things, statistics, official reports, and so on—but shall we ever get histories of the *real* things?" (13; 22). Dropped in the version of "A Night Battle" published in *Specimen Days* (*PW*, 45), this questioning sentence appears to have been the ancestor of the famous clause about the real war never getting in the books.[7] The italicizing of "real" signaled the charge this question had for Whitman, and after one of his idiosyncratic seven-dot ellipses, he implicitly proceeded to answer the question by undertaking the narration of "part of the late battle of Chancellorsville," narration that included the paragraph above.[8]

A recent commentator, writing for the *New Republic*, found this paragraph quite moving: "Why did such scenes cut me so deeply?" she mused after quoting the version from *Specimen Days* through "draperied night above, around," a version that dropped the initial "Such" and "the round, maternal queen," while inserting "silently and languidly" between "coming" and "out."[9] The answers to her question, which arose in the course of thoughts about the beautiful weather in New York on September 11, 2001, could be many, but they could not include the reality or authenticity of Whitman's account of the night battle at Chancellorsville. Although scholars and critics of Whitman have let the accuracy of this account pass unexamined, his narration of the night of May 2, 1863, substituted nothing but well-worn literary conventions for the authenticity of personally witnessed scenes, and as a result it still falls embarrassingly short of written representation worthy of the real war.[10]

To begin with, Whitman's account showed a very dim grasp of who did what where at Chancellorsville.[11] True, even many participants in the battle would still have had a similarly dim grasp only a week afterward, but they presumably would have known to which units they belonged and whether or not they were involved in combat. Among Whitman's more glaring errors, which he had more than ten years to correct and which may have come from garbled newspaper reports or his own imperfect listening to soldiers' stories, on which he often relied, were the location of divisions of Sedgwick's Sixth Corps in burning woods around Chancellorsville on May 2 (14; 24), when in fact Sedgwick's Corps was still at Fredericksburg, and the assignment to the Second Division of the Third Corps, led, according to Whitman, by "Hooker himself" (15; 26), of an advance actually carried out by David Birney's First Division. Whitman also showed no sense of the limited scale of Birney's advance, which resulted in 196 casualties, many of them from friendly fire (an unpleasant detail Whitman did not mention in "A Night Battle" or anywhere else in *Memoranda*). Although Whitman insisted the midnight attack planned by Third Corps general Dan Sickles, who went unnamed in "A Night Battle," was "quite a general engagement" (14; 23) with "both parties now in force" (15; 25), in fact it was evidently small enough to pass unnoticed by Edward Porter Alexander, who was on the spot "hunting out our line of battle in the woods from the extreme right to the extreme left" and whose account of Whitman's night battle occupied only two sentences: "Several times during the night there occurred false alarms on the enemy's line. There would be a musket shot or two, & then several, & then whole brigades would fire tremendous volleys in our direction, & I would get behind a tree & wait for them to quiet down."[12]

The one detail that Whitman got right, and the one that obviously enchanted him in the writing of his account, was the detail about a large moon casting bright light over Chancellorsville on the night of May 2.[13] Alexander noted the moonlight, too, as did many other participants in the battle. But although the moonlight may have been a real feature of the battle of Chancellorsville, where its efficacy in the thick woods of the Wilderness remains doubtful, it proved to be the undoing of Whitman's attempt at writing the history of "real things," since it seduced him into the stock literary conventions and motifs of romance and sentimentality. That such conventions and motifs were operating with little restraint in Whitman's account shows clearly in his use of one of the stalest images in poetic treatments of battle, that of blood on grass: "the red life-blood oozing out from heads or trunks or limbs upon that green and dew-cool grass" (14; 24). Of many contemporary examples of the same image, let one, housed in an iambic tetrameter couplet from Mary Hunt McCaleb's *Lenare: A Story of the Southern Revolution, and Other Poems* (1866), suffice: "Their rigid forms now cold in death, / Their hearts' blood crimsoning the heath."[14] Even if Whitman had invented this image, however, it still betrayed ignorance of the distinct conditions of flora in the Wilderness, or of woods in general, since grass has a hard time growing where dense second-growth forest dominates.

Returning to the paragraph above, which has moved at least one reader so deeply, we can use manuscript evidence and our own ears to confirm that the only reality present in Whitman's account was the reality of poetic form. In its autograph manuscript version the sentence that became "Such, amid the woods, that scene of flitting souls—amid the crack and crash and yelling sounds" reads, "And that was war, and such its scene of flitting souls that night, that beauteous gorgeous night." Recast into lines and formatted like a poem, this sentence reads as perfectly regular iambic verse many people would not associate with the founding father of American free verse:

> And *that* was *war*, and *such* its *scene*
> Of *flit*ting *souls* that *night*,
> That *beaut*eous *gorg*eous *night*.[15]

The iambic imperative governs the final version as well, both in *Memoranda* and in *Specimen Days*. And that was war? Probably not. But it was certainly Whitman's literary substitute for war when he had nothing personal to go on. The literary fraud of "A Night Battle" then culminated in a fulsome fantasy about the death of an unknown soldier, "the Bravest Soldier," who crawled off to die in a secluded spot, undiscovered by burial squads (16; 27), a fantasy quite likely inspired by that other notorious fraud on the same subject, Alexander Gardner's fictional caption about the staged photograph subsequently published in *Gardner's Photographic Sketch Book of the Civil War* (1866) as "Home of a Rebel Sharpshooter, Gettysburg, July 1863," a photograph in a book Whitman, given his love of the new medium, most likely would have known.[16]

Painful as it is for those who admire Whitman to acknowledge the fraud of "A Night Battle," especially when he himself presented it as his contribution to histories of real things, doing so clears the way for describing the genuine achievements of *Memoranda*, achievements that anticipated much we now take for granted in the writing of Civil War history and the perpetuation of Civil War memory. Having considered Whitman's convention of personal presence, I want to focus the rest of this discussion on two additional features of his method, beginning with that of representing the war from the bottom up rather than the top down. We have already noted the dismissive references to "the official surface-courteousness of the Generals" and "technical histories of some things, statistics, official reports, and so on," but now we can consider Whitman's alternative to such things. As though reacting against his own excesses, he immediately followed "A Night Battle" with the names (or initials) of specific men and their conditions, beginning with "Thomas Haley, Co. M, Fourth New York Cavalry—a regular Irish boy" and continuing through Amer Moore, who preceded Whitman's self-description in what became "My Preparation for Visits." Along the way we come upon this passage:

> In one bed a young man, Marcus Small, Co. K, Seventh
> Maine—sick with dysentery and typhoid fever—pretty
> critical, too—I talk with him often—he thinks he will
> die—looks like it indeed. I write a letter for him home to
> East Livermore, Maine—I let him talk to me a little, but
> not much, advise him to keep very quiet—do most of the
> talking myself—stay quite a while with him, as he holds on
> to my hand—talk to him in a cheering, but slow, low, and
> measured manner, talk about his furlough, and going home
> as soon as he is able to travel. (17; 29)

Although the authority of personal witness and presence informed this passage, we should guard against naively accepting it as nothing but raw material "written on the spot." Compared to the stylistic excesses of "A Night Battle," the simple, informal, understated rhetoric has the trustworthy sound of ordinary reality, but in fact this low-voltage style also represented a verbal experiment, one that succeeded where the other failed. What Whitman actually wrote in his notebook, and whether or not he wrote it at Small's bedside or sometime after this visit we cannot know, was this: "ward C bed 25 Marcus M Small co K 7th Maine Cynthia C Small East Livermore Androscoggin co Maine Sept 17) father Dr Wm B Small took sick about 4 weeks in reg hos—has diarrhea."[17] Somehow the diarrhea mentioned in the notebook entry worsened into dysentery and typhoid fever in the *Memoranda* passage, which focused on Whitman's ministrations to the Maine soldier, among them his sustaining of the fiction that Small would recover and return home, when, according to both patient and visitor, the death of the former looked much more likely. Particularly noteworthy here is the description contained in "talk to him in a cheering, but slow, low, and measured manner," a description both of Whitman's self-consciously adopted verbal manner with Small and, by implication, of his self-consciously adopted manner with his reader, for whom he slowed and measured his language with commas, rhyme, and alliteration.

To argue that even Whitman's most real representations of the real war also involved verbal tailoring is not really the point, however. Anyone who has ever written a second draft of any representation of reality has also tailored that reality. Instead, the point is that Whitman's experiment in the passage about Marcus Small involved not simply the presentation of some details and the withholding of others, or not simply the mannered measuring of sentences and parts of sentences; it involved the selection of such a passage at all, a passage that surely anticipated, if I read him correctly, what David Blight calls "telling the stories of real people." Marcus Small? A real person with real parents, a real hometown, a real company and regiment, a real bed, and real illness. His story? That he thought he would die, that he looked "pretty critical," that he could not write a letter home for himself, that Whitman visited and talked with him. What Whitman left unsaid here was an assumption that he would have shared with Blight: telling the story of this real person in a single short paragraph is as much a part of getting the real war in a book as telling the story of a night battle at Chancellorsville, which the writer never witnessed. In fact, considering that the story of the night battle at Chancellorsville was the only one of its kind in *Memoranda* (unless we include the extended account of Lincoln's assassination, which Whitman did not witness either), whereas passages like the one about Marcus Small recur throughout, we may reasonably conclude Whitman came to believe that getting the real war in a book depended more heavily on telling the stories of real people than on imagining battle descriptions.

Whitman was not the only person who told the stories of real people between the 1860s and the 1870s or 1880s, when the generals began publishing so many stories told from the top. Much to Whitman's chagrin, Louisa May Alcott anticipated him with her *Hospital Sketches*, published in 1863, and Sam Watkins, subsequently the representative Confederate private for Ken Burns's acclaimed documentary *The Civil War* (1990), obviously shared a commitment to telling the stories of real people in *"Co. Aytch": A Side Show of the Big Show*, based on newspaper articles that appeared in 1881 and 1882. But what distinguishes Whitman from these two examples, and what marks him as a pioneer in the formation of Civil War memory, was his refusal to accept that the stories he told were merely sideshows of the big show. Whether that refusal merely confirmed his egotism or instead reflected a radically innovative reassessment of what Civil War history was and what Civil War historiography should do, the fact remains that any subsequent historian who has worked under the assumption that getting the real war in books necessitates focusing also on black soldiers or common white soldiers or enslaved army servants or plantation mistresses or small farmers or female factory workers or members of various immigrant or ethnic groups in different roles and capacities follows Whitman and extends his method.

To be sure, Whitman's experimentation included hedges and disclaimers that occasionally sound like Watkins, as when the former suggested, "The present Memoranda may furnish a few stray glimpses in that life and into those lurid interiors of the period, never to be fully convey'd to the future" (5; 7), and the latter echoed, "I only give a few sketches and incidents that came under the observation of a 'high private' in the rear ranks of the rebel army."[18] A few stray glimpses, a few sketches and incidents, nothing too comprehensive or ambitious. But then Whitman also could make statements that neither Alcott nor Watkins ever would have, statements such as "I now doubt whether one can get a fair idea of what this War practically is, or what genuine America is, and her character, without some such experience as this I am having" (25; 43). Contemporary Civil War historians may wince at the notion of something called "genuine America," but the general trend of their work since the Civil War centennial shows that the collective activity of representing the war, and of publishing those representations, confirms Whitman's doubt that we can afford to dispense with the stray glimpses of individuals in our efforts to arrive at some sense of what the war practically was.

We have seen that Whitman's *Memoranda During the War* experimented with the convention of personal presence. We have seen that his achievement in the book relied in part on the convention of opposing the top-down narrations of courteous generals, in ever-widening circulation, with the bottom-up narrations of ordinary people, people whose importance to the writing of Civil War history he asserted with a strenuous outspokenness ahead of his time. Now let us turn finally to another convention, that of claiming to represent the general with the particular. As we can quickly appreciate, this convention follows closely from the previous one, since it is a very short step from saying the real war involves the lives of ordinary people to saying this particular ordinary person represents ordinary people in general. Many of Whitman's best readers have recognized that *Memoranda* took as one of its central concerns the problem of how to represent the war, which some then abstract into the problem of how to represent in general. In the process of this abstraction, a few have argued that Whitman carried out his representation by substituting the part for the whole, a rhetorical move that literary people call synecdoche.[19] But this description of Whitman's practice is not quite adequate. In substituting "head" for a bovine in the phrase "two hundred head of cattle," one is substituting a significant part of that bovine for the whole creature, who will not be going anywhere without its head. But when Whitman "specialize[d]" (11; 18) one of the soldiers he visited, Thomas Haley or Amer Moore or Marcus Small, it did not necessarily follow that this specimen soldier was truly representative.

This, of course, is the point. Although Whitman would have liked to convince us that a given "specimen"—which comes from the Latin verb *specere*, meaning "to look at," and claims etymological kinship with "spectacle" and "spectacles"—was a true synecdoche, a true substitution of a representative, important part for the whole, in fact his spectacles may have been, if not rose-colored, then certainly tinted red, white, and blue. When he claimed that "the Common People" were "emblemised in thousands of specimens of first-class Heroism" (4; 5–6), or when he described a soldier as "a typic one" (16; 27), he was not merely substituting a recognizable part for the whole, such as "head" for the bovine attached to it. Instead, he was urging his readers to accept a given sample as emblematic or typical. Such urging belongs to the realm of argument, if not propaganda, rather than to the realm of rhetorical substitution practiced by poets and orators. Without doubt the armies of both North and South included thousands of specimens of first-class heroism, for example. But without doubt they also included thousands of specimens of cowardice, and yet in his imaginative account of the night battle at Chancellorsville Whitman himself told his readers that he chose to ignore these: "(We hear of some poor fighting, episodes, skedaddling on our part. I think not of it. I think of the fierce bravery, the general rule)" (14; 23).

What is "the general rule"? How does it relate to the "real" war? At this point established conventions of selective remembering, along with contested definitions and expressions of loyalty, patriotism, and nationalism, come sharply into the foreground. In the course of *Memoranda During the War* Whitman made some sweeping statements on the basis of the specimen soldiers he visited and described, statements such as, "It may have been odd, but I never before so realized the majesty and reality of the American common people proper," and this realization "fell upon me like a great awe" (29; 50–51). Even more extreme, especially coming from a man who never left North America, was the unsettling pronouncement he encased in parentheses, "(The Americans are the handsomest race that ever trod the earth)" (52; 93). Other readers of *Memoranda* have commented on the reconciliationist impulse of the book, as Whitman was careful to include both white northerners and white southerners under the heading "American," but none, to my knowledge, has pointed out Whitman's deliberate tampering with his specimens, his suppression of certain samples in order to produce his emblems and types of what he calls the general rule.

In the closing pages of *Memoranda*, before the lengthy notes that followed, Whitman summarized his experiences in the Washington hospitals with some statistics: "During my past three years in Hospital, camp or field, I made over 600 visits or tours, and went, as I estimate, among from 80,000 to 100,000 of the wounded and sick, as sustainer of spirit and body in some degree, in time of need" (55–56; 100–101). He also claimed that he went among "the black soldiers, wounded or sick, and in the contraband camps" (56; 101). It is not clear if these visits or tours among black soldiers were included in the total of six hundred, but what is clear is that Whitman's list of hospitals—Finley, Campbell, Carver, Lincoln, Emory, Harewood, Mount Pleasant, Armory Square, Judiciary (27; 46–47)—did not include, for example, the L'Ouverture Hospital for black soldiers, located in Alexandria, despite his claim, "I am in the habit of going to all, and to Fairfax Seminary, Alexandria" (26; 45). More to the point, even if Whitman did visit black soldiers in L'Ouverture Hospital, he did not give his readers a single specimen of a black soldier anywhere in *Memoranda*. This omission should not come as a large surprise to anyone familiar with Whitman's views on race, which tended to reflect his identification with white workingmen in Brooklyn and Manhattan and led him to decry slavery on economic grounds, rather than on moral or spiritual ones. For Whitman the chief evil of slavery lay in the competition of black slave labor with white wage labor, not in any philosophical problems it posed.[20] Given this view, many will find the exclusion of black soldiers from Whitman's specimens predictable.

More surprising is his treatment of foreigners fighting in the Civil War. To make the arithmetic easy, we can take Whitman's upper estimate of a hundred thousand soldiers visited and calculate that if 90 percent of these were Union and 10 percent Confederate, then he should have encountered approximately twenty-two thousand foreigners fighting for the North and a thousand fighting for the South.[21] Even if he encountered a higher percentage of Confederates, and consequently fewer foreigners, the arithmetic still suggests that he would have visited thousands and thousands of foreign-born men, and yet *Memoranda* is conspicuously lacking in specimens of them. At one point early in the book, Whitman confronted this issue head-on, claiming that the soldiers were "far more American than is generally supposed—I should say nine-tenths are native born" (18; 31). Although much closer to true for the Confederate army than the Union, even this low estimate would yield visits with eight to ten thousand foreigners, only one of whom appears among his "typic" soldiers. In the first few pages we encounter "M. de F., of the Seventeenth Connecticut," who is "an intelligent looking man, has a foreign accent, black-eyed and hair'd, a Hebraic appearance" (9; 14). But this soldier, identified elsewhere as Maximilian de Fisheur, turns out to be a lone exception to the general rule of *Memoranda*, depending on whether we read Thomas Haley, described as "a regular Irish boy" (16; 27), as Irish-born or of Irish descent.[22] All we have to do is listen to the last names of other soldiers mentioned in Whitman's published works—Holmes, Giles, Lilly, Boardman, Haskell, Wilber, Miller, Mahay, Monk, Elliott, Brooks, Smith, Sawyer, Cunningham, Farwell, Babbitt, Byrd, Morgan, Williams—and to consider the omission of, for example, Henry Thurer ("Wants to see a German Lutheran clergyman") and John Grundke ("German") to hear that for Whitman the general rule of specimen cases tended to include white soldiers of Anglo-Irish-Scottish descent and exclude others.

Although we might feel considerable dismay at the manipulation behind Whitman's would-be synecdoches, we should be careful not to settle for pointing out the mote in his method while ignoring the beam in our own. If no historical writer can get all of the real war in a book, it follows that all books about the war, even the most ambitiously comprehensive, must proceed by a method of sampling bits and pieces of its reality. Some of these samplings acknowledge their incompleteness straightforwardly, as Sam Watkins's book did, although that book also contained enough irony to make readers suspect that its author had a higher opinion of his "few sketches and incidents" than he let on. But other books, though they necessarily proceed by sampling, adopt a much different strategy and proceed not merely by sampling but by making large claims for the significance of a particular sample, the representativeness of that sample, the contribution of this sample to an understanding of the real war. In other words, they follow Whitman rather than Watkins.[23]

Well of course they do, the response might go; how could they do otherwise? But this question simply reveals the extent to which Whitman's method, which writes from the bottom up while making large claims about the real war based on the asserted representativeness of a particular sampling or specimen of the war, has become naturalized into invisibility by subsequent Civil War historiography, especially in the latter part of the twentieth century. As a matter of fact, books about the war could proceed in many different ways. They could, for example, make no large claims at all, simply presenting instead their specimens, as photographs without captions do. They could abandon the rhetoric of argument and persuasion, along with theses to support, evidence to interpret, conversations to summarize and intervene in. What would such books look like? How would they fit into our picture of professional historiography? Would they no longer be books at all? Would these alternatives quickly move us beyond the technology of printed books into the realm of electronic archives and digital projects? The answers to such questions are not immediately apparent or conclusive.

What is apparent is that despite what he said about the relation of real war to books, Whitman developed a method of representing the war that many subsequent books employ. To say that these subsequent books follow Whitman is not to make a claim about the influence of *Memoranda During the War* on later writers, not to use "follow" in the sense of what disciples do in relation to their master. Since Whitman's book appeared in a very limited, privately printed first edition, such a claim would be irresponsible. It is unlikely he had many followers among the first members of the American Historical Association, founded a few years after the publication of *Memoranda*. But to say that much subsequent Civil War historiography, particularly the kind that focuses on telling the real stories of real people, as opposed to the general-centered narratives Whitman criticized in his little book, follows him in another sense is to make a claim about the history of Civil War history, and through that history a claim about Civil War memory. It is to say that before Whitman published his articles, the first of which appeared in the *New York Times* in February 1863 (*PW* 296), and then his little book about the war, people writing about the wartime lives of those who were not generals, whether they wrote in letters or diaries or newspapers, did not make the same large claim Whitman made in the same large way in which he made it, often implicitly, sometimes explicitly, the claim that my story and the stories of people around me are as real a part of the real war as any general's story. Some might wish for Whitman to be more humble, especially those unfamiliar with "Song of Myself" and other poems in *Leaves of Grass* (1855; 1891–92), but few twenty-first-century students of the Civil War now would say he was wrong. Humble or not, he got there first, and establishing an accurate history of the artistry of Civil War history requires saying so.

CHAPTER THREE

Sherman the Writer

You know Eisenhower has a hell of a good head and is a fine man.
Many mistakes last summer and fall but a good man and a fairly good
general. Bradley a much better General I think probably as good as
Sherman. Patton, if not such an impossible histrionic character and
an unmitigated liar is an excellent General officer. It will be fun to read
the shit that will come out after this war when they all publish their
memoirs. It will be fun and it will not be fun too.
—*Ernest Hemingway to Maxwell Perkins, July 23, 1945[1]*

To open *Memoirs of General William T. Sherman*, "Written by
Himself," as the cover of the 1875 first edition announced, is to
take a seat in a verbal theater. This formulation has special relevance in the case of Sherman, whose passion for theater began
in New York in June 1836, when he, then sixteen, was traveling
to begin his study at West Point and attended his first plays and
concerts.[2] Edmund Wilson, in his chapter on Sherman in *Patriotic
Gore* (1962), published during the Civil War centennial and the
first major study to identify the *Memoirs* as "literature," borrowed
from Lloyd Lewis's biography, *Sherman, Fighting Prophet* (1932),
a story of Sherman's persuading Ulysses S. Grant and two other
officers to attend a performance of *Hamlet* in Nashville in 1863.
During the performance Sherman became so disgusted by the bad
production of Shakespeare's play, lines from which he quoted in a
letter written to J. A. Rawlins earlier the same year and included
in the Vicksburg chapter of the *Memoirs*, that he erupted into
loud complaints, obliging Grant to make the party leave before the

performance ended.[3] After the war, when newly elected President Grant asked Sherman, who succeeded him as general-in-chief of the army, "Sherman, what special hobby do you intend to adopt?," in order to preempt newspaper reporters' inventions of anything "less acceptable," Sherman answered that he "would stick to 'theatre and balls'" (*Memoirs*, 928–29).

While Sherman's love of theater provided him with an acceptable hobby, one that afforded him many hours of pleasurable distraction and relief from the turbulence of his eventful and exhausting life, it also helped to shape his sense of himself, both as a man dedicated to an active life of service and as a writer deliberately crafting a narrative of that life. For the 1886 second edition of the *Memoirs*, Sherman added two new chapters, a first and a last, framing his original memoir with a prologue and an epilogue. The latter ended Sherman's thousand-page narrative with this revealing paragraph:

> This I construe as the end of my military career. In looking back upon the past I can only say, with millions of others, that I have done many things I should not have done, and have left undone still more which ought to have been done; that I can see where hundreds of opportunities have been neglected, but on the whole am content; and feel sure that I can travel this broad country of ours, and be each night the welcome guest in palace or cabin; and, as
>
> > "all the world's a stage,
> > And all the men and women merely players,"
>
> I claim the privilege to ring down the curtain.
> (*Memoirs*, 955)

In this moment of dramatic closure Sherman identified himself primarily as retiring soldier, forgoing any final references to his other careers as surveyor, banker, lawyer, professor of engineering, superintendent of Louisiana State Seminary, and street railway president. With his quotation of the melancholy Jaques in the Forest of Arden in *As You Like It* (II.vii.139–40)—*1 Henry IV*, *Macbeth*, and *Hamlet* are the other Shakespearean plays quoted or alluded to in the *Memoirs*—Sherman in turn appeared to concede that even the illustrious career of a famous soldier did not distinguish him essentially from any actor temporarily performing a part, making exits and entrances, moving through the seven acts or ages of life, including, fittingly enough, the soldier's, "Seeking the bubble reputation / Even in the cannon's mouth" (II.vii.152–53).

This closing identification of himself as soldier with himself as actor echoed a phrase he had published a decade earlier in the first edition and subsequently retained in the chapter titled "Capture of Atlanta." Describing there the "angry correspondence" between himself and Confederate general John Bell Hood about the victor's controversial order to evacuate the citizens of Atlanta, Sherman explained his publication of that correspondence "as illustrative of the events referred to, and of the feelings of the actors in the game of war at that particular crisis" (*Memoirs*, 585–86). References to war as a game recur throughout the *Memoirs* (for example, in a letter to Grant dated September 20, 1864, which appeared two pages later), and here Sherman mixed in the theatrical metaphor for good measure.

In addition to soldier and actor, at least two other identities suggested themselves in the final paragraph of the 1886 *Memoirs*. One is that of Sherman the traveler, confident of welcome in many a palace or cabin across the United States; the role of travel in shaping the *Memoirs* will return shortly. The other is that of a religious penitent confessing things done and left undone, a familiar formula originating in Matthew 23:23: "Woe unto you, scribes and Pharisees, hypocrites! for ye pay tithe of mint and anise and cummin, and have omitted the weightier matters of the law, judgment, mercy, and faith; these ought ye to have done, and not to leave the other undone" (King James Version). Along with quotations from Shakespeare, the *Memoirs* included quotations from the Bible, as in the case of Sherman's turn to Luke 3:14 when asserting, in what was the final chapter of the first edition, that "the soldier must be trained to obedience, and should be 'content with his wages'" (*Memoirs*, 879). But Sherman's ambivalence toward the Catholicism of his wife, Ellen, and his bitter disappointment when his son, Thomas, chose, in March 1878, the Jesuit priesthood over the practice of law, shaded the closing echo of the confession with irony, conscious or unconscious.

By contrast, irony does not appear to complicate the power Sherman claimed for himself in the final line of the *Memoirs*: "I claim the privilege to ring down the curtain." One might reasonably question the logic of his transition from conceding himself a mere player on the world stage to claiming for himself the privilege to decide when the play should end, but one cannot reasonably doubt the implications. In the *Memoirs* Sherman was leading actor, director, playwright, and theater-manager all in one. Furthermore, various aspects of the *Memoirs*, both in their published editions and in the manuscript drafts housed in the Library of Congress, suggest that he carried out these combined functions deliberately, self-consciously, and with a highly developed aesthetic sense of artistry.

This last statement may make some, or many, uncomfortable. Understandably, the bulk of published work that has discussed Sherman's *Memoirs* has done so in the service of biography or historiography, using the general's narrative as documentary evidence. In the context of such documentary uses, considerations of Sherman's artistry might well seem not only out of place, but possibly frivolous and even unethical. Savoring the niceties of theatricality, quotation, tone, rhetorical mode, point of view, or narrative structure has no place, the argument would go, in examining a record of events that cost hundreds of thousands of people their lives and millions the sound minds and bodies they had as of early 1861. Furthermore, this line of thinking could continue, considerations of Sherman as a writer become even more troubling because he was not only a participant in the destructiveness of the Civil War (never capitalized in the *Memoirs*); he was the architect and engineer of much of that destructiveness.

To argue this way, or to turn from considering *Memoirs of General William T. Sherman* as an artistic achievement, is to risk overlooking the continuity between Sherman's representation of himself in prose and the image of himself he constructed and wielded effectively as an instrument of war. During the Civil War Sherman discovered that the ways others saw him were important and powerful. In a letter to Grant dated January 29, 1865, included in the chapter "Savannah and Pocotaligo," he closed with this candid statement: "I observe that the enemy has some respect for my name, for they gave up Pocotaligo without a fight when they heard that the attacking force belonged to my army." Then, in a sentence anticipating the practical consequences of this fresh observation, he added, "I will try and keep up that feeling, which is a real power" (*Memoirs*, 741). It is instructive to compare these sentences with a passage in Grant's *Personal Memoirs* (1885–86), one in which Grant narrated his leading the Twenty-first Illinois regiment against Colonel Thomas Harris at Florida, Missouri, in the summer of 1861. Having advanced against Harris's camp and found it abandoned, Grant commented, "It occurred to me at once that Harris had been as much afraid of me as I had been of him. . . . The lesson was valuable."[4] Grant's revelation about the fears of an enemy occurred at the beginning of the war and served to free him from "trepidation upon confronting an enemy, though I always felt more or less anxiety"; Sherman's revelation about the fears of an enemy occurred late in the war and served to arm him with another weapon to brandish against that enemy. To Grant the revelation brought relief, to Sherman new ideas for controlling others.

During the war, and especially during the campaigns of 1864 and 1865, Sherman discovered, in other words, a second meaning behind the phrase "the theater of war." The word "theater" descends into English from a Greek verb meaning "to look at" or "to watch." When Sherman found himself looked at and watched, he found, too, that when he could not control the looking and the watching, his efforts did not advance, as in the instance of Samuel Wilkerson's publication in the *New York Tribune*, October 30, 1861, of an account of Sherman's statement to Secretary of War Simon Cameron that he would need 200,000 soldiers for offensive operations in Kentucky, an account that led subsequently to assessments of Sherman as unbalanced and insane.[5] This was the main reason he so hated "the dogs of the press," whom he denigrated as "the world's gossips" in the final paragraph of the 1875 first edition of the *Memoirs* (856, 899). The full title of John Marszalek's study *Sherman's Other War: The General and the Civil War Press* (1981) succinctly encapsulates Sherman's charged and ambivalent attitude toward what he considered pernicious abuses of the freedom of the press. Although his control over his image faltered at many points during the war, most bitterly in his dispute with Cameron's successor, Edwin M. Stanton, about the terms of surrender he offered to Joseph Johnston near Durham Station in North Carolina nine days after Grant accepted the surrender of Robert E. Lee at Appomattox, it strengthened him at other crucial moments and periods. Much of the control he achieved, he achieved by successes in the game of war, but he also achieved and maintained another kind of control through his prolific writing—of letters, orders, official reports. When he came to write his memoirs, he worked hard to establish and preserve a similar control. By paying attention to the methods and strategies of the *Memoirs*, one can begin to comprehend the continuity between the soldier and the writer, even as one acknowledges, in the words of the epigraph from Hemingway, paying this kind of attention to war memoirs "will be fun and it will not be fun too."

Another difference between Grant and Sherman is that the former undertook to write his memoirs, with the encouragement of Mark Twain, because in 1884 he lost his life savings to the fraudulent ventures of Wall Street financier Ferdinand Ward and badly needed to earn money. There is no evidence to suggest that if Grant's investment in the brokerage partnership between his son, Ulysses Jr., and Ward had prospered, Grant's earlier resistance to pressures to write for the public would not have continued or that *Personal Memoirs of U. S. Grant* would have appeared. Sherman's was an entirely different case. Evidence of aesthetic sensibility and artistic ambition appeared in him early on. Like every West Point cadet, the young man from Lancaster, Ohio, who graduated sixth of forty-three in the class of 1840, studied drawing, in which he ranked first in 1838 (Lewis, *Fighting Prophet*, 59). But it was not until his assignment to Fort Moultrie, outside Charleston, South

Carolina, from June 1842 until the spring of 1846 that, according to Lewis, "the artist awakened in Sherman" (*Fighting Prophet*, 71). In support of this claim, Lewis quoted most of one sentence from a letter to Ellen, dated November 28, 1842. The longer excerpt from this letter, included in *Home Letters of General Sherman* (1909), rewards reading in full (quotation marks and ellipses in original):

> ". . . Not long since I took a notion into my head that
> I could paint. I went to the city and laid in a full set of
> artist's equipments, prepared my studio, and without any
> instructions whatever have finished a couple [of] landscapes
> and faces which they tell me are very good. I have great love
> for painting and find that sometimes I am so fascinated
> that it amounts to pain to lay down the brush, placing me
> in doubt whether I had better stop now before it swallows
> all attention, to the neglect of my duties, and discard it
> altogether, or keep on. What would you advise? . . ."[6]

Here we have a revealing, even poignant, portrait of the artist as a young man, twenty-two years old, on fire with new inspiration and discovery, proud of his creative independence ("without any instructions"), gratified by encouragement from an anonymous "they," uneasy about the potentially disruptive effect of this new avocation on his professional duties, and eagerly solicitous of the young woman who, becoming his wife, would have to live with the consequences of his choice of vocation. In his biography Lewis shut the door on this moment quickly, following his excerpt from the letter to Ellen with the terse summary, "His brushes were laid by, never to be taken up again, after the summer of 1843, when he came home to Lancaster on a three months' leave" (*Fighting Prophet*, 71). The implication of this sentence is that the return home, not only to Ellen but to her family, with whom the fatherless Sherman had begun living at the age of nine, proved somehow decisive in ending his painting.

But if he laid aside the brushes in 1843, he was still thinking about them thirty years later in the midst of composing the chapter "Campaign of the Carolinas" for the second volume of the *Memoirs*.

In the pages before he turned to the burning of Columbia, South Carolina, during the night of Friday, February 17, 1865, Sherman described two visits to citizens of Columbia, both ladies, who were former acquaintances of his, in part, no doubt, to establish for his readers his sympathetic ties with civilians living in the city he stoutly maintained he played no part in destroying. During his years at Fort Moultrie, Sherman had visited the house of the first lady, whose maiden name was Poyas, described in the *Memoirs* this way: "One of the ladies was very fond of painting in water-colors, which was one of my weaknesses, and on one occasion I had presented her with a volume treating of water-colors" (*Memoirs*, 764). Because he had inscribed the book to Miss Poyas "with the compliments of W. T. Sherman, First-lieutenant, Third Artillery," and because the former Miss Poyas still owned the book and was able to show it to United States soldiers during the occupation of Columbia, "they had not handled her house and premises as roughly as was their wont" (*Memoirs*, 765). Whether or not the former Miss Poyas, who had requested that Sherman visit her house in Columbia so she could thank him for its safety, was one of the "they" who had encouraged the young artist twenty years before, Sherman did not say. What this lone reference in the *Memoirs* to his painting does reveal, however, is that during the thirty years after he laid aside his brushes in 1843, Sherman had managed to demote his earlier "love of painting" to a mere and safely contained weakness.

This demotion did not end the story of art and aesthetics in Sherman's life and career. For Lewis the image of Sherman as artist manqué became powerfully suggestive, if at times impressionistic and conjectural, and that image shaped much of his biography. Describing Sherman's unhappiness in the New Orleans commissary depot during the fall of 1852, for example, Lewis gave this image center stage: "He could not understand himself. Perhaps he remembered, at these times, the one period in his life when he had been swallowed up in the bliss of absorbed interest, the days when he had sat painting pictures hour after hour, lost to the flight of the sun as it passed over Fort Moultrie and sank behind the mists of South Carolina. His fingers, long and pointed, were those of an artist, his imagination was continually reconstructing the world as it ought to be. He was an artist without an art" (*Fighting Prophet*, 87–88).

"He was an artist without an art." One does not have to swoon over this heady depiction of the unhappy Sherman to appreciate that Lewis, a popular and colorful writer for the *Chicago Daily News*, one who numbered Sherwood Anderson, Sinclair Lewis, Carl Sandburg, and Frank Lloyd Wright among his friends, recognized something important about Sherman: an aesthetic sensibility contributed to the ways he perceived and imagined the world. In this moment Lewis risked overstating the importance of aesthetics in Sherman's life and career, possibly recreating Sherman in his own image. Sherman had many other sensibilities, too, among them the logistical, the legalistic, the mercantile, the didactic, the historical, the traveling or touristic, the historical, and the ethical (upon graduation he ranked seventh in his West Point class in the study of ethics; by comparison, Hood ranked fifty-second in the same course, dead last in the class of 1853), the last of which often shaded into self-defensiveness, self-justification, and self-righteousness.

In Lewis's biographical narrative the fulfillment of Sherman's artistic ambitions came not with the art of painting but with the art of war, recalling the title of the classic Chinese military treatise attributed to Sun Tzu. Imagining Sherman's insomnia during the Atlanta Campaign, Lewis celebrated this fulfillment: "Sherman had become, indeed, a friend of night. In it he found himself the complete artist, letting his imagination roam across space and time unhampered by the distractions of the daytime. On the walls of darkness he could picture what was happening far off, and what impended. Night hours, he said, were his favorites, because then his ears could tell him what the enemy was doing" (*Fighting Prophet*, 358). Not all readers will find either persuasive or acceptable the notion that Sherman, the thwarted painter, found his true artistic outlet in the art of waging war. At the very least, many might wonder how the impulse to paint landscapes and faces could find its satisfactory fulfillment in the work of destroying railroads, buildings, and people, even if that destruction was carried out in the name of preserving the Union.

An alternative claim, one I want to make here, is the claim that the artistic sensibility described by Lewis did fulfill itself in Sherman's life, not in the art of waging war but in the art of writing about waging war. Many moments in the *Memoirs* offer strong support for this claim, but one that stands out, both because of the quality of the writing and because of the historical significance of the moment the writing describes, narrated Sherman's departure from Atlanta with his army of sixty thousand, as it began the March to the Sea, about 7:00 A.M., November 16, 1864:

> Behind us lay Atlanta, smouldering and in ruins, the black
> smoke rising high in air, and hanging like a pall over the
> ruined city. Away off in the distance, on the McDonough
> road, was the rear of Howard's column, the gun-barrels
> glistening in the sun, the white-topped wagons stretching
> away to the south; and right before us the Fourteenth
> Corps, marching steadily and rapidly, with a cheery look
> and swinging pace, that made light of the thousand
> miles that lay between us and Richmond. Some band, by
> accident, struck up the anthem of "John Brown's soul goes
> marching on"; the men caught up the strain, and never
> before or since have I heard the chorus of "Glory, glory,
> hallelujah!" done with more spirit, or in better harmony of
> time and place. (*Memoirs*, 655–56)

Although Lewis did not quote these three sentences, their evocative power struck him, too, eliciting a sentence beginning, "The artist in him wished for canvas upon which to paint the stupendous scene—the 'extremely beautiful day,'" and continuing with his paraphrase of Sherman's vision of the glistening gun-barrels and white-topped wagons stretching out before him (*Fighting Prophet*, 436). Lewis gave no source for the statement that the artist in Sherman "wished for canvas"; it appears the general wrote no letters during the March to the Sea, which he could not have posted anyway, and most likely the source was Lewis himself. In one of the last letters Sherman did write before this period of silence, one to Ellen dated November 12, 1864, the day he started from Kingston, Georgia, to Atlanta, the taciturn contrast with the rich description in the *Memoirs* could hardly be greater:

> Mrs. W. T. Sherman
> Lancaster, Ohio
> We start today. My arm is quite well. The box of clothing came last night. I have all your letters too including Novr. 3. Write no more till you hear of me. Good bye.
> W. T. Sherman[7]

Three weeks earlier, in a much longer letter to his wife, one beginning with his characteristic "Dearest Ellen," Sherman told her he hoped that none of his letters, "sought after like hot cakes" since the capture of Atlanta, would be published "as sample [*sic*] of literary composition" (*Sherman's Civil War*, 738). Whatever the truth of this claim, it reflected an awareness that his writing had become increasingly public and an awareness of a particular category of writing he labeled "literary composition," one to which his hurried, telegraphic letter to "Mrs. W. T. Sherman," which reads like something dashed off and handed to an aid to post in the haste of departure, presumably did not belong, although later readers, schooled by Hemingway and those he influenced, might disagree. By contrast the three sentences describing Sherman's last look at Atlanta clearly belong to the category of "literary composition," or the category of aesthetically self-conscious writing, a category that Lewis's imagination of Sherman's artistic wish for canvas indirectly invoked and acknowledged. After all, in his description of the army leaving Atlanta, visual images dominate and suggest a kind of pictorial, painterly attention to the scene: black smoke; the "glistening gun-barrels and white-topped wagons" of the distant rear of the right wing of the army, heading toward Macon under the command of O. O. Howard and consisting of the Fifteenth and Seventeenth Corps; the cheery look of soldiers in Jefferson C. Davis's Fourteenth Corps, marching immediately before him and combining with the Twentieth to make up the left wing, with which he traveled as it feinted toward Augusta.

But then, in his third sentence, Sherman turned from the visual, pictorial mode of the verbal painter to the realm of sound and the soldiers' spirited rendition of "John Brown's Body." The sudden prominence of sound in Sherman's description not only pushed that description beyond the visual boundaries of Lewis's wished-for canvas; it signaled the operation of an auditory sensibility, one that pointed beyond music to the carefully orchestrated sounds of Sherman's own sentences, to the repetitions of assonance and alliteration (smouldering [Sherman's spelling]-ruins-smoke-rising, gun-barrels glistening, white-topped wagons) and the rhythms of syntactic pacing, as sentences unfold under the careful management of inserted phrases, especially participial ones, which dominate and prolong the first two sentences. In other words, it was not Sherman the erstwhile painter, wishing for canvas, who marshaled his descriptive powers for a last look at Atlanta; it was Sherman the writer, describing both sights and sounds in skillfully controlled language belonging to the opposite end of the writing spectrum from the hurried, telegraphic letter of November 12, 1864, to Mrs. W. T. Sherman.

The descriptive mode was not the only one Sherman attempted and mastered, but it makes sense to begin with it because it surfaced early in his development as a writer. In 1825, at age five, he entered Lancaster Academy, where his studies consisted of "all the common branches of knowledge, including Latin, Greek, and French" (*Memoirs*, 14). At some point his study of the classics may have involved examples of, if not exercises in, detailed description of an image, most often visual, known in Greek as *ekphrasis* and in Latin as *descriptio*. If not, he may have studied and practiced the writing of description in his rhetoric course at West Point, taken in 1839, a course he did not include among those in which he ranked among the best students: "drawing, chemistry, mathematics, and natural philosophy [physics]" (*Memoirs*, 16). In a letter to his brother John, however, dated January 14, 1840, he summarized the successful results of his recent examinations, including the one in rhetoric: "In Engineering I am fourth in my class, in Geology and Rhetoric and Moral Philosophy each sixth; as to demerits, I have a respectable number, about one hundred."[8] But it is also possible that Sherman's powers of verbal description, like his painting, developed without extensive formal instruction.

Whatever the origin of Sherman's descriptive mode, it surfaced, gradually, in the genre he took up energetically at West Point, the letter. Introducing her edition of her father's letters to his brother John, Sherman's daughter Rachel commented frankly, "His earliest letters are labored and boyish. He had not yet acquired a vocabulary or the fluency of pen which later developed itself to an almost wonderful degree" (*Sherman Letters*, 1). The primary recipients of Sherman's letters from West Point were Ellen and John, and it was in his correspondence with his future wife that he began to develop descriptive fluency, apparently as part of a strategy to make a visit to the academy attractive to her, as early as a letter dated May 4, 1839, the same year he took the course in rhetoric:

> I am delighted that there is a probability of your coming
> here during the coming summer, and why shouldn't you?
> Will you ever have a better opportunity? Is not West Point
> worth visiting? Is not the scenery of the finest order in the
> world in its vicinity? Are there not incidents in its history
> that render it dear to us all? I might ask a hundred such
> questions which any individual who has ever been here
> would be compelled to answer in the affirmative. Here's
> Old Fort Put, in itself a curiosity, with its damp and gloomy
> cells, and Kosciuszko's Garden, with its jet of water and
> marble basin on which is inscribed the Pole's name, as also
> a large monument erected a long time ago by the Corps of
> Cadets to the same person. I might go on and enumerate
> many more things which have attracted every summer and
> probably will continue to attract crowds of visitors, and I
> hope soon to learn that you and your father will be of the
> number next summer. (*Home Letters*, 7)

One could argue that there was still something labored and boyish about the breathless volley of rhetorical questions unleashed at Ellen, and something a little stiff and artificial about the subjunctive flourishes of attempted persuasion ("I might ask a hundred such questions," "I might go on and enumerate many more things"), but this early letter makes two things clear. The first is that a self-conscious rhetorician was emerging in his epistolary medium; the second is that his attempts at description were linked with travel, in this case with the prospect of Ellen's visit to West Point.

In a letter written to John during his last term at West Point, dated March 7, 1840, Sherman raised the subject of travel and travelers as he discussed his options upon graduation, explaining to his brother, "To be stationed in the east or west, to be in the artillery, infantry, or dragoons, depends entirely on my choice." He thought it "probable that the Indians will break out again, in which case I should have an opportunity of seeing some active service" in Florida, but at the same moment war with England over disputed boundaries between Canada and Maine was a possibility, in which case, "I should prefer the artillery, for the reason that it is stationed east of the mountains, which would be the seat of war, and it is an arm of service which I would prefer in a war against a civilized people" (*Sherman Letters*, 12). He did not say why he preferred to fight with artillery against civilized people, but in sharing his choice with John, he revealed the role that "descriptions of travellers" played in his decision: "This choice will be, unless war breaks out with England, the Fifth Regiment of Infantry, because it is stationed on the northwestern frontier, a country which I have always felt a strong inclination to see; and if it meets my ideas, formed from descriptions of travellers and officers, it must be the finest spot on the continent" (*Sherman Letters*, 12).

In 1840 the Fifth United States Infantry Regiment, headquartered in Detroit, was operating across a broad area between Michigan, recently admitted to the Union in 1837, and what became, thirty years later, the state of Nebraska. Sherman did not name for his brother the descriptions he had been reading; nine years before the appearance of Francis Parkman's *The Oregon Trail* (1849), they may have included Nicholas Biddle's two-volume *History of the Expedition under the Command of Captains Lewis and Clark*

(1814) or something comparable. But he did show the importance of travel writing—a genre with roots in the classical worlds of, among others, Homer, Xenophon, Lucian, and Pausanias—in shaping his imaginative response to his own.

With his assignment to Company A, Third Artillery Regiment, rather than to the Fifth Infantry on the northwestern frontier, and with the assignment of his unit to Fort Pierce, Florida, Sherman became a travel writer, too, as in the first two paragraphs of a letter dated March 30, 1841, written to John: "The peninsula of Florida is of the latest geological formation, one mass of sand, with few rocks of the softest consistency, and, were it not for its delightful climate, would be as barren as the deserts of Africa" (*Sherman Letters*, 13). As the topographic description continued, however, it focused not on the charms of the climate in a new land but on the strategic implications and tactical possibilities of the ground:

> It is cut up by innumerable rivers, streams, and rivulets, which, watering the soil, nourish a rank growth of weeds and grass, which, continually decomposing, gives a rich soil, and gives rise in time to a heavy growth of live oak, palmetto, and scrub of every kind. These are the dreaded hummocks, the stronghold of Indians. . . . The thick growth conceals his little fire and hut, secures his escape. . . . In a word, the deep streams, bordered by the dense hummock, have enabled the Indians thus far to elude the pursuit of our army. (*Sherman Letters*, 13)

In the rhythms of the first sentence ("It is cut up by innumerable rivers"), with its ramified syntax of relative clauses, participial phrases, and parallel structures, one can hear an early version of the rhetorical periods that marked Sherman's mature style, exemplified by his description of the army marching away from the ruins of Atlanta. The mechanics of description, particularly description of a landscape, had much to do with shaping that style, as accumulations of visual detail and inventories of specific features necessitated, at least in Sherman's hands, the grammatical patterns of carefully wrought, intricately segmented, complex sentences.

Adapting the structure of Lewis's formulation that the artist in Sherman awoke during his years at Fort Moultrie, I want to suggest here that the travel writer in Sherman may have awakened in Florida but developed aboard the USS *Lexington* during its voyage from New York around Cape Horn to Monterey, California, July 14, 1846, to January 26, 1847. This six-and-a-half-month voyage has received relatively little attention from Sherman's many biographers, who have been understandably eager to get Sherman from land to land—the major exception is John Marszalek, who gave the voyage eight pages—but in light of his careers as both soldier and writer, it is hard to avoid the conclusion that this voyage was formative.[9] For one thing, it forced Sherman the soldier to work closely with officers of the United States Navy, laying the foundation for his effective cooperation with the them during the Civil War, beginning with his assignment to command the District of Cairo at Paducah, Kentucky, February 13, 1862, and his subsequent movements by water during March toward the battle of Shiloh. Meanwhile, for Sherman the writer the voyage aboard the *Lexington* had some of the same significance that Herman Melville's Ishmael, in the words that close the chapter "The Advocate" in *Moby-Dick* (1851), discovered in his time aboard the *Pequod*: "For a whale-ship was my Yale College and my Harvard."

Unlike Ishmael or Melville, Sherman had been to college, not at Yale or Harvard but at West Point, where he had just missed graduating among the top five, whose names were distinguished with asterisks in the annual *Register of the Officers and Cadets*.[10] But the library records at West Point suggest that Cadet Sherman may not have read widely beyond the requirements for his courses. During 1836 the library records showed no books checked out to him. For three weeks in March 1837 he checked out one volume of the *Museum of Literature and Science*, an eclectic weekly paper published in Philadelphia by Eliakim Littell, beginning in July 1822, under the motto "Carpere et Colligere," to seize and collect. The following month Sherman borrowed Louis Antoine Fauvelet de Bourrienne's *Life of Napoleon Bonaparte*, published in London in 1831; the records do not say whether he borrowed all three volumes for the two weeks the title appeared on his record. The next titles, volumes 2–4 of *Niles' Weekly Register*, one of the most widely circulated political magazines in the United States from 1811 until 1849, did not appear until January and February 1838, and when they did, they appeared for three weeks. Finally, for two weeks during his last term at West Point, one in January, the other in March, Sherman borrowed two of the four volumes of Wilhelm Müller's *Elements of the Science of War*, published in London in 1811.[11]

Seven volumes borrowed for a total of ten weeks over nearly four years do not suggest a bookworm, although it is certainly possible that he devoured books he owned or borrowed from fellow cadets. With the voyage of the *Lexington* Sherman's reading life intensified, as he described in a letter to Ellen, dated August 3, 1846: "The spar deck is divided also into two parts like the berth deck, the forward part assigned to the men, and the after part or quarter-deck to the officers. Over this when the sun is hot are awnings spread, rendering a most pleasant place to read. We have many books aboard of all kinds, but our voyage will be so long that we will be forced to read even the tables in Bowditch" (*Home Letters*, 40). Citing the unpublished 112-page autobiographical manuscript the general drafted in 1868, John Marszalek pictured young Sherman avidly reading "travel, history, novels, Shakespeare and Sir Walter Scott" (*Passion for Order*, 12).[12] Aboard the *Lexington* Sherman's schoolboy avidity returned. In a letter to Ellen dated November 6, in which for the first time he included the navigational location of the ship, "Lat. 58° S., Long. 76° W. of Greenwich, or 1° E. of Washington" (after the date of the August 3 letter, he had written simply, "Ship *Lexington*, at Sea"), he named the books he had read in under four months: "I have read all of Washington Irving's works that are aboard, Pickwick, Barnaby Rudge, Shakespeare, everything I could get, and yesterday cast about to determine which I should attempt next—the Bible, History of the Reformation or the Wandering Jew, but have postponed such a task till even a time more urgent than the present" (*Home Letters*, 68).

There may have been something tongue-in-cheek about suggesting to Ellen that reading the Bible was a task only greater urgency could make him take up, a task ranking lower than reading the tables in Nathaniel Bowditch's *New American Practical Navigator*, first published in 1802, as the inclusion of the coordinates of his position suggested he may have been doing. Whatever the tone behind the sentence, it came from a serious reader, one who also made his way through Emerich de Vattel's *Law of Nations* (published in 1758 and the only book he brought with him); travel books such as *Narrative of the United States Exploring Expedition* (1844; five volumes and an atlas) by Charles Wilkes, future precipitator of the *Trent* affair, and Richard Henry Dana's *Two Years Before the Mast* (1840); and books about California to prepare himself for landing there more than two and a half months later (*Passion for Order*, 56). At other moments in his life, according to Charles Royster, Sherman also read "Walter Scott, Robert Burns, Captain Frederick Marryat, Charles Lever, William Makepeace Thackeray, and later, Bret Harte and Mark Twain" (*Memoirs*, 1089).

The range of Sherman's reading is richly impressive, although it behooves twenty-first-century onlookers to remember that much of what he read fell under the heading of what in 1846 was recent or contemporary fiction rather than canonical literature aglow with the nimbus imparted to it by subsequent literary history. What matters as much as the sudden plunge into extensive reading, as the *Lexington* rounded stormy Cape Horn and the calendar rounded the new year into 1847, is Sherman's occasionally critical, even complex response to much of what he read. In a letter written to his sister Elizabeth (Mrs. William James Reese as of October 29, 1829), dated only four days after the November one to Ellen, he included two important sentences about his responses as a reader, each of which hinged on an antithetical "but" and both of which had larger implications for his development as a writer:

> Travellers always allude to the strangeness of seeing the sun to the north, new constellations in the sky, etc., but education explains causes, removes mystery, and strips travelling of nearly all its ancient zest.
> (*Home Letters*, 32)

These mountains [the Andes] are from seventeen to twenty-two thousand feet in height, and may be seen at the distance of one hundred and fifty miles; but so accustomed have I been to read accounts of them and to see and dream pictures of snow-clad mountains, that these seem more like a representation than reality. (*Home Letters*, 36)

In the first sentence one may be tempted to hear only the regretful shrug of a traveler whose zestful pleasure in what he experienced had been drained by the rise of scientific empiricism in the eighteenth and early nineteenth centuries, and Sherman's regret may have been genuine. Whether it was genuine, and not the passing rhetorical pose of a younger brother adopted for the benefit of his older sister at home, it showed him aligning his sensibility with the realistic explanations of education rather than with the romantic attractions of mystery, at least in his writing. Working through his memoirs, driven as they were by a powerful didactic impulse to educate his readers in practical matters great and small, whether those readers be "the rising generation, who therefrom may learn that a country and government such as ours are worth fighting for, and dying for, if need be," as he put it in the introductory note to the first edition (*Memoirs*, 3), or novices in need of step-by-step instruction in the business of destroying railroad tracks (*Memoirs*, 579), one would not necessarily guess the book was the work of a devoted reader of the literary knight of romance, Sir Walter Scott. Yes, he would continue to travel and describe his experiences, but his descriptions would be informed by the explanations of education, not the obfuscations of mystery.

In the second sentence from the letter to his sister, Sherman recorded the grasping of a crucial lesson, one that the developing writer later put to sweepingly effective use in his *Memoirs*: written accounts of things can seem more real than the things themselves. The admission that, faced with the real Andes, he could only see them as secondary representations of what he had read about them followed predictably from the admission to John, more than six and half years earlier, that his idealization of the Northwest as "the finest spot on the continent" had been formed by descriptions of travelers and officers. Many readers have had their ideas of places formed by written accounts of those places, and some of those readers have been subsequently disappointed when they visited the places themselves, the realities failing to meet their expectations. But it is a much smaller subset of these readers who then resolve to become the writers who will shape the realities of others, providing them with representations of reality that will make reality seem like the representation.[13]

During his voyage on the *Lexington*, Sherman, reader and traveler, not only realized something profound about the powers of written representation that would shape his memoirs when he came to write them almost thirty years later; on board the ship he began the writing that led directly to the memoirs themselves. This statement is indirectly true in respect to his letters, which grew in length, some of them approaching the size of short essays, as his powers of description developed and strengthened. But it is directly true in respect to his experience with a second genre, the journal. Beginning with an entry dated July 16, 1846, two days after the *Lexington* set sail from New York, and continuing for sixty-one pages—each measuring eight inches by thirteen, the first three appearing to have been written in pencil, the rest in ink—through an entry dated "Monterey Cal.," August 27, 1847, seven months after the *Lexington* arrived, and on through a twenty-five-page draft of a letter to General George Gibson on military matters in California, Sherman kept his journal, which has been neither transcribed nor published. What makes the journal important is not the quality of the writing, which, when legible, one finds to be simpler and rawer than the more polished prose of the long letters. In an entry dated "Christmas day, 1846," for example, Sherman recorded his participation, or lack thereof, in festivities involving eggnog: "I am under the weather and couldn't indulge farther than one glass—the rest are very cheery indeed." This unembellished straightforwardness continued in the next entry, dated "January 19, 1846" [*sic*], when he caught up on the intervening weeks, noting another party: "We crossed the line Long 117 and had a real New Years spree. The weather was then fine and continued all the time so till the 15th when we lost the N. E. trades and got into variables and a heavy sea."[14]

What makes the journal valuable to students of Sherman is that it represents an attempt to narrate a series of events in a continuous form.[15] Grant also made an early experiment with journal-keeping, but he used his journal primarily to help him remember all that he read, which included "many valuable historical works, besides an occasional novel," as he prepared for an assistant professorship of mathematics at West Point (*Personal Memoirs*, 24). When Grant's regiment was ordered away en route to Mexico, the journal was lost and never found. According to his own account, he never kept another, "except for a portion of the time while travelling abroad" (*Personal Memoirs*, 25), so he could not have drawn on a journal when he began writing his memoirs, as Sherman could draw on his record of the voyage of the *Lexington*. Moreover, as he finished shaping the first edition of his memoirs, ten years before Grant began writing his, Sherman did not begin as Grant did, with his ancestry, birth, and childhood. Having opened his 1868 autobiographical manuscript that way, he subsequently discarded this material and did not return to it until he added the first chapter for the second edition. Instead he narrowed his focus to the story he was most eager to tell, one that had to begin with the voyage to California, first recorded in his journal.

In building a narrative any narrator must make decisions about how to select and shape material, decisions that recall the original meaning of "fiction" (from Latin *fictus*, past participle of *fingere*, to touch, form, mold). In the first edition of his memoirs, Sherman followed the lead of many epic poets and began his narrative in medias res, although unlike those epic poets he then rarely flashed back to the earlier part of the story, which in his case consisted of more than a third of his life and almost half of it at the time of writing. A telling exception to this general rule did not come until the first chapter of the second volume, when the narrative returned briefly to the "early days" of 1844 and a trip Sherman made from

Charleston, South Carolina, to Marietta, Georgia, during which he "noted well the topography of the country" over which he directed the Atlanta Campaign twenty years later (*Memoirs*, 511). But this flashback is unique. It was not that the first third of his life contained nothing of significance—his experiences at West Point, in Florida, and at Fort Moultrie belong to this third—but Sherman did not consider earlier experiences germane to the narrative he was shaping.

Instead, he wasted no time getting his readers aboard the *Lexington*, by the third page of the first edition, and landing them, after another page and a half—during which he described the ship, introduced his shipmates, most important among them fellow lieutenants Henry Halleck and E. O. C. Ord, and dissembled that he passed "the humdrum of a long voyage, reading some, not much" (*Memoirs*, 39)—sixty days later at Rio Janeiro, as he referred to the city, dropping the "de": "Sugar-loaf Mountain, on the south of the entrance, is very remarkable and well named; is almost conical, with a slight lean. The man-of-war anchorage is about five miles inside the heads, directly in front of the city of Rio Janeiro. Words will not describe the beauty of this perfect harbor, nor the delightful feeling after a long voyage of its fragrant airs, and the entire contrast between all things there and what we had left in New York" (*Memoirs*, 39). Although this first instance of his published travel writing fell back on the conventional formula "Words will not describe," a familiar rhetorical feature of descriptions by classical writers, sometimes called adynaton, sometimes aporia, Sherman established himself at this early moment as a knowing guide, naturally curious, intensely excited, infinitely interested, who would scoop up his readers, transport them across vast distances, describe to them notable features of landscape and culture, and infuse his descriptions with strong traces of his particular sensibility, marked here by his stirred response to "the beauty" of the scene, the first of many appearances of the words "beauty" and "beautiful" throughout the *Memoirs*.

The raw material for this passage appeared in the journal entry for Friday, September 11, 1846: "We are now at anchor, 11 A.M.

expecting the sea breeze to take us in—Rasa island is a large rock with a castle upon it and a fine lighthouse—Pay and May farther north are mere rocks that loom up through the thick haze or smoke that so obscures the atmosphere that we shall not see the Sugar Loaf and forts that stand at the entrance of this most beautiful harbor of the world" (Journal). Despite the airbrushing of haze or smoke from the published version, along with the deletion of the gushing superlative "most beautiful harbor of the world," hardly earned by someone entering his first foreign port, the continuity between the passages is palpable, as Sherman at twenty-six and Sherman in his early fifties both exerted themselves to put into words the new scenes and "magnificent vistas" (*Memoirs*, 14) traveling showed them.

Sherman's choice to begin his memoirs originally with the voyage of the *Lexington* suggests that his characteristic, and often acknowledged, impatience may have been at work. Rather than trudging dutifully through his ancestry, birth, and childhood, according to the conventions of full-blown autobiography, he wanted to get on with the business of narrating the parts of his life that had given him reason to think the public would be interested in his story in the first place. But to say he was thinking only of what his readers wanted may not be accurate. His utter disregard for the importance of narrating the first third of his life also reflected his own impulse to focus on what interested him most: travel, adventure, and various logistical and moral challenges to confront and overcome. In other words, he began with the voyage of the *Lexington* because he needed that voyage, and subsequent events in California up to his departure from San Francisco on July 3, 1858, to establish his courage far from the fighting of the Mexican War (as when he tracked and captured deserters or remained on board with the last of the passengers during a shipwreck) and integrity (in confronting a committee of vigilantes or steering his bank through financial crisis) for the narrative to follow, the heart of which recounted the Atlanta Campaign and the March to the Sea over an eight-month period that occupied more than one-quarter of the 1875 *Memoirs*. Although it would be irresponsible oversimplification to reduce Sherman's monumental narrative to an instance of travel literature—despite the recurrence of such moments as a paragraph that followed the March to the Sea and opened the chapter "Savannah and Pocotaligo" with language that reads as though it had wandered into his narrative from a guidebook to Savannah (*Memoirs*, 708)—evidence shows that he never outgrew his early impulse to write descriptively about traveling.

That evidence appears in the general's unpublished correspondence with Mark Twain, whom he addressed as Samuel Clemens, initiated by Sherman on September 15, 1885, on stationery from 912 Garrison Avenue, St. Louis, Missouri:

My Dear Friend,

You are in the "business," and I approach you as a business man.

In 1871–2 I made the tour of Europe and took notes in the form of entries at the chief stopping places. Several of my friends have seen these notes, and insist that they should be published—During this summer in my absence my clerk Mr. Barrett has copied them from my original m/ ss—and I have gone over the whole. 294 pages of foolscap— very plainly written and reasonably correct—If I should send these pages to you, will you read them, give me your *honest* opinion of their merits, and your advice as to their disposition.

I have been offered tempting prices to contribute to the "Century", the "North American Review" &c &c—but have been obstinate, and have never received a cent except for the "Memoirs," a sum far below the popular estimate. Indeed all I have done in the way of writing and printing has been on the other side of the ledger at my own cost.

Now if these notes of travel have any value, I do not need the money, but my grand children and old soldier dependants and beggars do,—so that if they have any money value, these dependants might share the profits even during my life-time.

I would sell outright, or take the excess on cost of publication.

This letter is meant merely to sound you, in a matter where you are familiar, and I am not—

> With real respect I am
> Your Friend,
> W. T. Sherman[16]

If the letter of November 28, 1842, to Ellen about his new passion for painting presented a portrait of the painter as a young man, this letter to an expert in the business of publishing presented a portrait of the writer as a middle-aged professional with an eye on the literary marketplace.

The timing of Sherman's correspondence with Twain, which ran from September 18 through October 16, 1885 (five letters from Sherman, three from Twain) and resumed from December 7, 1885, through February 6, 1886 (three letters from Sherman, one from Twain) points to important aspects of the composition of the *Memoirs*. The first is that the production of a final draft followed the return from Sherman's trip to Europe and the writing of his notes about that trip. Although any direct narrative of the trip itself did not appear until the chapter "After the War," added to the second edition and, according to his fourth letter to Twain, dated October 9, already completed by that date, readers of the first edition will detect references to recent experiences in Europe, such as, "I saw, recently, in Aldershot, England, a very complete pontoon-train" (*Memoirs*, 892). As for the brief narrative of the trip included in "After the War," it demonstrated quite clearly how laconically minimalist Sherman could sound when he included none of the descriptive, anecdotal, argumentative, didactic, or moralizing material abundantly displayed elsewhere. Beginning, "I have very full notes of the whole trip, and here need only state," three short paragraphs, consisting of little more than place names in his itinerary through Europe and Egypt, closed with the statement, "I refrain from dwelling on this trip, because it would swell this chapter beyond my purpose" (*Memoirs*, 942–43).

The October 9 letter to Twain also showed that Sherman's revisions to the *Memoirs* preceded his reading of Grant's *Personal Memoirs*:

> I have revised my "Memoirs" prefixing a chapter, and another in conclusion, with some maps & illustrations which are in the hands of the Appletons with injunctions to take their own time as there is no hurry. I would like to obtain Grants two volumes at the earliest possible moment, although I had his own assurance as well as that of Fred Grant that on all the controverted points he sustained me perfectly.
>
> I am taking things easy, and have plenty of leisure to read the current literature, even the sensational novels, so that if you come across anything extra-fine let me have it, or a catalogue which will enable me to purchase it.[17]

For Sherman the chief value of his friend's memoirs lay in their forensic potential to corroborate his version of "the controverted points." It did not lie in providing a fellow-writer with other models for narrative, Sherman's new first chapter on his ancestry, birth, and childhood having evolved independently of Grant's.

By contrast, Sherman's correspondence with Twain reflected not only the former's respect for the latter's business sense; it reflected his admiration for Twain as a writer who did provide him with models for narrative. By the time Sherman initiated the correspondence with Twain, the latter had published two books that helped set the standard for American travel narratives of the late nineteenth century, *The Innocents Abroad* (1869), about a trip through Europe and the Holy Land during 1867 (advertisements for this trip named Sherman as a celebrity passenger, but other duties prevented him from sailing with Twain on the *Quaker City*), and *Roughing It* (1872), based on Twain's earlier travels west through the Nevada Territory to San Francisco and Hawaii. The American appetite for travel narratives, at least in the northern states where more people still had money to travel after the Civil War, grew rapidly during the second half of the nineteenth century as three technological breakthroughs altered the way many Americans imagined the world: the completion of the transcontinental railroad in 1869 (in which Sherman played an important role; see, for example, Marszalek, *Passion for Order*, 391–93), the opening of the Suez Canal the same year, and the linking of railways across the Indian subcontinent in 1870. With these developments, trips such as Sherman's around Cape Horn (or his subsequent voyages to California abridged by arduous trips overland across Nicaragua) and comparable trips around the Cape of Good Hope were no longer necessary for travelers circumnavigating the globe or traveling large parts of it. Those Americans who could not afford to travel by means of any of the newly available routes still could travel vicariously by means of books such as Twain's or the accounts of Grant's world travels, from 1877–79, published in the *New York Herald* by John Russell Young, who accompanied Grant, and subsequently made available, with eight hundred illustrations, as *Around the World with General Grant*, published by Young in 1879.

Sherman's *Memoirs* emerged against this backdrop, and his first letter to Twain showed clearly that he was aiming the European travel narrative, envisioned as a money-making sequel to the *Memoirs*, at the market prepared by the narratives of Twain, Young, and others. Twain's response to Sherman's letter came in two parts, the first in a letter of September 19 agreeing to read the manuscript:

> Indeed I will read that MS with the greatest pleasure & give as square & honest an opinion as I possibly can; & I will also advise as to its disposition. I know I am competent & at home in the latter matter. I know even better how to advise, now, than I did when I advised General Grant; for at first I did not advise him to publish with any particular house, but only to require certain just & high terms; but *now* I should say "require just & high terms, but publish with Charles L. Webster & Co, *anyhow*." [I am Charles L. Webster & Co.— at last I am 90 percent of that firm.] And I should say it with a conscience clear & void of guile; for good generalship

is as necessary in the publishing field as in the military
field; & Webster has shown much the best generalship I
have ever seen in the former—both in the handling of my
last book & now General Grant's.[18]

Although his comparison of military generalship on a battlefield
with self-promoting savvy in the publishing marketplace may have
strained too hard, in this first letter Twain adopted the tone of
someone wooing a famous author for the privilege of handling
his next work. The frank admissions of having learned since giving Grant advice and of his own financial interest in Webster and
Company must have been particularly disarming and attractive.
In the second letter, written a little more than two weeks later,
over October 5 and 6, the tone changed, even as Twain continued
his military metaphor, brandishing his own military credentials,
minimal though they were:

You tempt me pretty nearly beyond my capacity to resist.
You offer me, at my own terms, a book which would sell
a great many thousand copies & make a large amount of
money for your old soldiers & other beneficiaries, & also for
me; but you have given me permission to advise, & I regard
the permission as a command: in fact, by old military
custom & habit, you *did* command—& as I have been a
soldier myself, once, it comes easy to obey. My distinct &
well-considered advice is, *do not publish it*; & do not allow
affection-blinded friends to persuade you that I am wrong.
I am not wrong; I am right.[19]

If Sherman could have read Twain's "The Private History of a
Campaign That Failed," published in *Century* two months after
this letter was written, he might have met this bid for authority
conferred by military service with stiffer resistance.[20] Not only was
Twain's service laughably minor and inglorious; his humorous account of it parodied in not so subtle ways many of the war memoirs published by *Century* in the series "Battles and Leaders of the
Civil War," not to mention aspects of Sherman's and Grant's own

memoirs. Despite, or because of, the bald-faced effrontery of this inconsistency, Twain's letter was a bravura performance, a model for any rejection letter, a shrewd assessment of the fragility of literary reputation, and an acute piece of literary criticism:

> If you had never written a book at all, I would still advise against the publication of this one; I advise against it all the more strongly in view of the fact that you *have* written one before this; & with it this one would be brought into instant comparison. Your "Memoirs" are rich [*bottom of page torn away to cancel one line*] [*one word canceled*] in incident, anecdote, fact, history; it is a book which is all food, & all nutricious—it is *fat*, there is no lean, there is no waste matter; its interest is unflagging & absorbing; it is a model narrative, & will last as long as the narrative language lasts. If I had read my own books half as many times as I have read these Memoirs, I should be a wiser & better man than I am. *There's* the true test of a book!—to be able to read it over & over & over again—& that is the kind of book the Memoirs are. I wish I had it; for in spite of the fact that it is not new, I think I could sell a large edition.[21]

No doubt some of Twain's fulsome praise should be discounted as intended to moderate Sherman's disappointment by the advice he was giving, advice the latter graciously accepted in his response of October 9. But even with such a discount, and despite the metaphoric slippage that equates pure fat with nutritiousness, Twain's assessment of the *Memoirs* leads usefully to fuller consideration of Sherman's remarkably effective mixing of "incident, anecdote, fact, history." By comparison, Twain continued, turning to a corporeal metaphor, the manuscript of Sherman's European trip offered "a thousand *texts* from which to write a book of travels; they are valuable texts, a skeleton is valuable, but it must have the meat on it, & the muscle, & the beating heart, & the blood in the veins before it can march." Because the *Memoirs* marched so well on narrative meat, muscle, heartbeat, and blood, Sherman had set a standard by which any later publications would be judged. He himself realized the complexity of his situation, referring to himself from the objective distance of the third person in his letter to Twain of September 22: "I am perfectly conscious that General Sherman occupies an official position which should not be imperilled by injudicious publication."[22] Closing his October 6 postscript, Twain confirmed Sherman's intuition by adding for good measure, "But don't forget this: Tom, Dick or Harry can reduce the size of his footprint if he wants to, but Hercules can't. He must leave a No. 19 track behind him all the time."

Twain was right in saying that incident, anecdote, fact, and history provided the meat, muscle, heartbeat, and blood of the *Memoirs*. One could divide much, if not most, of Sherman's book into these four categories. But incident, anecdote, fact, and history also provide the meat, muscle, heartbeat, and blood of much of the best travel literature, such as Twain's own, whereas in his *Memoirs*, inclined as he was to the reading and writing of travel literature, Sherman added a significant new component, and not just a little of it; he added the presentation of primary documents in the form of many, many letters, telegrams, dispatches, reports, and tables produced by himself and others. Twain remained silent on this aspect of Sherman's narrative, and any later reader's appreciation of its "unflagging & absorbing" interest will stand or fall on a response to these documents. The first inserted letter, written by Sherman to Louisiana governor Thomas O. Moore, January 18, 1861, did not appear until the chapter "Louisiana," sixth in the first edition, seventh in the second (*Memoirs*, 174), and the first inserted dispatch, from Postmaster General Montgomery Blair to Sherman, April 6, 1861, followed in the next chapter, "Missouri" (*Memoirs*, 188). From this moment on the primary documents followed thickly, some of them quite long, as in the case of Sherman's report to John A. Rawlins, December 19, 1863, which runs twenty pages of small or very small print, depending on the edition (*Memoirs*, 394–413).

By contrast, Grant's *Personal Memoirs* contained many fewer documents, and many of the ones included appeared at the bottoms of pages as footnotes. Sherman's *Memoirs* cannot help but suffer by comparison in the eyes of those readers who share the opinion of William S. McFeely: "Sherman's narrative skills are formidable, but he does make the mistake of interrupting his voice of reminiscence, the voice of 1875, with too many wartime letters and reports."[23] Did Sherman make a mistake in interrupting the "voice of reminiscence"? Many readers of Melville's *Moby-Dick* have made similar criticisms of that book: Melville should have cut all the cetology chapters, which focus on the particulars of whales and the business of whaling, in order to concentrate solely on the romance of Captain Ahab's monomaniacal quest for the White Whale. One cannot argue an individual reader out of his or her taste for a certain kind of reading, and abridgements of *Moby-Dick* cater to readers who want nothing beyond the romance of the quest. But one can argue that it is mistaken to assume the point of Sherman's *Memoirs* was only to reminisce about the years 1846–65 from the vantage point of 1875.

Here the nature of genre becomes an issue because the generic identity of a work amounts to a contract between writer and reader. If a work presents itself as full-blown conventional autobiography, a reader has a right to expect the writer to deliver the details of ancestry, birth, and childhood, especially after the emergence of Freudian psychoanalysis asserted the primary significance of parentage and childhood experiences. If a work presents itself as a memoir, a reader has a right to expect that the writer's reminiscences will narrow to focus predominantly on his or her involvement in particular events or experiences that constitute an unusually significant slice of a life.[24] In Sherman's case the difference between the first and second editions reflected some of the differences between memoir and autobiography, although bookending the first edition with autobiographical chapters, each surveying many years, did not alter the core of the book. But whether memoir or autobiography, Sherman's memoirs have much in common with another genre, the formal defense or "apology," a word that comes from Greek *apologiā*, or speech in defense.

A paradox of Sherman's *Memoirs* is that one of the great offensive campaigners of military history should have written a book in which he constantly put himself on the defensive. His inclusion of so many of his own letters and reports also may have had a narcissistic aspect, to be sure; with respect to the battle of Shiloh, for example, he stated bluntly, "I think my several reports of that battle are condensed and good, made on the spot, when all the names and facts were fresh in my memory, and are herewith given entire" (*Memoirs*, 250). It is difficult to imagine the modest Grant making such a statement, and he did not include one in his *Personal Memoirs*. But then Grant, though hardly without his share of criticism and controversy, as after the battle of Shiloh, did not find himself the subject of such constant criticism and controversy, real or imagined, as Sherman. As Lewis pointed out in a shrewd formulation, "There was irony in the fact that as a general thing Grant did not share the hatred given Sherman by the South. . . . Both sections came to praise if not revere those enemies who had destroyed human life [Grant and Lee] and to execrate those enemies who had destroyed barns [Sherman and Confederate raider John Morgan]" (*Fighting Prophet*, 620). Moreover, unlike Grant, Sherman was a lawyer, and he met the charges against him as a lawyer would meet charges against a client, with abundant documentary evidence. The word "documentary," now associated primarily with a genre of filmmaking, in fact appeared first in the early nineteenth century in the context of jurisprudence and "documentary evidence" (*Oxford English Dictionary*).

The first spate of documentary evidence ran through Sherman's chapter "Louisiana," and he justified it explicitly as rebutting a charge against him: "I have given the above at some length, because, during the civil war, it was in Southern circles asserted that I was guilty of a breach of hospitality in taking up arms against the South" (*Memoirs*, 180). It would be much harder to charge Grant with breaching prewar southern hospitality because he did not enjoy the same extent of it that Sherman did, despite the former's agreeable recollections of "much pleasant intercourse between the inhabitants and the officers of the army" during the summer of 1844, when his regiment was at Camp Salubrity, Natchitoches Parish, Louisiana (*Personal Memoirs*, 27). Finding himself in a more complicated position, and having been charged with such a breach, what should Sherman have done? Would those who criticize him for including too many letters and reports have advised him to ignore the charge altogether or to mention it without attempting to refute it?

Sherman could not have narrated his involvement in the Civil War fully without narrating controversy, which dogged him from Louisiana to Kentucky, where he was called insane. It then blew up in Memphis, where newspapers accused him of "cruelty to the sick" (*Memoirs*, 296). Next came responses to his failed attack on the bluffs north of Vicksburg near Chickasaw Bayou, December 29, 1862 (*Memoirs*, 318). Then followed Chattanooga and reports that he was repulsed on the left, which he denied in the long report to Rawlins of December 19, 1863 (*Memoirs*, 403). After the Meridian Campaign, subject of the chapter that completed volume one, criticism surfaced that he should have continued to Mobile (*Memoirs*, 421). Then came in swift succession the charges of cruelty toward the citizens of Atlanta and the correspondence with Hood, the howls of Georgia during the March to the Sea, accusations following the burning of Columbia, and the storm over the terms of surrender offered Johnston after Bentonville. He received criticism for his harshness and criticism for his leniency. And controversy did not end for Sherman with the war. Despite the naive confidence expressed to his brother John, in a letter of January 23, 1875, that he had "carefully eliminated everything calculated to raise controversy, except where sustained by documents embraced in the work itself" (*Sherman Letters*, 343), the publication of the first edition of the *Memoirs* set many southern tempers boiling, among them those of Jefferson Davis and Pierre Gustave Toutant Beauregard (Lewis, *Fighting Prophet*, 619).

One could argue that even if Sherman the soldier was too thin-skinned and hotheaded when it came to taking criticism, much of which he brought down on himself, Sherman the writer should have devoted less space to rebutting that criticism in order to focus on the voice of reminiscence. But to argue this way is to argue that the *Memoirs* should have resigned from one genre and joined another. Again and again in his narrative, Sherman demonstrated clearly that preserving the Union may have been his larger reason for fighting the war but that preserving his good name was concurrently his private goal.[25] He explicitly said so, for example, after narrating the events in Kentucky behind the charges of his insanity: "Indeed, it was not until the following April that the battle of Shiloh gave me personally the chance to redeem my good name" (*Memoirs*, 233). As Joan Waugh has shown in *U. S. Grant: American Hero, American Myth* (2009), Grant's good name was in no danger when in 1884 he began to write his memoirs in order to recuperate the financial losses he had suffered.[26] Although he enjoyed his share of celebrity, Sherman, by contrast, could never free from criticism and controversy his most famous military achievements, the Atlanta campaign and the March to the Sea, although he downplayed the latter, perhaps disingenuously, as nothing more than a pragmatic "shift of base" (*Memoirs*, 697). The criticism and controversy have continued to persist, as in the case of Edmund Wilson's provocative, if simplistic, comparison of Sherman's "policy of deliberate intimidation" of the citizens of Atlanta to the *Blitzkrieg* of the Second World War.[27]

Sherman was not uniformly self-righteous, however. He included abundant documentation in his own self-defense, true, but when he realized he was at fault, he admitted so. "I think I made a mistake there," he stated bluntly in recounting his order to the "ever rash" General Joseph Mower to abandon his advance on Bentonville on March 21, 1865 (*Memoirs*, 786). Two pages later he returned to this mistake: "With the knowledge now possessed of his small force, of course I committed an error in not overwhelming Johnston's army on the 21st of March 1865" (*Memoirs*, 786). More charged and ambivalent was the admission to Stanton, in a letter of April 25, 1865, included in the chapter "End of the War," "I admit my folly in embracing in a military convention any civil matters" (*Memoirs*, 850). And then there was the self-aware candor of the comparison he drew between himself and Grant, posed as a question to President Andrew Johnson in a letter of January 31, 1868: "If this political atmosphere can disturb the equanimity of one so guarded and so prudent as he is, what will be the result with me, so careless, so outspoken as I am?" (*Memoirs*, 917).

Such moments may have been rare in Sherman's apology, but they remain rhetorically effective, for they help to establish an ethical persona behind the narrative, one who is not merely a compulsive hoarder of documents, displayed relentlessly for the sake of narcissistic exhibitionism. Furthermore, Sherman did not include every document he might well have, referring his reader several times to testimony before the Committee on the Conduct of the War (*Memoirs*, 486, for example) or acknowledging that earlier narratives of the war, John William Draper's *History of the Civil War in America* (1867-70) and Adam Badeau's *Military History of Ulysses S. Grant* (volume 1, 1868), had freed him to offer only "additional details" about Vicksburg (*Memoirs*, 326). Finally, and most important, unlike Grant, Sherman wrote his first edition before the Government Printing Office began publication of *The War of the Rebellion: A Compilation of the Official Records of the Union and Confederate Armies* (1880-1901). In the absence of published records, to which he might have referred his readers, Sherman had to act as his own compiler.

Those opposed to Sherman's constant documentation may remain unconvinced by these arguments, although reading the manuscript drafts of the *Memoirs*, instead of printed editions that set the documents in small type, might make them appreciate more the oases of legible penmanship provided by the many different clerks who copied the documents. But before we conclude by turning to examples of how Sherman the writer reworked the drafts of his reminiscences to strengthen the presentation, even the theatricality, of certain key incidents, it is important to note that in the *Memoirs* the many modes of reminiscence—"incident, anecdote, fact, history," along with didactic instruction, pervasive throughout but especially obvious in the original final chapter ("Conclusion—Military Lessons of the War")—did not remain wholly cut off from the many modes of documentation. Sherman engineered abundant continuity between them.

Let one small example suffice. Toward the middle of the December 19, 1863, report to Rawlins, the longest document included in the book, Sherman introduced this sentence into his narrative of the battle of Chattanooga, which had reached a moment when Jefferson C. Davis's division had arrived at the city depot: "The depot presented a scene of desolation that war alone exhibits—corn-meal and corn in huge burning piles, broken wagons, abandoned caissons, two thirty-two-pounder rifled-guns with carriages burned, pieces of pontoons, balks and chesses, etc., destined doubtless for the famous invasion of Kentucky, and all manner of things, burning and broken" (*Memoirs*, 404–5). With the words "burning," "burned," and "broken" returning rhythmically in the manner of a refrain, this sonorous verbal painting was vintage Sherman, Sherman in the descriptive vein he developed while traveling, the vein that made Lewis imagine the artist-turned-soldier wishing for canvas. What business did such a sentence have in an official report, especially with its didactic opening, "The depot presented a scene of desolation that war alone exhibits"? Did Sherman believe that Rawlins needed such a caption?

He did not always dilate his reports with such description, and he could be tersely tight-lipped, particularly in moments of what he called "intense feelings" (*Memoirs*, 374), as when, earlier in the same chapter, he briefly narrated the death of his son Willie from typhoid fever in camp, October 3, 1863, a little more than a year and a half after Lincoln's son of the same name died of the same cause: "Being in the very midst of an important military enterprise, I had hardly time to pause and think of my personal loss" (*Memoirs*, 374). Even more starkly austere was the account he gave of the death of General James McPherson, July 22, 1864, a close friend over whose body Sherman wept while continuing to direct the fighting in progress (Marszalek, *Passion for Order*, 277). In the final one-paragraph sentence of his report on the battle of Atlanta, he anticipated the powerful understatements later perfected by Ambrose Bierce and Ernest Hemingway: "General McPherson, when arranging his troops about 11 A.M., and passing from one column to another, incautiously rode upon an ambuscade without apprehension, at some distance ahead of his staff and orderlies, and was shot dead" (*Memoirs*, 556). "And was shot dead" exhibited the same compressed mastery as Lincoln's "And the war came." Sherman commanded both these abilities, to expand and to contract, along with many shadings in between, and he could produce any of them at any time, whether in the midst of narrative reminiscence or in an official report.

In looking closely at drafts of particular moments of reminiscence, one can see the writer at work, deliberately crafting. Although he could render the panoramic, open-air scenes and landscapes of war with proto-cinematic skill, as in the burning depot at Chattanooga or the smoldering ruins of Atlanta, it was in the small spaces of private encounters with other people that his powers matched those of playwrights and novelists he admired. In narrating, for example, his meeting with Johnston on April 17, 1865, to arrange the surrender of Johnston's army on terms that would soon have him reviled in northern papers, Sherman intensified the drama of his account by sharing beforehand with his reader the news of Lincoln's assassination, just arrived that morning and deliberately hidden from everyone else but the telegraph operator who deciphered the message. "Dreading the effect of such a message at that critical instant of time," he met Johnston, whom he had not encountered before: "We shook hands, and introduced our respective attendants. I asked if there was a place convenient where we could be private, and General Johnston said he had passed a small farm-house a short distance back, when we rode back to it together side by side, our staff-officers and escorts following" (*Memoirs*, 836–37).

Having described this arrangement of a private interview with his adversary at the farmhouse of James and Nancy Bennett, Sherman continued in a new paragraph: "As soon as we were alone together I showed him the dispatch announcing Mr. Lincoln's assassination, and watched him closely" (*Memoirs*, 837). The four-word phrase "and watched him closely" added no significant information whatever to the narrative; it was pure theatricality, in the root sense of "theater" as action staged for the benefit of people who are looking and watching. The phrase functioned as a parenthetical stage direction and anticipated moments in screenplays that call for close-up shots. By directing attention to his own watching, Sherman made his reader watch him watch, much as productions of *Hamlet* make us watch Hamlet watch Claudius watch the players. Having directed his reader's attention so forcefully, his manuscript draft then focused on Johnston's reaction this way: "The perspiration came out on his forehead, and he did not attempt to conceal his distress." It was an evocative detail, Johnston's sudden anxiety forcing him to sweat on a spring morning, and Sherman could have left it there. But he did not. Instead, he inserted above the line, and over a caret mark after "out," the small prepositional phrase, retained in the published version, "in large drops."[28]

Against the backdrop of a thousand-page narrative, the insertion added little. But it strengthened the image of Johnston's intense feelings and the theatricality of Sherman's watching Johnston as the reader watches him. Sherman may have been thinking of another moment of intense feeling and equally intense watching, one in Shakespeare's *1 Henry IV*, a play he alluded to elsewhere in his narrative (*Memoirs*, 132), when Lady Percy questions Hotspur, "For what offence have I this fortnight been / A banish'd woman from my Harry's bed?" In that speech (scene 3, lines 40–67), she continues by describing times when she has watched her warrior husband sleeping ("In thy faint slumbers I by thee have watch'd, / And heard thee murmur tales of iron war") and then comes to lines that must have had particular resonance for Sherman, as perhaps for Ellen, too: "Thy spirit within thee hath been so at war / And thus hath so bestirr'd thee in thy sleep, / That beads of sweat have stood upon thy brow / Like bubbles in a late disturbed-stream." Sherman may have read or reread this scene aboard the *Lexington*, where he also may have read its great precursor, when he finally turned to the Bible, Luke's gripping image, not found in the other gospels, of the perspiration of the doomed Jesus in the garden at Gethsemane: "And being in an agony he prayed more earnestly: and his sweat was as it were great drops of blood falling down to the ground" (Luke 22:44, King James Version).

Whatever the inspiration for Sherman's insertion of "in large drops," the addition improved the narrative, however slightly. But not all revisions, Sherman's or anyone else's, necessarily improve a narrative. Another dramatically rendered meeting with a few people in a small space appeared earlier in the same chapter, when Sherman recounted his meeting with Lincoln, Grant, and Admiral David Porter aboard the *River Queen*, March 28, 1865. Sherman began the account of what turned out to be his last meeting with Lincoln with nearly a page of social comedy, in which Julia Grant chastised her husband and Sherman for neglecting to ask after "*Mrs.* Lincoln" on a visit to the *River Queen* the day before, exclaiming over this breach of manners, "'Well, you are a pretty pair!'" (*Memoirs*, 811). In the next paragraph the two returned to the boat, along with Porter; attempted to make amends by asking after *Mrs.* Lincoln (wryly italicized twice by Sherman in the paragraph), who was indisposed and did not see them; and settled down to the business of discussing with the president the likelihood of "one more bloody battle," which the generals thought would be the last. Having shown Lincoln as distressed by the prospect of yet more bloodshed, Sherman turned to discussion of what should be done with Confederate political leaders who might be captured, chief among them Jefferson Davis. Although "hardly at liberty to speak his mind fully," Lincoln intimated that Davis should be allowed to "clear out, 'escape the country'" (*Memoirs*, 812). Sherman's manuscript draft completed the paragraph as follows: "As usual he illustrated his meaning by a story. A man once had taken the total abstinence pledge. When visiting a friend he was invited to take a drink, but declined on the score of his pledge, when his friend suggested a lemonade, to which he consented. When his friend was mixing the lemonade, he pointed to the Brandy bottle + said the lemonade would be more palatable if he were to pour in a little brandy, when he said if he could do so 'unbeknown to him' he would not object."[29]

Anecdote within an anecdote, Sherman's representation of the president both reflected and contributed to the posthumous image of Lincoln as political sage with a knack for folksy parables. The first glimpse of Lincoln in the *Memoirs* had come in the chapter "Missouri," in which Sherman recounted being introduced to the newly installed president by his brother John, a United States senator, in March 1861. From Sherman's point of view the meeting did not go well: "I was sadly disappointed, and remember that I broke out on John, d-mning the politicians generally" (*Memoirs*, 186). Lincoln soon returned in the following chapter, after "our late disaster at Bull Run," this time more attractively, delivering to dispirited United States soldiers "one of the neatest, best, and most feeling addresses I ever listened to" (*Memoirs*, 207). Two paragraphs later Sherman narrated an incident in which one of his captains complained to the president about Sherman's threat to shoot him if he attempted to leave because the term of his three-month enlistment had expired. Sherman gave Lincoln's response with full appreciation of the president's own flair for theatricality: "Mr. Lincoln looked at him, then at me, and stooping his tall, spare form toward the officer, said to him in a loud stage-whisper, easily heard for some yards around: 'Well, if I were you, and he threatened to shoot, I would not trust him, for I believe he would do it'" (*Memoirs*, 208).

With this second appearance of Lincoln, the *Memoirs* inscribed within the narrative a subtle story of conversion—Sherman, initially disappointed by the president, now won over and grateful to him "for his confidence" (*Memoirs*, 208). The anecdote of March 28, 1865, aboard the *River Queen* brought Lincoln on stage for a third and final time, but elsewhere in the *Memoirs* Sherman had some trouble blending Lincoln's offstage presence into the smooth chronological flow of his own story. In working to establish once and for all that the March to the Sea was his own idea and not Grant's, for example, Sherman flashed forward from Grant's order authorizing the march, dated November 2, 1864, to Lincoln's congratulatory telegram, dated December 26, 1864, and sent to Savannah after the march had been completed (*Memoirs*, 641). As elsewhere in the *Memoirs*, Sherman introduced the documentation in his own defense, but here it disrupted the narrative sequence. More problematic was the later inclusion of a letter from

Admiral John A. Dahlgren, dated April 10, 1865, which, in the course of affirmative remarks about Sherman's march through the Carolinas, referred to the assassination of Lincoln more than thirty pages before Sherman turned to it in preparation for his meeting with Johnston.

These examples show that Sherman could not wholly contain or manage the significance of Lincoln's omnipresence, both during the war as commander-in-chief and after the war as a national icon. A last, especially telling example appeared in the manuscript draft of the paragraph that closed the narration of the March 1865 meeting aboard the *River Queen*, the published version of which ends, "Of all the men I ever met, he seemed to possess more of the elements of greatness, combined with goodness, than any other" (*Memoirs*, 813). In the course of this paragraph Sherman asserted that in "the language of his second inaugural address, he seemed to have 'charity for all, malice toward none.'" Not only did Sherman misquote the opening of Lincoln's final paragraph, "With malice toward none; with charity for all"; in the manuscript he attributed the language to "his most extraordinary and eloquent speech at Gettysburg." This mistake, canceled and corrected in the manuscript, had about it more than a little irony, since the general required his son, Philemon Tecumseh, to study Lincoln's speeches "as models of lucidity and conciseness."[30]

Lincoln's is a large presence for any director to manage, and the revision Sherman made for the published version of Lincoln's anecdote about the man who, despite his abstinence pledge, hoped to have his lemonade spiked showed Sherman's *Memoirs* working hard to manage it. In the published version Sherman went on to gloss the president's parable by adding the sentence, "From this illustration I inferred that Mr. Lincoln wanted Davis to escape, 'unbeknown' to him" (*Memoirs*, 812). Here Sherman's didactic, managerial impulses got the better of him, and his revision pushed the anecdote one step too far, dissipating the power of Lincoln's sly indirectness with obvious interpretation of it. By contrast, when Grant presented a very similar version of Lincoln's parable in his *Personal Memoirs*, although he did not set it aboard the

River Queen with Sherman and Porter present, he wisely let the president have the last word: "'Doctor, couldn't you drop a bit of brandy in that unbeknownst to myself'" (*Personal Memoirs*, 628). Given Grant's suffering from throat cancer during the writing of his memoirs, and his prescribed regimen of cocaine and morphine use, one should be cautious about attributing too much aesthetic self-consciousness to particular moments, especially late in the book. But Grant's unannotated version stayed truer to the spirit of Lincoln's own suggestive roundaboutness.[31]

A third and final example from Sherman's manuscript comes with its version of a conversation between Grant and Sherman after the occupation of Corinth, Mississippi, by United States forces in May 1862. Grant mentioned nothing of the conversation in his *Personal Memoirs*, but he opened his corresponding chapter with a crisply direct and businesslike sentence that provided the background: "General Halleck arrived at Pittsburg Landing on the 11th of April [1862] and immediately assumed command in the field." The result was that Grant was demoted to "second in command of the whole, and was also supposed to be in command of the right wing and reserve" (*Personal Memoirs*, 200). A few pages later he added, "My position was so embarrassing in fact that I made several applications during the siege to be relieved" (*Personal Memoirs*, 203). Enter Sherman, whose version of events, in its published form, began with learning from Halleck "that General Grant was going away next morning": "Of course we all knew that he was chafing under the slights of his anomalous position, and I determined to see him on my way back" (*Memoirs*, 275). In his manuscript Sherman first cast this sentence as "I was aware that General Grant was not satisfied with his position and concluded to visit him on my way back to my camp."[32] Otherwise, up through the recounting of their conversation, the manuscript differed only slightly in particular details from the published version, which then quoted Grant this way: "After passing the usual compliments, I inquired if it were true that he was going away. He said, 'Yes.' I then inquired the reason, and he said: 'Sherman, you know. You know that I am in the way here. I have stood it as long as I can, and can endure it no longer.' I inquired where he was going to go, and he said, 'St. Louis.' I then asked if he had any business there, and he said, 'Not a bit.' I then begged him to stay, illustrating his case by my own" (*Memoirs*, 275–76).

Sherman's management of other people's voices is worth close scrutiny. He let people speak for themselves in their letters and reports, especially if they were saying things that reflected well on him. But outside such documents he tended to screen other people's voices with indirect discourse. There were exceptions, of course, but they often had to do with letting someone else speak for comic effect, as in Lincoln's stage-whisper reply to the disgruntled captain or Sherman's attempt at blackface mimicry when describing his meeting with "an old negro" in the chapter "The March to the Sea": "I inquired, 'What do you want, old man?' He answered, 'Dey say you is Massa Sherman.' I answered that such was the case, and inquired what he wanted. He only wanted to look at me, and kept muttering, 'Dis nigger can't sleep dis night'" (*Memoirs*, 662). In the narrative of meetings with Johnston, by contrast, he let Johnston speak only one word for himself, and both the italicizing of that word and the placement of it in quotation marks were changes made to the original draft: "He plainly and repeatedly admitted this, and added that any further fighting would be '*murder*'" (*Memoirs*, 837). Even Lincoln's remarks in the meeting aboard the *River Queen* were muffled by indirect discourse, until the anecdote about the man who took the abstinence pledge, not encased by quotation marks in the manuscript. It was a strong sign of Sherman's respect and affection for Grant that he quoted his friend directly but quieted into indirectness his own part of the conversation, which provided the minimal rhythmic frame "I inquired. . . . I then inquired. . . . I inquired. . . . I then asked . . . . I then begged," a frame within which Grant's short, staccato replies sounded even sharper. This simplified representation of the dialogue generated some of the same effects as classical stichomythia, the alternating of single lines by speakers in a play, and suggested Sherman's awareness of its inherent dramatic power.

In the light of subsequent events, this proved to be one of the most important conversations of the war. Sherman knew it, and his handling of the following narrative showed humility and deference to the magnitude of the moment. In the published version he continued with a long, intricately coordinated sentence: "Before the battle of Shiloh, I had been cast down by a mere newspaper assertion of 'crazy'; but that single battle had given me new life, and now I was in high feather; and I argued with him that, if he went away, events would go right along, and he would be left out; whereas, if he remained, some happy accident might restore him to favor and his true place" (*Memoirs*, 276). The manuscript version was more condensed—Sherman later added the clause "and now I was in high feather"—but it corresponds basically to the published version until this commentary in the manuscript: "He did remain, and most luckily for him it was, for had he gone to the rear then, his after career so brilliant might never have occurred— I have always believed that my personal visit to him that evening changed his purpose, for his trunks + boxes were already packed, ready for a start to St. Louis the next morning."[33] Again the didactic interpreter leapt forward to point his reader toward the significance of an event, as well as to his own prominent role in it. But this time Sherman had second thoughts and trusted his reader to draw the obvious conclusion. The published version omitted these two sentences and followed instead with "He certainly appreciated my friendly advice, and promised to wait awhile; at all events, not to go without seeing me again, or communicating with me" (*Memoirs*, 276). In this instance he bowed out in favor of the capabilities of implication.

If all narrative must select what to include and what to omit, then the best narrative is that which balances inclusion with omission most effectively and most memorably. Fifty years after the first edition of Sherman's *Memoirs*, Ernest Hemingway pushed the art of omission to new levels, claiming that a writer of prose who knows enough about a subject "may omit things," adding, "The dignity of movement of an ice-berg is due to only one-eighth of it being above water."[34] Neither his own temperament nor the expectations of nineteenth-century American readers would have permitted Sherman to leave seven-eighths of his story below the surface of his writing. It would take the magisterial obliqueness of Henry James, particularly in his great trilogy of late novels published in the first years of the twentieth century, to begin to sharpen readers' attention to the unspoken and prepare them for Hemingway's more radical modernist experiments.[35] Even those readers who appreciate and endorse Sherman's inclusion of abundant documentation throughout the *Memoirs* must recognize what he himself recognized: he was outspoken, he liked center stage, he liked to talk, often at length, and he liked to be heard. His characteristic thoroughness in logistical preparations for war-making had its counterpart in the thoroughness with which he narrated and documented the signal events of his military career. The very structure of his carefully jointed sentences reflected the operations of a mind inclined to qualify, elaborate, and supplement simple statements with additional material.

But Sherman could omit, too. In a short nonfictional piece entitled "The Crime at Pickett's Mill," Ambrose Bierce acerbically noted, for example, Sherman's omission of any reference to the disastrous attack of March 27, 1864, during the Atlanta Campaign: "It is ignored by General Sherman in his memoirs, yet Sherman ordered it."[36] With this omission Sherman opted for a narrative strategy different from Grant's frank admission after another disaster: "I have always regretted that the last assault at Cold Harbor was ever made" (*Personal Memoirs*, 477). Whether or not the attack at Pickett's Mill filled Sherman with similar regret, he did not say. But beyond the omission of a particular event, to which he might well have preferred not to call the reader's attention, one of his largest omissions in the *Memoirs* was the writing of his memoirs. In the final chapter of the 1886 edition he passed directly from the removal of his headquarters to St. Louis in the fall of 1874 to the scandal over Secretary of War W. W. Belknap's selling of sutlerships in the army, reported by newspapers in March 1876. There was no mention in the narrative itself of completing his memoirs in 1874 and publishing them in 1875, although he included abundant correspondence about his book, much of it laudatory, in an appendix to the second volume of the second edition. We began by noting that in the final paragraph of the 1886 edition, Sherman waived references to the other roles he played in his book, those of surveyor, banker, lawyer, professor of engineering, superintendent of Louisiana State Seminary, and street railway president. But readers who watch him all the way through his narrative will see him performing them nevertheless. What they will not see is a man who spent long hours at a desk generating a thousand pages of print based on prolific notes, letters, an early journal, dispatches, reports, and a previous attempt at autobiography. Reading about Sherman from 1861 on, they will see only the soldier, loyal, relentless, decisive, triumphant, just as he meant them to see.

CHAPTER FOUR

Ambrose Bierce, Chickamauga, and Ways to Write History

Valor, *n. A soldierly compound of vanity, duty and the gambler's hope.*

"Why have you halted?" roared the commander of a division at Chickamauga, who had ordered a charge; "move forward, sir, at once." "General," said the commander of the delinquent brigade, "I am persuaded that any further display of valor by my troops will bring them into collision with the enemy."
—The Devil's Dictionary *(1911)*

Writing on August 17, 1892, to Blanche Partington, one of his many disciples, from St. Helena, California, the Napa Valley town where he sought relief from chronic asthma and where one can stay where he did, now the Ambrose Bierce House Bed and Breakfast, a structure built on Main Street in 1872, Bierce, at the age of fifty, responded to the young woman's request for a list of books to read with, among others, this sentence: "Read Longinus, Herbert Spencer on Style, Pope's 'Essay on Criticism' (don't groan—the detractors of Pope are not always to have things their own way)[,] Lucian on the writing of history—though you need not write history."[1] Even this small sample of recommended works reveals much about Bierce's literary sensibility, its layers of neoclassicism and admiration for British models, the latter fueled in part by his residence in England from 1872 to 1875 and the former the impressive result of his autodidactic exertions, which led him to brandish his familiarity with Latin, though not with Greek.

Although consideration of any of the authors in his list could lead productively to discussion of Bierce the writer, the last name, that of Lucian, offers the swiftest access to Bierce's complicated dual relation as both participant in and subsequent chronicler of the events of September 19 and 20, 1863, near Chickamauga Creek in northwestern Georgia. Bierce wrote repeatedly about the battle of Chickamauga, in both published work and private correspondence, and his writings about the Confederate victory there are especially important because they illuminate his understanding of the art of writing history in general and Civil War military history in particular.

Bierce wrote one fictional treatment of the battle, a short story about a deaf-mute boy who wanders away from home during the fighting, falls asleep in the woods, awakes to a nightmarish procession of wounded soldiers retreating to a creek from which some of them drink, and returns to his house to find it on fire and his mother killed. Published under the simple title "Chickamauga" in the *San Francisco Examiner* on January 20, 1889, the story will occupy the final part of this discussion. But those unfamiliar with the narrative contours of the battle will get little help from Bierce's story, and no book or movie has yet lodged Chickamauga (second only to Gettysburg in casualties produced) in popular awareness, as Michael Shaara's novel *Killer Angels* (1974), Ken Burns's documentary *The Civil War* (1990), and Ronald Maxwell's feature film *Gettysburg* (1993) have done for the Pennsylvania battle, fought two and a half months earlier. Many brief summaries, available in reference books or on line, sketch the major phases of Chickamauga, but few are clearer and more concise than that offered by the National Park Service:

> After the Tullahoma Campaign [in Tennessee, June 23–30, 1863], [Union major general William] Rosecrans renewed his offensive, aiming to force the Confederates out of Chattanooga. The three army corps comprising Rosecrans's army split and set out for Chattanooga by separate routes. In early September, Rosecrans consolidated his

forces scattered in Tennessee and Georgia and forced
[Confederate general Braxton] Bragg's army out of
Chattanooga, heading south. The Union troops followed
it and brushed with it at Davis' Cross Roads. Bragg was
determined to reoccupy Chattanooga and decided to meet a
part of Rosecrans's army, defeat them, and then move back
into the city. On the 17th [of September, 1863] he headed
north, intending to meet and beat the XXI Army Corps. As
Bragg marched north on the 18th, his cavalry and infantry
fought with Union cavalry and mounted infantry which
were armed with Spencer repeating rifles. Fighting began
in earnest on the morning of the 19th, and Bragg's men
hammered but did not break the Union line. The next day,
Bragg continued his assault on the Union line on the left,
and in late morning, Rosecrans was informed that he had
a gap in this line. In moving units to shore up the supposed
gap, Rosecrans created one, and [Confederate lieutenant
general] James Longstreet's men promptly exploited it,
driving one-third of the Union army, including Rosecrans
himself, from the field. [Union major general] George
H. Thomas took over command and began consolidating
forces on Horseshoe Ridge and Snodgrass Hill. Although
the Rebels launched determined assaults on these forces,
they held until after dark. Thomas then led these men
from the field[,] leaving it to the Confederates. The Union
retired to Chattanooga while the Rebels occupied the
surrounding heights.[2]

With this summary as background to Bierce's several narrations
of Chickamauga, we can return to his suggestion to his young dis-
ciple that she consult Lucian on the writing of history. Footnotes to
the contrary notwithstanding (e.g., *Selected Letters*, 27–28), Lucian
was not a Greek, though he wrote in Greek, nor was he merely a
satirist, any more than was Alexander Pope or Bierce himself, if by
"satirist" one means a writer who only attacks and lampoons. Born
in Syria in the second century A.D., Lucian of Samosata lived in

the Roman Empire at its height, under Marcus Aurelius, and the work to which Bierce refers in his letter to Blanche Partington—its Greek title is *Pōs dei historian syngraphein*, which means literally "How it is binding to write history together" or "How one must compose history" and which is usually translated "How to Write History" or "The Way to Write History"—considers the writing of history in the context of recent warring with the Parthians over Armenia. The history of history around the Mediterranean shows it to be the offspring of war, and the recent conflict with the Parthians, according to Lucian, uncorked a spate of new histories of the fighting, so many of which are bad that he must first show his addressee, Philo, in what ways they offend and then give his prescriptions for writing good history: *"Well, I may be told, you have now a clear field; the thorns and brambles have all been extirpated, the débris of others' buildings has been carted off, the rough places have been made smooth; come, do a little construction yourself, and show that you are not only good at destroying, but capable of yourself planning a model, in which criticism itself shall find nothing to criticize."*[3]

Come, do a little construction yourself, and show that you are not only good at destroying. This is the ethos of true satire, as practiced by Lucian and his student Ambrose Bierce, and it explains much of what readers of Bierce describe under the heading of his contradictions. If in his writings—epistolary, journalistic, fictional—he was a fierce and feared destroyer, he was also a tirelessly productive builder. But this congruence of Lucian and Bierce as constructive satirists is not the only one. When it comes to presenting the ingredients of good history, Lucian not only prescribes ingredients Bierce uses; he describes traits Bierce embodies. Although no one who has published a book on Bierce seems to have taken his advice to Blanche Partington and read Lucian's twenty-five pages on the writing of history in order to understand Brigadier General William B. Hazen's young topographical officer at the battle of Chickamauga, or the older man who later wrote about that battle in a number of ways, Lucian's short work contains passage after passage that resonates sonorously with Bierce's historical outlook and authorial credo. Let three brief examples suffice:

> Well then, my perfect historian must start with two indispensable qualifications; the one is political insight, the other the faculty of expression; the first is the gift of nature, which can never be learnt; the second should have been acquired by long practice, unremitting toil, and loving study of the classics. (*Lucian*, 126)

> He must not be weak either at understanding or at making himself understood, but a man of penetration, a capable administrator—potentially, that is,—with a soldierly spirit (which does not however exclude the civil spirit), and some military experience; at the least he must have been in camp, seen troops drilled or manœuvred, know a little about weapons and military engines, the differences between line and column, cavalry and infantry tactics (with the reasons for them), frontal and flank attacks; in a word, none of your armchair strategists relying wholly on hearsay. (*Lucian*, 127)

> For history, I say again, has this and this only for its own; if a man will start upon it, he must sacrifice to no God but Truth; he must neglect all else; his sole rule and unerring guide is this—to think not of those who are listening to him now, but of the yet unborn who shall seek his converse. (*Lucian*, 128–29)

Bierce's qualification that Blanche should read Lucian "though you need not write history" suggests that, for her, the value of reading the ancient author would reside in his exhortations to seek truth, to ignore the self-interested responses of a contemporary audience, and to cultivate the faculty of expression, especially important to Bierce, who in 1909 published a little book entitled *Write It Right: A Little Blacklist of Literary Faults*. All these exhortations would have spoken to Bierce, too, of course, but Lucian's requirement that the historian also have some military experience would have excluded Bierce's young female correspondent and endorsed her mentor's own soldierly credentials. Bierce liked to flash those credentials, as we shall see shortly, and many of his biographers and literary critics have been somewhat hypnotized by them, as though his presence as a Union staff officer near the northern end of Poe Field on the long afternoon of Saturday, September 19, 1863, and on Snodgrass Hill during the even longer afternoon of the next day, Sunday, sufficed to put his various representations of Chickamauga beyond the reach of the kind of exacting historical cross-examination to which Lucian, like Bierce himself, put so many other historical writings. But if we are to honor the rigorous historiographic ethic that Lucian urged and Bierce endorsed, then we must sacrifice to no god but truth, even when truth complicates the image of Bierce as unimpeachably truthful witness.

A little more than two weeks before he wrote her to recommend Lucian, Bierce wrote Blanche from Angwin, California, also in Napa County, to lecture her on the difference between literature as art, in which he firmly believed, and literature as an instrument of social reform, which he just as firmly rejected. His lecture included this Lucian-worthy declaration: "The love of truth is good enough motive for me when I wrote of my fellow men" (*Selected Letters*, 23). As it subsequently turned out, Bierce's unapologetic identification of his own motives with truthfulness anticipated that of historian Archibald Gracie, whose painstakingly meticulous study *The Truth about Chickamauga* appeared in December 1911. What makes these two versions of self-proclaimed truthfulness more than coincidental is that Bierce corresponded with Gracie during the writing of his book, and their correspondence, only one item of which has received any appreciable attention from Bierce scholars, is worth a closer look.

Son of Brigadier General Archibald Gracie III, who commanded Gracie's Brigade of Preston's Division of Buckner's Corps of Longstreet's Left Wing of Bragg's Army of Tennessee and who was later killed at Petersburg, the younger Gracie made clear from the outset that he was a man on a mission and that his mission was to "show how the history of Chickamauga has ever since the day it was fought been made a conspiracy for the silencing and suppression of truth."[4] According to Gracie, this historiographic conspiracy included "the fact that the Confederate soldier's testimony was thus thrown out and no attempt made to reconcile his statements with the truth" (*Truth*, 5). In his opening chapter, which he titled "Elimination of False History," Gracie continued, "and (*hinc illæ lachrymæ* ['hence those tears': quotation from Roman playwright Terence]) it was due thereto that my work was undertaken, and an effort made to find the truth, first, from the Federal reports themselves, then from the Confederate, and reconcile the two" (*Truth*, 5). As Ralph Waldo Emerson proclaimed in 1841 in his essay "Self-Reliance," "If I know your sect I anticipate your argument," and anyone reading only this far in Gracie's book could be excused for anticipating that an author lamenting the suppression of Confederate testimony, who was also the son of a Confederate general, had probably written a book devoted to tipping the balance back toward a Confederate perspective, especially when the reader finds, twenty-five pages later, that "the heart of this hydra-headed monster of untruth . . . comes from the newspaper writings and similar publications of Colonel Henry V. Boynton" (*Truth*, 30), who at Chickamauga commanded the Thirty-fifth Ohio, Third Brigade (Van Derveer), Third Division (Brannan) of Thomas's Fourteenth Army Corps.

But Gracie turned out to be a truer student of the truth, and his book, which contains foldout maps that anticipated Peter Cozzens's later designation of the three hills comprising Horseshoe Ridge as Numbers One, Two, and Three, although Cozzens does not credit Gracie with the designation,[5] undertook to correct Boynton, author of *The National Military Park, Chickamauga-Chattanooga: An Historical Guide* (1895) and later "called upon to fill the office of Historian of the Park Commission" (*Truth*, 32), not to promote a Confederate perspective but rather to clean up the "awful mess" Boynton made because of his desire to promote the importance of the Thirty-fifth Ohio on Horseshoe Ridge (*Truth*, 33). Furthermore, in the process of making such an awful historiographic mess, Boynton distracted attention from units that actually deserved credit, as Gracie proposed to demonstrate by careful examination of *The War of the Rebellion: A Compilation of the Official Records of the Union and Confederate Armies (OR)*, recently completed in 1901.[6] According to Gracie, Boynton's chief fault as historian was that he did not bother to consult the *OR*.

Among the units receiving considerable attention from Gracie were the Ninth Indiana (Suman), Bierce's own original regiment in Hazen's Second Brigade of the Second Division (Palmer) of Crittenden's Twenty-first Army Corps (see, for example, *Truth*, 407–9), and the Ohio Light Artillery, Eighteenth Battery (Aleshire), belonging to the First Brigade (Whitaker) of the First Division (Steedman) of Gordon Granger's Reserve Corps.[7] This battery included Lieutenant Albert Sherwood Bierce, Bierce's immediately older sibling in a family of thirteen children, the last three of whom did not survive childhood. In his preface Gracie thanked "surviving comrades of the Army of the Cumberland with whom I have had an exhaustive correspondence" (*Truth*, xii), and the two Bierce brothers contributed to that exhaustive correspondence. A portion of a letter from Albert appeared among the endnotes to Gracie's book (*Truth*, 405–6), and Ambrose wrote Gracie a letter, dated March 9, 1911, that found its way into a published book only in 1998, though it was subsequently reprinted in two others.[8] It is to this letter that we now turn.

At first glance, and considered out of context as it appears in the books that contain it, Bierce's letter to Gracie would seem to offer champions of Bierce many familiar satisfactions, as the veteran who had read Lucian undertook to set the younger historian straight without troubling to do so gently. Including in his first sentence the bold opening gambit, "I infer that you are really desirous of the truth" (*Selected Letters*, 210), Bierce proceeded to deliver that truth, in the process condescending to admonish Gracie about the need for good historiographic sportsmanship: "The historians who have found, and will continue to find, general acceptance are those who have most generously affirmed the good faith and valor of their enemies. All this, however, you have of course considered. But consider it again" (*Selected Letters*, 211). Many readers of Bierce know him as so dazzlingly offensive, in both senses, that they may not always consider how sometimes his aggressive offensiveness also may have functioned to defend his own limitations and shortcomings. Examined a little more closely, and in conjunction with other documents, Bierce's letter to Gracie turns out to be not a shining moment of historical instruction but something of an embarrassment.

First, if ever there has been a military historian who needed no lecture on how to affirm the good faith and valor of his enemies generously, it is Archibald Gracie. We do not know the nature of all his consultations with Bierce, and Bierce probably would not have read everything Gracie wrote about Chickamauga before he published it, but subsequent letters from Gracie to Bierce clearly show the former working strenuously to give full credit where credit was due, as does this representative sentence from Gracie's book: "This my first volume, while intended to preserve the truth and record of great deeds, is also devoted to the memories of those Federal soldiers whose records have suffered by most undeserved aspersions cast upon their conduct and character" (*Truth*, xi). Bierce saw things differently, however, and warning Gracie against history written by "bad losers" (his phrase), he continued, "your strange views of Thomas, Granger and Brannan, and some of the events in which they figured, are (to me) so obviously erroneous that I find myself unable to account for them on the hypothesis of an entirely open mind" (*Selected Letters*, 210).

But the mind not entirely open appears to have been Bierce's, when one considers, for one example, that Gracie thought enough of his enemies to use a photograph of Thomas, the "Rock of Chickamauga," as the frontispiece to his book and, for another, that with respect to the question of Granger's presence or absence on Horseshoe Ridge during the afternoon of September 20, Gracie worked diligently to supplement the *OR* with extensive correspondence documented in long endnotes (see *Truth*, 228–29, 428–37, 448–49). Furthermore, more recent accounts of Granger's behavior, after marching his troops to Thomas's support, suggest that this balanced statement by Gracie is wholly justified: "After General Granger had performed his great service in saving the army under Thomas by his timely arrival, it does not appear from our study of the Records and from our information from authoritative sources, that his subsequent services were at all creditable" (*Truth*, 157).[9]

This kind of criticism of Granger could have posed problems for Bierce. For one thing, not only was Granger Albert Bierce's corps commander; according to Cozzens, the general helped Albert's battery "place his pieces and then set to work aiming and firing them" (*Terrible Sound*, 450). With his own commanding general pitching eagerly into the same gritty work he was doing, how could Albert avoid the conclusion in his unpublished letter to his brother, dated March 29, 1911, "I believe there were some officers in high command who did not do their whole duty at Chickamauga but Thomas, Granger and Brannan were not in that class surely" (see Appendix)? That Granger might have been better employed closer to his own troops extending the precarious Union right on Horseshoe Ridge does not seem to have occurred to either Bierce. For another thing, criticism of Granger could have taken some of the shine off Bierce's "happy distinction of a discoverer" of Granger's approach toward Snodgrass Hill (Bierce was the only person on Snodgrass Hill to notice the approach of James B. Steedman's two-brigade division, or in the midst of so many intensities could be sure he was the first to do so?), a distinction he later represented in the "little unmilitary sketch" he lent Gracie (*Selected Letters*, 211), "A Little of Chickamauga," first published in the *San Francisco Examiner* (April 24, 1898).[10] To be sure, it is a far better distinction to discover an approaching hero, or to claim that one has, than it is to discover an approaching commander whose record later turns out to be mixed.

A second questionable aspect of Bierce's letter to Gracie involves place-naming and topography, the veteran's specialty, as he was quick to remind Gracie with his credentials: "I passed almost the entire afternoon at and near the Snodgrass house, with nothing to do but look on, and, as a topographical officer, with some natural interest in, and knowledge of, 'the lay of the land'" (*Selected Letters*, 211). The point in question was the identification of the three-hill ridge to the south and west of the Snodgrass house: "Hazen's fire was at no time directed toward what I think you call Horse-shoe Ridge," then after an intervening sentence, "The ridge immediately south of the Snodgrass house (I do not know if that is the one that you call Horse-shoe Ridge) was at no time, until after nightfall, occupied by the Confederates, nor was any other part of the ridges that our forces held" (*Selected Letters*, 211).

What these two sentences show is that Bierce's credentials as a witness to events on Snodgrass Hill did not also make him a thorough reader of writings about those events. In fairness to him, the ridge now designated as Horseshoe Ridge on most recent maps of the battle did not have that name at the time of the battle, or Bierce most certainly would have known it. It was the battle of Chickamauga that christened this particular topographic feature, as so many other battles produced so many other capitalized names of topographic features on other fields in both the eastern and western theaters. But when did the name emerge? Cozzens comments, "From the Snodgrass hill west to the Dry Valley road was a series of hills and ridges that after the battle become known collectively as Horseshoe Ridge" (*Terrible Sound*, 417–18). But how long after? Was it in 1911, when Gracie took a long paragraph's worth of pains to warn his reader against "the pitfalls of nomenclature": "Let him not be misled by any such general terms as 'Snodgrass Hill,' or the 'Snodgrass Hill Line.'" Instead, "Let him use the term '*Horseshoe Ridge*'" (*Truth*, 33). If this moment marked the birth of the name, certainly Bierce could be excused for not knowing it. But it did not.

The name "Horseshoe Ridge" appeared in Granger's reports of the battle, dated September 30, 1863, and his handling of it with quotation marks showed the freshness of the designation:

At about 1 P.M. I reported to General Thomas. His forces were at that time stationed upon the brow of and holding a "horseshoe ridge." The enemy were pressing him hard in front and endeavoring to turn both of his flanks.

To the right of this position was a ridge running east and west, and nearly at right angles therewith. Upon this the enemy were just forming. They also had possession of a gorge in the same, through which they were rapidly moving in large masses, with the design of falling upon the right flank and rear of the forces upon the Horseshoe Ridge.[11]

We cannot know for sure, though perhaps we can imagine, when the first soldier or officer pointed to the ridge line and compared it to a horseshoe, but we can and do know that the name was in official circulation ten days after the battle. Again in fairness to Bierce, he could not have had access to Granger's reports in the *OR* until 1890, but that date still would have given him twenty-one years until his correspondence with Gracie. Meanwhile, Granger need not have been Bierce's only source for the name. Brigadier General John B. Turchin, Third Brigade, Fourth Division, Fourteenth Army Corps, used it throughout his 1888 book *Chickamauga*, for example, and seven years later it appeared in Boynton's historical guide to the newly created national military park.[12]

Whatever the written antecedents of the name "Horseshoe Ridge," one cannot help wondering what a self-described topographical officer, "with nothing to do but look on" in the vicinity of two generals, Thomas and Granger, was doing with his "natural interest in, and knowledge of, 'the lay of the land,'" if he was not seizing immediately on every scrap of newly minted nomenclature adhering to the lay of that land. But behind this wondering looms a larger question about Bierce and his ways of writing, and judging the writing of, history: Is it enough to have been there? In his letter to Gracie, he assumed the posture of affirming that it is, and many of his readers and critics seem to concur, if their ready acceptance of his versions of events is any indication. But Bierce himself has written one of the great passages on the limitations that inevitably circumscribe the perceptions of an eyewitness during a Civil War battle, and the passage appeared in the piece that follows "A Little of Chickamauga" in his *Collected Works*, "The Crime at Pickett's Mill," first published in the *San Francisco Examiner*, May 27, 1888. This long passage ends with the summary sentence, "It may be said, generally, that a soldier's knowledge of what is going on about him is coterminous with his official relation to it and his personal connection with it; what is going on in front of him he does not know at all until he learns it afterward" (*CW*, 1:281).

To think otherwise would be naive, and there was something uncharacteristically naive about Bierce's response to Gracie, who clearly had read much more about Chickamauga than he had. How did a Civil War soldier learn afterward about what had gone on in front of him? He read. Bierce read, too, of course, but his letter to Gracie showed that he read rather selectively. One of the things he did read, which he mentions twice in his letter to Gracie, was Lieutenant General Daniel Harvey Hill's "Chickamauga—The Great Battle of the West," first published in *Century Magazine* in April 1887 and reprinted in the third volume of *Battles and Leaders of the Civil War* (1888). In his first reference to Hill's account, Bierce pointed to the Confederate general as an example of "the 'good loser'" of the war "and, with reference to the battle of Chickamauga, the good winner," someone who pays the "tribute of admiration to some of the men whom he fought" (*Selected Letters*, 210–11). In the second reference, Bierce concurred with Hill on the time of Granger's arrival as about two hours later than the 1:00 P.M. time in Granger's official report. But although Hill's account contains much of undisputed value for the student of Chickamauga, Bierce again appears to have been somewhat naive in holding Hill up as the standard of judicious and accurate historiography. Moreover, a closer look at Hill's account sheds some light on Bierce's own writings about Chickamauga.

Whatever else one can say of Hill's battlefield record, which included his leadership in Bloody Lane at Sharpsburg (Antietam), one cannot say that the battle of Chickamauga was his shining hour, and whatever else one can say about his account of Chickamauga, one cannot say that it was free from all taint of bad losing. In the case of his contribution to *Century Magazine*, Hill did not come across as a bad loser of the war; he came across as a bad loser to Braxton Bragg, who after the battle requested that Hill be relieved from duty, as he subsequently was. For all its other virtues as a piece of historical narrative, some of which clearly impressed

Bierce, "Chickamauga—The Great Battle of the West" was about blaming Bragg for failure: "As the failure of Bragg to beat Rosecrans in detail has been the subject of much criticism, it may be well to look into the causes of the failure."[13]

Not surprisingly, Hill's account did not receive much attention in Gracie's book, which mentioned Hill only once in four hundred and fifty pages and cited his article only four times, once to correct it, since Gracie's judgment of Bragg's performance differed markedly from Hill's: "In the course of my study, however, I have awakened to the fact that, whatever may have been his faults before or immediately after the Battle of Chickamauga, there is no evidence in the Official Reports of any action or order of his, particularly on September 20, which I can find deserving of anything but the greatest of praise. The worst that can be said against him is that he was unfortunate,—therefore unsuccessful as a leader" (*Truth*, 31–32). Some may feel that this assessment lets Bragg off too easily, but recent historians of Chickamauga confirm that having Hill as a subordinate was among Bragg's misfortunes. Glenn Tucker asserts that Bragg was "poorly served" by Hill, who before the battle failed, in Bragg's judgment, to "bag Negley in McLemore's Cove" (*Bloody Battle*, 67, 214). Cozzens judges that "Bragg erred both in giving Polk only oral attack orders on the night of the nineteenth and then in failing to see they were implemented," and he gives Hill's account the last word in his book, but he also paints Hill throughout as a sulker who carried out his orders "with the energy of a sloth" (*Terrible Sound*, 309–10, 489).

Although students of Chickamauga may apportion blame to Bragg and Hill in different proportions, if blaming is what they incline toward, no informed student of the battle now can see Hill, in his capacity as general, as trustingly as Bierce did. But in his capacity as writer, Hill deserves more attention, particularly with respect to the visible effects of his writing on Bierce's own treatments of Chickamauga, the first of which, "On Chickamauga," appeared in the *San Francisco Examiner* on November 11, 1888, or just nineteen months after Hill's piece in magazine form. Then, two months later, came the famous story "Chickamauga."

One can make different arguments about the timing of Bierce's Civil War writings; in 1888 he published eight pieces, in 1889 six, and these two years rank first and second in his output of material about the war (*Phantoms*, 344–46). In a letter of August 13, 1887, to Sergeant Abe Dills, Bierce expressed gratitude for an invitation to a reunion of the Ninth Indiana, which he did not accept, and then continued, "Your letter has called up all manner of memories—men and things that had not for years been in my mind" (*Selected Letters*, 20). Exerting itself throughout the United States in the 1880s, the memory-stirring power of reunions corresponded to copious publication of Civil War writings as well, and the timing of Bierce's contributions certainly reflected this larger trend. Another stimulus could have been Boynton's visit to the Chickamauga battlefield with Ferdinand Van Derveer, his former brigade commander, in June 1888, a visit about which Boynton, Washington correspondent of the *Cincinnati Commercial Gazette* at the time, wrote a series of letters published in the newspaper. According to Boynton, these letters represented the first step toward development of the national military park.[14] Meanwhile, one reader of Bierce has linked his story "Chickamauga" to coverage by the *San Francisco Examiner* of the volatile situation in Samoa, where, until an agreement reached in 1899, Germany, Great Britain, and the United States were vying for influence and trade privileges.[15] Biographical pressures may have been driving Bierce as well, with the winter of 1888–89 bringing separation from his wife Mollie after his discovery of what he took for love letters from another man.[16] But whatever the promptings that pushed him to write about Chickamauga at a particular moment, Bierce still needed to figure out the way to write his versions of history, and it appears that Hill helped him do so.

In "The Way to Write History" Lucian advised the historian that "his attention should be for the generals first of all" (*Lucian*, 131). Despite a contemporary counter-current of attention paid to common soldiers—in, for example, Walt Whitman's *Memoranda During the War* (1875) or Sam Watkins's *"Co. Aytch"* (1882)—and despite moments in his own Civil War writings when he did focus on soldiers below the rank of general, Bierce certainly took Lucian's advice, especially in his nonfictional writings about Chickamauga. In particular, these writings show that he paid special attention to how generals talked and wrote. In "On Chickamauga," for example, Bierce attended to his division commander, John Palmer, whose "perfectly ghastly frankness" clearly impressed him and whose honesty in admitting error, in the general's later writing, clearly distinguished him in Bierce's mind (*Sole Survivor*, 35–36). In "A Little of Chickamauga" he singled out, through indirect discourse, the incivility, and implicit cowardice, of Major General James S. Negley, Second Division, Fourteenth Army Corps, and, by contrast, the tough single-mindedness of Hazen, whom Bierce admired (*CW*, 1:275–77). In a piece published in 1882, he quoted Brigadier General Thomas J. Wood's command, delivered "with marked impatience, 'General, send a couple of regiments and your battery out there and put an end to that fighting'" (*Sole Survivor*, 64). In attending so closely to the utterances of generals, Bierce appears to have been fascinated not only by what generals said and the consequences of their utterances—many of Bierce's war writings, fictional and nonfictional, pivot on the giving and following of particular orders—but also by how they said the things they said, by the tones, phrases, and formulas that reflect individual character and sensibility.

The only generals Bierce would have heard during Chickamauga would have been Union ones, but twenty-five years later he read Hill's narrative, and in that narrative he would have heard the tones of a kindred spirit, one who admired many of the same qualities he did and taught him ways to show his admiration in the manner of a West Point professional. Take, for example, Hill's description of Longstreet's breakthrough at the Brotherton farm during the late morning of September 20: "Discovering, with the true instinct of a soldier, that he could do more by turning to the right, he disregarded the order to wheel to the left and wheeled the other way" ("Great Battle," 655). Hill's reference to "the true instinct of a soldier" not only praised and endorsed Longstreet, a fellow member of the West Point class of 1842; it consolidated Hill's own authority as someone in a position to recognize and determine what constitutes true soldierly instinct in a general.

Neither a general, nor a professional, nor even a college graduate, Bierce struggled, according to one biographer, with feelings of inferiority in relation to West Pointers, and Hill's rhetorical move still reverberates with a confidence and authority Bierce apparently coveted.[17] In his depictions of Granger marching toward Snodgrass Hill, Bierce used versions of Hill's formula twice, first in "A Little of Chickamauga" and next in "War Topics," published in the *San Francisco Examiner* two weeks later, on May 8, 1898. In the former he described Granger as "moving soldier-like toward the sound of heavy firing" (*CW*, 1:276), and in the latter the phrasing was even closer to Hill's: "As to who saved the army there can be no two intelligent opinions: it was saved by the superb obstinacy of Thomas and the soldierly instinct of Gordon Granger in marching toward the sound of cannon" (*Sole Survivor*, 33–34). Necessarily limited by his relatively low rank in the chain of command and, consequently, by the restricted scope of his understanding, a young lieutenant's opinion of his corps commander would not necessarily carry on its own the same ring of unquestionable authority that Bierce established here with the help of Hill's professional tone, as though, like Hill on Longstreet, Bierce were praising his peers rather than his superiors.

Hill's narrative of Chickamauga contained many other tones and rhetorical flourishes that anticipated Bierce's war writings and may sound familiar to many of his readers. There was, for example, the drily civil understatement of "My interview with General Bragg at Chattanooga was not satisfactory" ("Great Battle," 639); the praise for coolness under fire, specifically with reference to Bushrod Johnson ("Great Battle," 655n); and moments of amused irony, such as this description of Thomas Crittenden, which appeared to consist of more praise for coolness but turned into subtle mockery of the kind Bierce came to master: "Surely in the annals of warfare there is no parallel to the coolness and nonchalance with which General Crittenden marched and counter-marched for a week with a delightful unconsciousness that he was in the presence of a force of superior strength" ("Great Battle," 643).

As for the faculty of expression extolled by Lucian, Hill's narration also provided models of compelling rhythmic variations, whether in the use of short sentences or clauses to puncture and deflate, a technique Bierce also employed (compare Hill's "but Bragg had other plans" with Bierce's "Chickamauga was a fight for possession of a road" ["Great Battle," 651; *CW*, 1:271]), or in the alternation of specific details of battle with sweeping, authoritative-sounding generalizations about leadership in warfare, such as a sentence by Hill beginning, "The one thing that a soldier never fails to understand is victory" or the sentence, "The great commander is he who makes his antagonist keep step with him" ("Great Battle," 639, 651). With such magisterial pronouncements as these, compare Bierce's dicta to Gracie about good historians or the statement about eyewitness perspectives in "The Crime at Pickett's Mill." Given the blind spots we have discovered in Bierce's view of Chickamauga, we might think a more circumspect, qualified tone appropriate for his letter to Gracie, but a circumspect, qualified tone would not have become the voice of military professionalism he admired in Hill, and this was the voice, or one of the voices, Bierce worked to develop in his war writings.

Hill's narrative of Chickamauga may also have influenced Bierce's fictional treatment of the battle, but before leaving the letter to Gracie and turning to that fiction on the way toward conclusion, we can glance fruitfully at two other sets of unpublished documents, one that illuminates Bierce's fascination with the giving of orders and one that raises some more questions about his accuracy as a historical witness.

On September 25, 1908, when he lived in Washington, D.C., Bierce wrote a letter to the adjutant general of the army, a letter the adjutant general then referred to Brigadier General William Wallace Wotherspoon, president of the Army War College. Wotherspoon's side of the correspondence soon makes it clear that "Major Bierce," as Wotherspoon addressed him (Bierce was commissioned Brevet Major as of March 13, 1865, "for distinguished

service during the war," the commission signed by Andrew Johnson and Edwin M. Stanton, August 3, 1866), had written the adjutant general seeking an opportunity "to explain and illustrate"
his "theory and system of giving oral commands." In his letter of
September 29, 1908, Wotherspoon invited Bierce "to come to the
War College at 1:30 p.m., Saturday, October 3rd, and either lecture
or explain and illustrate before the officers connected therewith,
your theory and system." In a letter of October 1, 1908, the general
expressed gratification at Bierce's acceptance of the invitation, invited him to "a very simple luncheon which we have daily at 12:30,"
and told him his talk could be "just as informal as you please." Subsequently, in a letter dated October 16, 1908, answering a letter of
Bierce's dated three days earlier, Wotherspoon summed up Bierce's
apparently successful visit: "Both I and the officers who listened
to you were so convinced of the correctness of your position in all
respects as to deem a field demonstration as unnecessary."[18]

According to biographer Walter Neale, "Bierce said that he
thought oral commands in the field should be given slowly, in rolling tones, as carrying several times farther than sharp and crisp
orders."[19] From this information, which Neale gave in the course of
illustrating Bierce's sense of inferiority with respect to West Point
officers, one may infer that Major Bierce went to the Army War
College to demonstrate the giving of orders in slow, rolling tones.
One might hear in Wotherspoon's third letter either the genuine
endorsement of someone wholly persuaded by Bierce's demonstration or the polite but firm refusal to humor the old veteran any
further (Bierce was then sixty-six). Either way, what is significant
and revealing about this incident is that late in his life Bierce identified so clearly with the army, with the officers of the army, and
with the giving of orders that is their responsibility and power.
Where did this identification come from? Did it come from the
single year he spent at the Kentucky Military Institute at Frank-
lin Springs, beginning in the fall of 1859? Did it come from admiration of his uncle, Lucius Verus Bierce, who went by the title
"General" and who, according to Roy Morris Jr., on December 3,
1838, "led a contingent of volunteers across Lake Erie aboard a

captured passenger steamer and set fire to the British barracks at Windsor" (Ontario)?[20] Or did it come from his own experiences as sergeant and lieutenant in Company C, Ninth Indiana, before his appointment to Hazen's staff, after which he would have had fewer opportunities to give orders than to execute them? Wherever it came from, his identification with order-giving officers challenges any reductive description of Bierce as so embittered and appalled by his military service that his attitudes toward the military, and toward the war-waging function of the military, turned wholly toward revulsion and cynicism.[21]

The second set of unpublished documents, those that raise more questions about Bierce's accuracy as historical witness, return us to his correspondence with Archibald Gracie, specifically to Gracie's side of that correspondence. In a letter of July 1, 1911, written not quite four months after Bierce's corrective letter to him, Gracie asked Bierce to examine a photograph of General Steedman with his staff "and state whether you recognize the members of the Staff and can give me their names. If so, please simply mark on the back of the picture, designating each Staff officer and whether he was with Steedman in the battle of Chickamauga." The painstaking carefulness reflected in this letter was typical of Gracie's procedure, and in a subsequent letter of July 22, 1911, he questioned Bierce's identification of himself in a photograph because Isaac Suman, Colonel of the Ninth Indiana at Chickamauga, had said, "you are mistaken." In his reply of July 24, 1911, Bierce admitted his error: "If you are in correspondence with Suman kindly make to him my acknowledgment of my error and convey my greeting. (Confidentially, I may say to you that he and I never loved each other as all are commanded by your Holy Scriptures to do.)"

A letter from Suman to Bierce, dated March 25, 1894, and addressed to "My Esteemed Capt. A. G. Bierce," was perfectly friendly and cordial, even nostalgic, in tone, culminating in the closing "Your comrade in the Ninth," so it remains unclear what animosity toward his old commander Bierce was still nursing seventeen years later in the summer of 1911.[22] What is clear is that, once again, Bierce's status as participant in the battle of Chickamauga did not guarantee the reliability of his testimony. This episode of his mistaken identification of himself in a photograph becomes especially interesting when one turns to page 318 of Gracie's *The Truth about Chickamauga* and recognizes the familiar and widely reproduced picture of the mustachioed Bierce in uniform, but then reads the caption "Jun. 1st Lieut. A. S. Bierce" and, at the bottom of the page, "18th Ohio Battery Officers." Is this a photograph of Ambrose Bierce or his brother Albert? The Elkhart County Historical Museum, in Bristol, Indiana, claims the former, as does everyone else who has reproduced the photograph, with the exception of Gracie, who sought Bierce's help in identifying the subjects of photographs he used. But even with an allowance for the indeterminacy of black-and-white contrast, the man in this photograph does not look blond, as Bierce has been described so frequently as being. Did he commit another error, mistaking his own young face for his brother's? Did Gracie make a mistake once Bierce had made the correct identification? Is the photograph really one of Albert, despite its wide dissemination as an image of Ambrose?

The mystery here, with its tantalizing evasion of verifiable factuality, leads easily and finally to Bierce's other way to write history, his short fiction. In many discussions of his story "Chickamauga," Bierce's readers have felt called upon, for reasons of their own, to describe it as one of his two greatest Civil War stories, the other being "An Occurrence at Owl Creek Bridge." This judgment, which is unnecessary, risks foreclosing full appreciation of the thirteen other stories in the "Soldiers" section of the second volume of Bierce's *Collected Works*, but it does testify to the power of Bierce's story of a deaf-mute boy wandering the edges of the Chickamauga battlefield during the fighting, as does the decision of French director Robert Enrico to make a film of the story, released in black and white in 1962. (Enrico also made films of Bierce's stories "The Mocking-Bird" and "An Occurrence at Owl Creek Bridge," the latter airing in the United States on *The Twilight Zone*, February 28, 1964.) Somewhat less predictable but still common are attempts by both professional and amateur readers of "Chickamauga" to identify the factual aspects of Bierce's fiction. In a letter of July

18, 1975, for example, one visitor to the Chickamauga and Chattanooga National Military Park wrote the superintendent, Robert L. Deskins, to ask about "parallels between the story and fact," anticipating by many years professional readers of Bierce interested in the same parallels.[23]

In his reply of July 24, 1975, Deskins summarized several facts that one could construe as connected to Bierce's story:

> Mr. George W. Snodgrass who lived on Chickamauga Battlefield, had two sons, Charles and Joh[n]. Charles was killed during the battle, but John managed to survive the battle and the war as he was a cripple.
>
> At the time of the Battle in 1863, there were 24 families living on the land which was to become Chickamauga Battlefield. The Glenn and Poe houses were destroyed by direct shell fire. It is possible that most of the other houses were destroyed or damaged by shell or musketry fire. This area in 1863 suffered one of the worse [sic] droughts that the State has ever had. The fields and woods were literally tinderboxes. Hot shot from the cannon set the woods afire and many soldiers burned to death.[24]

Deskins misread the ending of Bierce's story—he opened his letter by referring to "the death of the child" in it, though the deaf-mute child does not die—but he did point his correspondent to James A. Sartain's *History of Walker County, Georgia* (1932), also a source for Tucker and Cozzens (whose bibliography mistakes the author's name as "Sartrain") and those who have relied on them.

The section of Sartain's book devoted to the families living on the battlefield in fact was not written by Sartain; it was, according to his headnote, a reprint of an article by Charles W. Lusk, first published in the *Chattanooga Times* in September 1923. Lusk's article apparently provided Deskins with several of the details he gave his correspondent, such as the severe drought and the burning of the Poe and Glenn houses. But Lusk also provided details that Deskins did not mention: that the Poe house was burned by Confederate shells, not Union ones; that more than sixty local people left their houses at the start of the battle and spent eight days in a ravine northwest of the Snodgrass house; that these people suffered greatly both from overnight frost and from lack of water, since they were behind Union lines, until the Union retreat, and had no access to Chickamauga Creek; that the death of Charles Snodgrass was not that of a civilian, since he was a Confederate soldier who fought in the battle; that in addition to the two sons mentioned in Deskins's letter, the Snodgrass family included six younger children also at home when the battle began.[25]

Bierce had no access to Lusk's article, of course, and, to the extent that he drew on real topographic features, conditions, and events in writing "Chickamauga," he may have drawn on his own observations. Did he have any contact with local civilians before they withdrew to the ravine beyond the Snodgrass house? If so, did he encounter John Snodgrass and reimagine his disability as deaf-muteness? Did he see the Glenn or Poe house burning and use it as a model for the child's burning house at the end of the story? Perhaps so, but he could not have been omnipresent along a battle front of several miles, and two details in Hill's narrative suggest that it is just as likely that Bierce may have drawn on that narrative for some of his material. One detail appears in this sentence: "Wood's (Confederate) brigade on the left had almost reached Poe's house (the burning house) on the Chattanooga road, when he was subjected to a heavy enfilading and direct fire, and driven back with great loss" ("Great Battle," 656). The second appears in a caption beneath an image reproduced from a photograph of the sinkhole near the Glenn house: "This sink-hole contained the only water to be had in the central part of the battle-field. Colonel Wilder's brigade of mounted infantry at one time gained the pool after a hard contest and quenched their thirst. In the water were lying dead men and horses that had been wounded and had died while drinking" ("Great Battle," 656). A burning cabin and wounded men drowning while drinking from a water source (a creek in "Chickamauga," not a sinkhole; *CW*, 2:55) are two vivid images from a story full of them. Bierce could have encountered these images elsewhere, either in oral reportage or in print, if he did not see such sights himself, as would have been unlikely in the case of the men drinking at the sinkhole, since presumably he would have been with Hazen near the Kelly house when John Wilder was fighting at Bloody Pond around midday on September 20. But since we know that he read and admired Hill's narrative, it makes sense that Hill would have been, if not his only source for these images, then at least the most recent stimulus in recollecting them for his story.

Parallels between Bierce's story and the facts of the Chickamauga battlefield will be especially significant to those interested in how writers of historically based fiction go about the business of shaping their materials. That a few years after the publication of his story Bierce became acquainted with Elizabeth (Lily) Walsh, a young deaf-mute woman in whose life and writing he took keen interest before her early death in 1895 (see *Selected Letters*, 41, 45–48, 50, 54), might make some wish that chronology would permit the drawing of this parallel, too.[26] But to become preoccupied with drawing parallels between selected realities of Chickamauga and Bierce's fictionalization of Chickamauga is to risk missing at least one important point of that fictionalization: it is not realistic, and the ways in which it is not suggest that it never was intended to be.[27]

Bierce's departures from the realities of the battle are many and obvious: all the families had left the battlefield by the time the fighting erupted around their houses; the gradual arrival in the vicinity of more than 135,000 soldiers (*Terrible Sound*, 154)—a number exceeding that of the 1860 population of Chicago—with all their horses, mules, artillery, and wagons, could have taken no one by surprise, and no child would have been left alone to gambol through the woods during the gathering of the opposing armies; deafness does not preclude sensitivity to vibration, so the child's sleeping through the concussions of artillery fire, the advance of soldiers who "had almost trodden on him as he slept," and the fighting of a battle almost "within a stone's through of where he lay" (*CW*, 2:48–49, 54) suggest the magical sleep of Rip Van Winkle, rather than the real sleep of a real child;[28] and, finally, the topography of Bierce's plot does not agree at all with the real events of Chickamauga, since the only army that could have advanced and retreated near a creek would have been Bragg's, and any Confederate unit that both advanced and retreated did so well to the west of Chickamauga Creek.

Then there are all the details of the real conditions at Chickamauga about which Bierce's story is completely and inscrutably silent, such as the tinderbox dryness caused by drought; the resulting fires and immolation of wounded soldiers, as at Shiloh and the Wilderness (Bierce had written about the burning of soldiers at Shiloh in "What I Saw of Shiloh" [1881]; *CW*, 1:261–262); and the local families thirsting and shivering in the ravine northwest of the Snodgrass house. Given so many omissions, one might incline toward questioning, or at least, in the case of "Chickamauga," toward qualifying, the claims of those who have praised Bierce's realistic treatment of war, H. L. Mencken among them.[29] The one aspect of his story that some might associate with realism could be its graphic description of maimed bodies, especially those of a wounded soldier with "a face that lacked a lower jaw" (*CW*, 2:52) and of the child's dead mother, whose forehead has been torn away by a shell: "from the jagged hole the brain protruded, overflowing the temple, a frothy mass of gray, crowned with crimson bubbles" (*CW*, 2:57).[30] But do such graphic descriptions necessarily point toward realism? Some might call them pornographic instead. In itself, gory ghoulishness, a streak of which Bierce began showing early in his life, does not necessarily promote realism; it may lead instead toward violent fixation and gothic fantasy.[31]

If in "Chickamauga" Bierce was not trying to write realistically about the battle, what was he trying to do, and how does the story constitute a way of writing history? We can begin to answer these questions by looking at Bierce's little book *Write It Right*, his blacklist of literary faults, among which he included the mistaken use of "novel" for "romance": "In a novel there is at least an apparent attention to considerations of probability; it is a narrative of what might occur. Romance flies with a free wing and owns no allegiance to likelihood. Both are fiction, both works of imagination, but should not be confounded. They are as distinct as beast and bird."[32] According to his own definitions, Bierce's story is closer to the realm of romance than to that of the novel, and with "no allegiance to likelihood" it would seem to be the opposite of history. But the title, originally set in large bold type at the top of the leftmost column of the front page of the special Sunday section of the *San Francisco Examiner* for January 20, 1889, insisted to its first readers, as it still does, recalcitrant and unyielding, on linkage to a particular historical event.

One way to understand this insistence would be to say that for all his admiration of Lucian and Daniel Harvey Hill, for all his attentiveness to the words of generals and all his eagerness to correct Archibald Gracie's version of the truth about Chickamauga, for Bierce something about the battle clearly remained unspoken, both in the writings of others and in his own nonfictional efforts, which have furnished recent histories with colorful quotations (see, for example, *Bloody Battle*, 206; *Terrible Sound*, 257 and the title of chapter 13). In fact, the professional way of writing history, as exemplified by Hill, not only left much unspoken; it demonstrated that the true professional necessarily treated real aspects of war with a particular kind of decorous restraint, as when Hill described a wounded man, "his head partly supported by a tree," as "shockingly injured" ("Great Battle," 659). Hill's description was not a lie or an untruth. In its way it even may have been, and still be, more effectively suggestive, to some readers, than Bierce's graphic descriptions of wounds in "Chickamauga." But suggestive or not, it reflected the rhetorical code of an insider, someone who knew the reality of historical events so well that he could represent them adequately to other insiders, such as Bierce, with this kind of shorthand. Those insiders, in turn, knew how to decode the code.

But what about those who were not insiders? In Bierce's hands the decorous restraint of the military professional threatened to turn into, or converge with, what Edmund Wilson, in an ambivalent appraisal of Bierce's Civil War writing, called his "marble correctitude."[33] What Wilson may have missed, as in the case of the entry for "valor" in *The Devil's Dictionary* above, is that marble correctitude also provided Bierce with a target for mockery, especially in the context of combat. In other words, he, too, found something unsatisfactory about marble correctitude, particularly when it came to trying to convey to noncombatants, such as most readers of the *San Francisco Examiner*, the truth about the massive indecorousness of the battle of Chickamauga. In helping him get at this indecorous truth, neither Lucian of Samosata nor Daniel Harvey Hill could have been of much use. He needed something beyond the conventional codes of either the ancient historian or the professional general.

That something was fiction, by means of which Bierce also tried to write history from the opposite extreme of unlikely romance. In titling his unlikely romance "Chickamauga," Bierce in effect titled it "History" or "Real Historical Event." It is easy to say that fiction can tell truth in ways that nonfiction cannot, but it is not always so easy to say how. In his story about the battle, with "about" meaning both "with reference to" and "around," Bierce attempted to get at the truth, or another truth, of this historical event by disrupting the familiarity of conventional codes often used to represent it. The adjective "strange" appears five times in the story, piling up repetitions a stickling editor might question. But Bierce was severe in his self-justifying response to an early instance of editorial second-guessing: "Everything I send you is constructed with the utmost care; most of it being written three times over, and all of it twice" (*Selected Letters*, 5). If he used the word "strange" five times, he did so because he wanted to hammer a sense of strangeness into a reader's awareness, a strangeness nowhere to be found in, for example, Hill's account of Chickamauga, which worked to manage and contain strangeness with decorous professionalism and correctitude.

In choosing to filter a little of Chickamauga through the sensibility of a deaf-mute child, Bierce imagined a sensibility at the opposite end of the spectrum from that of a commanding general engaged in the battle. One, an insider, would have known as much about the battle as any person could know; the other, an outsider, would have known as little. Again and again in the story, Bierce represented these extremes by using the child's point of view to make strange what would be familiar to a veteran of Chickamauga and then dispelling the strangeness with a short, simple, matter-of-fact sentence, clause, or phrase: "They were men"; "He was dead"; "But that was blood"; "They were drowned"; "the work of a shell"; "The child was a deaf mute (*CW*, 2:50, 51, 55, 57)."[34] The last of these, "The child was a deaf mute" ("He was a deaf mute" in the *Examiner*), is the penultimate sentence of the story and springs a surprise ending, which some readers admire, while some do not. But the surprise of the ending cannot be separated from the chain of smaller surprises the story forges all along, the surprises of strange and unfamiliar things suddenly turned comprehensible, even if awfully so. Admittedly, surprise is not altogether foreign to the language of warfare, which includes the phrase "surprise attack." But the language of military history, whether written by a participant in events treated by that history or by someone narrating those events one hundred years later, tends to promote explanation over surprise. In doing so, however, it may be forfeiting a crucial connection to the strange and unprofessional, the inexplicable and indecorous, which also formed part of the historical truth, at least for Ambrose Bierce, of Chickamauga.

APPENDIX: Albert Bierce's letter to Ambrose Bierce, March 29, 1911 (Ambrose Bierce Collection, Albert and Shirley Small Special Collections Library, University of Virginia, Charlottesville, MSS 5992-a, Box 1, Item 41)

[This letter covers 13 sheets of 5 x 7.75-inch paper, 16 horizontal blue lines on each page. All spellings are Albert's. His writing is clear and legible, although not all punctuation marks and indentations are clear (e.g., some of his commas could be dashes or other marks). I have not included any of his crossings out, which are few.]

My dear Brother

This is my story of Chickamauga, all of which is true to the best of my recollection.

On the evening of the 18 of Sept. 1863 Whitaker's brigade to which Aleshires battery was attached was on the Ringgold road, probably about a mile east of McAfee's church where, first at dusk, we met the enemy and engaged in a sharp but short artillery duel in which infantry [p. 2] took no part. After dark the brigade was withdrawn to McAfee's church where Granger was, with the rest of his command. My section of the battery was left on picket-duty about a quarter of a mile in advance of this position with instructions to remain awake all night and take note of any sound which might indicate a movement of the enemy, for, as the staff officer said to me, they will either leave our front tonight or attack us in the morning. In the latter case [p. 3] when I was sure of his advance I was to fire one gun as a signal to prepare to receive the advance and then fall back to the main line near the church. At about daybreak I heard the rumble of his artillery in motion but waited till I saw him coming, fired the one shot and fell back as ordered and reported to Granger. The attack was made and repulsed, renewed about an hour later with the same result. In this attack Lieut. Roseburg of the battery was wounded. During the rest of the day there was only a [p. 4] succession of skirmishes. We remained in this position until the following day.

Now this brings us to the morning of the 20th[.] Historians tell us that Gen Rosecrans was overwhelmed and carried from the field in the rout at about 11 A.M. Rosecrans thinking his whole army in retreat would of course hasten to order Granger to fall back by the Rossville and Ringgold road which order he promptly sent and which was promptly disregarded by Granger. Whitaker and Mitchell were soon in column on [p. 5] their way to Thomas. This was, to my best recollection, about 12 m. The distance from McAfee's church to the Snodgrass [house or farm] is something like three miles and the column moved with but one short halt.

Some of the enemy's cavalry and a battery were seen on our left. The battery opened fire on our column and Granger halted for a few minutes, surveyed them with his field glasses, then ordered the column to advance. My section was detained here probably about twenty minutes by a shell from [p. 6] the enemy's battery on our left which broke the pole to one of my gun carriages. I repaired it by splicing a sapling on to it. This happened but a short distance before you met us. I remember your saying to me that Hazen had left the position that he held when you left him to go for the ammunition train and as you did not know where he was at the time you would stay with the battery. You remember that Granger reported to Thomas not far from the Snodgrass house and the battery went into position at the edge [p. 7] of a cornfield. Was there a cornfield in Hazens front at the Kelly farm? You probably remember that Lieut Chestnut was wounded only a short time before the battery got into position, and it seems to me that this happened near the Snodgrass house—a little east of it. I remember that we were agreeably surprised to find that the battery's position was with Hazen's troops. There were no breastworks of any kind there. The enemy made one assault on Hazen through the cornfield and we harvested the [p. 8] corn with canister. We left this position under the guidance of somebody's chief of artillery to be placed farther to the right, just where we, or at least I, never knew as the officer was wounded or killed before placing us. Aleshire asked me if I thought it possible to get the battery on that hill south of the Snodgrass house. I told him I could get my part of it there, and his reply was "Go ahead[.]" I got it there by taking the hill at an angle and the shoulders of the men at the wheels. On the crest, [p. 9] which was sharp, I found a line of infantry lying flat on their stomachs and a desperate conflict going on at its southern base, almost hand-to-hand. I could have killed an hundred men with one round of canister but some of them would have been wearing the blue. The officer in command of the troops on the hill—a col. whom I did not know—said to me, "This is no place for artillery, you cant do a thing." And he was right. He made no attempt to make room for my guns on the crest so I rode down and told [p. 10] Aleshire the condition of things and he ordered me to bring my guns down. You may remember that when I came down the battery passed near the Snodgrass house—a little to the east of it—and took a position in open ground after making a half circle to the right. In this place we remained until about dark when we got the order to retire by the McFarland Gap road.

You're right in your letter to Gracie when you say that the Confederates did not take possession of this hill till after [p. 11] our forces had withdrawn. I believe there were some officers in high command who did not do their whole duty at Chickamauga but Thomas, Granger and Brannan were not in that class surely.

I think that this whole muddle of placing the battery at the Kelly farm comes about by the mistake of Hazen putting the time of his arrival at the Snodgrass farm about two hours too late. Our loss was, in the three days, two Lieuts wounded, two men killed. [p. 12] Our loss of horses compelled us to abandon one caisson, which we destroyed.

I think that Col Gracie will get little satisfaction from your criticism of his work.

Yes, I have the fifth volume and shall be very glad to get the others; and doubtless you will be glad when your work is finished.

Affectionately

Alberto

March 29, 1911

[p. 13, unnumbered] P.S. On reading this over I find I've made a blunder. When the battery was first moved from Hazens line it was placed farther to the right, near the east base of the ridge, and it was from this position that we were moving when I took my guns up the hill.

CHAPTER FIVE

Joshua Lawrence Chamberlain Repeats Appomattox

In his *Personal Memoirs* (1885–86), Ulysses S. Grant, commenting on what he described as "the story of the famous apple tree" at Appomattox, offered by way of introduction this typically lean, efficient sentence: "Wars produce many stories of fiction, some of which are told until they are believed to be true."[1] Among the many stories of fiction produced by the Civil War, and by the events of Wednesday, April 12, 1865, at Appomattox Court House in particular, are those connected with Brigadier General Joshua Lawrence Chamberlain, subsequently breveted Major General, and his involvement in the surrender ceremony. Grant himself mentioned Chamberlain only once in his *Personal Memoirs*, in a paragraph about his promoting then Colonel Chamberlain "on the spot" after he was wounded near Petersburg in June 1864, but Grant nowhere mentioned Chamberlain in connection with the surrender ceremony at Appomattox, at which Grant himself was not present, having designated Generals John Gibbon, Charles Griffin, and Wesley Merritt to parole Lee's troops and then left for Washington to see Lincoln. In omitting Chamberlain's name in this context, Grant was not alone, as we shall see, but in giving us the somewhat wry formulation about how stories of fiction are "told until they are believed to be true," he provided us with a useful place to start thinking about Chamberlain's role at Appomattox, his subsequent representations of that role, and the willingness, even eagerness, of many people to believe his representations today.

What was Chamberlain's role in the surrender ceremony on that damp, chilly April Wednesday at Appomattox, named after the river, which in turn took its name from the Algonquin for "sinuous tidal estuary"?[2] Most of what we know about that role comes from Chamberlain himself, a fact that immediately puts many healthy skeptics on their guard. But even the most skeptical among them would be unlikely to quibble with some basics: at 5:00 A.M., almost four years to the minute after the first signal shot was fired at Fort Sumter, the officer from Maine, having requested a transfer from the First Brigade back to his old command for the surrender ceremony, began assembling the Third Brigade of Joseph Bartlett's Division of Griffin's Fifth Corps along the southern side of the Lynchburg stage road, the main street of Appomattox Court House. This location put his left somewhere just east of the courthouse building, with Chamberlain himself positioned at the other end of the line, about three hundred yards away toward the river, on the extreme right of the Fifth Corps, the only unit of the Army of the Potomac at Appomattox, the Second and Sixth Corps having been sent toward Burkeville. Wanting to start his own Twenty-Fourth Corps of the Army of the James on the road to Lynchburg, Gibbon had ordered Griffin to relieve John W. Turner's Division of the Twenty-Fourth Corps with one of his own, and Griffin had sent Bartlett's First Division into the village. Chamberlain was no stranger to extreme positions on a Federal flank, as we know from Gettysburg, where he earned the only Congressional Medal of Honor awarded to a soldier of the Fifth Corps, and this particular position put him closest to the surrendering southerners, led by the Confederate Second Corps under General John B. Gordon, who would soon be marching into the village from the north and east, or from Chamberlain's right.[3]

The next day, April 13, Chamberlain wrote a letter to his sister Sarah, nicknamed Sae, and from this letter, now in the possession of Bowdoin College, we know the disposition of the troops under Chamberlain's command, who, he claimed, numbered about six thousand, a figure more appropriate for the entire First Division than for the Third Brigade alone: on the extreme right he claimed he placed the Massachusetts 9th, 18th, 22nd, and 32 regiments; then the Maine 1st, 2nd, and 20th, Chamberlain's own original command; then the Michigan 1st, 4th, and 16th; and finally the Pennsylvania 82nd, 83rd, 91st, 118th, and 155th. Over the years of Chamberlain's subsequent retellings, this basic configuration of Massachusetts-Maine-Michigan-Pennsylvania remained consistent, although in a 1903 address a Maryland unit slipped into the picture. (Andrew W. Denison's Second Brigade of Romeyn B. Ayres's Second Division of the Fifth Corps consisted of four Maryland regiments, but Bartlett's First Division included none.)[4]

So far, so good. But as for subsequent events, when Gordon's Confederate Second Corps, marching in from Chamberlain's right, finally came abreast of these Federal soldiers, the simple truth is we just do not know for sure what happened. What we can be reasonably sure of is that some command was given (the passive voice here reflects the uncertainty), the Federal soldiers made some change in how they were standing, and that change in turn changed the tone of the surrender ceremony in some way, the meaningful significance of which many people are still willing and eager to believe. As Chamberlain came to represent the moment, he ordered his soldiers to "shoulder arms," and this order constituted a salute to the surrendering Confederates. But even this simple claim has stirred controversy and disagreement, some of which Chamberlain biographer John J. Pullen has summarized helpfully: "There is some question as to whether or not this was really a salute. In 'shouldered arms' as described in Casey's *Infantry Tactics* the musket was held vertically in the right hand and resting in the hollow of the right shoulder. A salute would have required that the piece be held by both hands at 'present arms' vertically opposite the center of the body."[5] In other words, a skeptic could argue, Chamberlain's famous salute to Gordon's troops may have consisted of nothing more than Chamberlain calling his own soldiers to attention for the sake of imposing stillness and silence on them, thereby assuring that there would be no exulting or taunting of the kind that Grant himself expressly wanted to avoid.

King of the Chamberlain skeptics and chief debunker of the salutation myth has been William Marvel, who has chided the man from Maine in not one, but two books, *A Place Called Appomattox* (2000) and *Lee's Last Retreat: The Flight to Appomattox* (2002). In the first Marvel described Chamberlain this way: "General Chamberlain proved as magnificent a soldier as he was a literary stylist, but while he was courageous and coolheaded he also tended to wrap life's little dramas in ribbons of romantic imagery in which he, himself, was somehow entwined." In the second book, showing some of the same tendency toward rhetorical embellishment for which he criticized his subject, Marvel had this to say: "A college professor from Maine just three years before this day, he saw the world as one grand romantic cavalcade in which he participated prominently, and if he did anything common, he seemed unable to remember it that way." Not everyone will find these patronizing dismissals of Chamberlain necessary or justifiable, and such dismissals can become even more unappealing as one tracks some of the minor errors in Marvel's own scholarship, not to mention his naive idea of what a magnificent literary stylist is (Chamberlain would be the first to admit he was no Dickens or Tolstoy). But the more important point to make here is that for Marvel the fact that Chamberlain revised and improved his subsequent narratives of the salute is the end of the story, whereas those later revisions and improvements are also the beginning of another story, one that has considerable historical, not just literary, importance.[6]

In fairness to Marvel, criticisms and counter-claims have dogged Chamberlain's accounts all along, both during his lifetime and since his death. Another Chamberlain biographer, Edward G. Longacre, summarized some of these criticisms and counter-claims: Chamberlain made it appear that his command alone took part in the ceremony, ignoring other elements of the Fifth Corps; he implied that his command received Confederate arms and flags all morning and afternoon, instead of during only a portion of the day; he maintained that he was designated by either Grant or Griffin (depending on the account) to receive the Confederate surrender, when, in fact, his division commander and superior officer, Bartlett, was really in charge but was summoned elsewhere; and, most important for this discussion, he insisted that he and Gordon exchanged salutes of some kind, although they may not actually have done so at all. Having summarized these criticisms and counter-claims, however, Longacre then drew an admirably judicious and levelheaded conclusion: "These criticisms notwithstanding, it seems clear that some gesture on Chamberlain's part that day made the surrender ceremony something other than the degrading, humiliating experience Lee's army might otherwise have found it."[7]

Since we cannot determine the exact nature of Chamberlain's gesture, let us focus instead on how his narratives of that gesture evolved over fifty years and on how subsequent students of history have interpreted that gesture. Six documents authored by Chamberlain can map this evolution, and for the sake of clarity we can refer to each by its number in the chronological sequence: (1) Chamberlain's letter to his sister, written the day after the surrender ceremony; (2) "The Surrender of Gen. Lee," published almost three years later, in January 1868; (3) "The Third Brigade at Appomattox," published in 1894; (4) "The Last Salute of the Army of Northern Virginia," first published in 1901; (5) "Appomattox," published in 1903; and, finally, (6) Chamberlain's book *The Passing of the Armies*, published posthumously in 1915, the year after Chamberlain died at the age of eighty-five, a few months before the outbreak of World War I.[8]

With these six chronological points at hand, one can trace quickly the progress of, for example, Chamberlain's narrative of his own thoughts about offering a salute to Gordon's troops. In the first version, that of April 13, 1865, he gave his sister only this bare reportage: "We received them with the honors due to troops—at a shoulder—in silence. They came to a shoulder on passing my flag + preserved perfect order." In this version he makes no mention of deciding to offer the salute or issuing orders for that salute. His only depiction of his own thoughts took this shape: "Poor fellows. I pitied them from the bottom of my heart."

In version two, that of 1868, new details emerge, details that caused a Maine newspaper reporter in Chamberlain's audience to rhapsodize:

> The large audience that assembled in City Hall on Thursday evening were entertained with one of the most thrilling narratives ever related to a Portland audience. It was the scholar narrating the deeds of the soldier, with all the grace and eloquence of the one, and the modesty and gallant bearing of the other. . . . In his description of this last scene he gave many incidents not heretofore known, and the narrative had all the interest of romance and the value of history. The audience sat spellbound during the entire discourse.

Chamberlain's spellbinding descriptions, which combine the interest of romance with the value of history, were precisely the kinds of touches that William Marvel, among others, would censure. But in fact Chamberlain's account of his own role in version two was still remarkably tame:

> Soon the rebels were seen slowly forming for the last time: on they they [*sic*] came with careless step, their ranks thick with banners. The bugle sounds. Our line shoulders arms— not present, as some of the histories have it; that would have been too much honor. On our side there is not a sound; the silence is as if the dead passed; it is a funeral salute we pay them. They move along our front, face inward towards our line, dress lines, fix bayonets, stack arms, take off their cartridge boxes and place them on the pile, and then reluctantly, painfully, furl their flags, and lay them down, some kneeling and kissing them with tears in their eyes.

Here Chamberlain showed the surrendering Confederates behaving in ways that could arouse the pity to which he confessed in version one, and here he added the epic image of saluting a procession of the dead, employing one of his favorite rhetorical techniques, the shift into the present tense. But even with these flourishes, he still did not take credit for issuing an order for the salute—the prompting bugle sounds on its own—and he already showed an awareness of potential confusion about, or misunderstanding of, the historical record of this moment, as we see in the careful distinction he drew between "shoulder arms" and "present arms," which would have been "too much honor." This last qualification suggests that Chamberlain knew very well what he was about; it implies a shrewd, canny recognition of limits not at all characteristic of some misty-eyed romantic sentimentally sloshing his way into unqualified reconciliation with a defeated enemy.

With version three, delivered in 1893 and published in 1894, things became more complicated:

> We could not content ourselves with simply standing in line and witnessing this crowning scene. So instructions were sent to the several commanders that at the given signal, as the head of each division of the surrendering column approached their right, they should in succession bring their men to "attention" and arms to the "carry," then resuming the "ordered arms" and the "parade rest." . . . As they came opposite our right our bugle sounds the signal and repeated along our line. Each organization comes to "attention," and thereupon takes up successively the "carry." (140)

Chamberlain's narrative now included a representation of the thought-process behind the order to salute, and a first-person pronoun had emerged to authorize that process. But the pronoun is a plural one, so it remains unclear who really was thinking this way. Chamberlain only? Chamberlain along with his fellow officers, including those in the First and Second Brigades, which Chamberlain mentioned in this version and placed across the Lynchburg stage road from the Third Brigade? Or did Bartlett, the division commander, say something to Chamberlain? Chamberlain's use of the passive voice ("So instructions were sent"), also characteristic of Lee's dispatches and reports throughout the war, further obscured the top link in the chain of command. Finally, a new detail emerged from the manual of arms. Instead of coming to shoulder arms and standing in that position silently throughout the surrender, Chamberlain's soldiers, as he now represented them, cycled through the sequence from "order arms," with musket butts resting on the ground (as they do in "parade rest"), to "carry" (which results in the same position as "shoulder arms"), and back, repeating the sequence as each Confederate division passed.

With version four, first published in the *Boston Journal* in April 1901, and subsequently picked up and circulated throughout the South by the *Southern Historical Society Papers* (1904), Chamberlain clearly positions himself as the originator of the salute to Gordon's troops: "At such a time and under such conditions I thought it eminently fitting to show some token of our feeling, and I therefore instructed my subordinate officers to come to the position of 'salute' in the manual of arms as each body of the Confederates passed before us" (362). In this iteration the first-person singular "I" has relieved the earlier "we," and the active voice has displaced the passive. Meanwhile, the ambiguous catchall term "salute" blurs the earlier specificity of "shoulder arms," "carry arms," and "order arms." Most important about this fourth version is the role it played in southern imaginations of the surrender, first in Gordon's *Reminiscences of the Civil War* (1903; but, given Gordon's connection with Chamberlain, discussed below, it is difficult to believe he would not have also seen the earlier 1894 version) and subsequently in Douglas Southall Freeman's *Lee's Lieutenants: A Study in Command* (1944), which spliced this fourth version with the sixth and final one in Chamberlain's *Passing of the Armies*, noting, without censure, that the account in the *Southern Historical Society Papers* gave "some details" not in *Passing of the Armies*.[9]

Version four also presented one other striking development in the narrative of the salute: "And it can well be imagined, too, that there was no lack of emotion on our side, but the Union men were held steady in their lines, without the least show of demonstration by word or by motion. There was, though, a twitching of muscles of their faces, and, be it said, their battle-bronzed cheeks were not altogether dry. Our men felt the import of the occasion, and realized how fully they would have been affected if defeat and surrender had been their lot after such a fearful struggle" (362–63). What the English Romantic poet William Wordsworth called "the spontaneous overflow of powerful feelings" tends not to be a favorite topic of conversation among many American males and especially not among many military historians. But clearly the surrender at Appomattox was emotionally charged for the men gathered there (consider Grant's small but telling detail in his *Personal Memoirs* of how his headache suddenly vanished as soon as he got word of Lee's intention to surrender), and clearly Chamberlain's many versions of his salute to Gordon wrestled with the problem of how to convey powerful feeling or affect without foundering in sentimentality. In version one, the letter to his sister, Chamberlain mentioned his pity, and in version two, delivered to an audience in Portland, Maine, he represented Confederate soldiers as weeping and kissing their surrendered flags. Here in version four, the emotions of the hour received their fullest, most compelling treatment, Chamberlain's feelings of pity for, and identification with, the Confederates before him now combined with their tears and projected onto his own soldiers. Although Marvel and others might cringe at the alliterating hyphenation of "battle-bronzed cheeks," Chamberlain's narrative here achieved something real, as it not only anticipated Hemingway's strategies for depicting men trying to steady themselves while under the influence of violent emotions produced by combat and war; it added another layer to the salute offered to Gordon. Instead of an officer's effective method for preserving discipline and preempting the potential taunts of victorious soldiers, Chamberlain's salute now became what it no doubt was for more than a few: a manly, even heroic, feat of unfaltering self-control under unusual emotional pressure.

In version five, published in 1903, Chamberlain consolidated his role as originator of the salute, although he did retain the passive voice when it came to the transmission of his order:

This was the last scene of such momentous history that I was impelled to render some token of recognition; some honor also to manhood so high.

Instructions had been given; and when the head of
each division column comes opposite our group, our bugle
sounds the signal and instantly our whole line from right to
left, regiment by regiment in succession, gives the soldier's
salutation,—from "order arms" to the old "carry"—the
marching salute. (16)

This version added nothing new to the representation of the salute itself, although this was where the stray Maryland unit made
its one appearance, but it did show Chamberlain straining toward
greater eloquence, with phrases such as "last scene of such momentous history" and "impelled to render some token of recognition" now strutting where the perfectly serviceable prose of version
four formerly did its work.

Finally, with version six, published posthumously in 1915 in
The Passing of the Armies, we get not only a new inconsistency, as
Chamberlain now placed the First Brigade behind the Third on
the south side of the Lynchburg stage road, facing only the Second
Brigade on the north side; we get Chamberlain's thoughts on General Bartlett's possible resentment that Chamberlain had charge
of the First Division for the parade, resentment that Chamberlain soothed with the statement, "but he was a manly and soldierly
man and made no comment" (194). More important, though, is
another new wrinkle: "The momentous meaning of this occasion
impressed me deeply. I resolved to mark it by some token of recognition, which could be no other than a salute of arms. Well aware
of the responsibility assumed, and of the criticisms that would follow, as the sequel proved, nothing of that kind could move me in
the least" (195). Here Chamberlain scaled back some of the straining eloquence of version five, but in its place we now have a feisty
self-righteousness absent from the other versions.

Coming at the end of his life, this defiant declaration sounds
like the proud hindsight of an old warrior who, having received
his share of wounds from both bullets and words, has tenaciously
survived both. But in fact this bit of valedictory bravado seems to
be little more than the old warrior's shadow-boxing, since there

is no evidence that anyone criticized Chamberlain's salute. Some have questioned his facts, but none that I can find has condemned whatever gesture he made. In fact, many do not even mention it. Among the principals who published memoirs, Grant said nothing, Longstreet said nothing, Edward Porter Alexander said nothing. Likewise, the *New York Times* said nothing, nor did any of the major papers that began publishing in the North or the West during the later decades of the nineteenth century, as Chamberlain released his various versions: not the *Washington Post*, not the *Wall Street Journal*, not the *Chicago Tribune*, not the *Los Angeles Times*. And the silence also extends to the last volume of *The Civil War* (1974) by Shelby Foote, who loved a good story as much as anyone.[10] (Bruce Catton's *A Stillness at Appomattox* [1953] ends before the surrender ceremony.) Two entire-war narrators who did tell the story of Chamberlain's salute are Allan Nevins and James McPherson, the latter of whom gave it most of one paragraph, which he based on Chamberlain's fourth version.

In other words, by the time of his death Chamberlain's narrative of the salute showed him spoiling for a fight he never got. Although it is pure conjecture to say so, it may be that his readiness to take on anybody who condemned the salute was a strategy for distracting potential critics from some of the inconsistencies among his many narratives. If so, that strategy certainly did not work in the case of Marvel, who in a long note near the end of *A Place Called Appomattox* (358 n. 38) explained the changes in Chamberlain's narratives by making the northern general out to be some kind of historiographic ambulance-chaser, promoting himself in the narrative as each of his superior or peer officers died. Again, Marvel's evidence is questionable here, since in fact Alfred Pearson, who had command of the Third Brigade until Chamberlain's transfer and command of the First Brigade as a consequence of that transfer, was still alive when Chamberlain's fourth version first appeared and represented him as the originator of the salute. (That version appeared in 1901, and Pearson died in 1903.)[11]

Furthermore, not only did Marvel's reasoning constitute an instance of the *post hoc, ergo propter hoc* fallacy (since some of

Chamberlain's claims appeared after other officers died, they necessarily appeared because those other officers died); it also risked oversimplifying the nature of memory and truth-telling. It is not necessarily true that because one memory of an event comes later than another, the later memory is less true than the earlier. If it were, psychoanalysis would be out of business. The letter Chamberlain wrote his sister the day after the surrender ceremony certainly had a raw immediacy that still makes it compelling, but its hurried, dashed-off quality may also have meant that it could not encompass all the details Chamberlain might have recovered later, when the eclipsing urgency of his immediate duties subsided. Nor is it necessarily true that just because Chamberlain may have embellished his accounts, those accounts have no veracity in them. Comparing the surrendering Confederates to a procession of the dead or describing his own soldiers' cheeks as battle-bronzed did not in itself negate the reliability of other claims he made. And, finally, it is not necessarily true that inconsistencies among his accounts negate the reliability of those claims either. Did he place the First Brigade with the Second Brigade on the north side of the Lynchburg stage road, as he claimed in version three, or behind his own Third Brigade on the south side, as he claimed in version six, published twenty-one years later? This kind of imperfection or flaw in recollection actually may be a sign of authenticity rather than falsehood, whereas exact, undeviating repetition of precisely the same details over fifty years could characterize the rigidly rehearsed consistency of a liar.

Then there is the whole matter of John B. Gordon's role in the story of the salute. If we say that Chamberlain made up the story, disregarding whatever claims to integrity his many years of service as a college teacher, military officer, college president, and state governor might have entitled him, must we then say the same of Gordon, subsequently a U.S. senator and governor of Georgia? It is easy to be cynical, especially where politicians are concerned and especially when one of them was associated with the Ku Klux Klan.[12] It would be easy, for example, to claim that Chamberlain merely brought his men to attention for the sake of imposing silence on them; Gordon, not to be outdone by Yankee chivalry, ordered his men to attention also; and then during the postwar period the two men consciously or unconsciously collaborated to spin out a reconciliationist yarn, each for his own political reasons and advantage. If we adopt this line of thinking, then the showmanship and duplicity of moments such as one on the night of November 25, 1893, when both men appeared on the same stage for a lecture by Gordon in New York, become deep indeed, as does the pathos of our gullibility:

> Around Gen. Gordon on the stage were gathered a number of prominent military men who had fought in the civil war, and during the course of his lecture he made mention of them. Gen. Chamberlain was one of those mentioned, and his name was introduced dramatically by the speaker.
>
> Gen. Gordon had been telling of how, after the surrender, the Confederate troops were marching behind their battle flags, under command of a Union officer. When he reached the point where the audience were waiting to hear the name of the officer, Gen. Gordon turned to the row of military men behind him and exclaimed:
>
> "And I now take a sincere pleasure in shaking the hand of that man, who was afterward Governor of the State of Maine—Gen. Chamberlain."[13]

If we take a cynical line on the story of the Appomattox salute, we might also see the artifice of this theatrical postwar moment in New York exceeded by that of Chamberlain's own successive representations of Gordon during the salute itself. Beginning with version three, which he prepared for the national encampment of the Grand Army of the Republic in Indianapolis eleven weeks before the 1893 meeting of the two men on the New York stage, Chamberlain began polishing his account of Gordon's response to his salute, and he polished it through versions four (1901) and five (1903), where it reached its final form (except for minor differences in punctuation), repeated subsequently in *The Passing of the Armies*:

> Gordon at the head of the column, riding with heavy spirit and downcast face, catches the sound of shifting arms, looks up, and, taking the meaning, wheels superbly, making with himself and his horse one uplifted figure, with profound salutation as he drops the point of his sword to his boot toe; then facing to his own command, gives word for his successive brigades to pass us with the same position of the manual,—honor answering honor. On our part not a sound of trumpet more, nor roll of drum; not a cheer, nor word nor whisper of vain-glorying, nor motion of man standing again at the order, but an awed stillness rather, and breath-holding, as if it were the passing of the dead! (195–96)

A typescript precursor of this passage, in the possession of the Bowdoin College Library, shows various interlinear alternatives written in Chamberlain's hand, alternatives such as "swordpoint to the boot-toe" (having used "the point of his sword" in version three, he adopted "swordpoint" in version four before returning to "the point of his sword" in version five). Since the difference between "swordpoint" and "the point of his sword" makes a difference only in prose rhythm, not in meaning, we could argue that here is an instance of verbal polishing all too characteristic of artifice and theatricality, an instance of what Marvel described as Chamberlain's tendency "to wrap life's little dramas in ribbons of romantic imagery."

Not all would agree that the surrender at Appomattox was merely one of life's little dramas, but most would accept, I suspect, the assertion that "honor answering honor," which in context described Gordon's response to Chamberlain's salute, not that salute itself, has become the most famous and frequently quoted phrase to come out of Chamberlain's many versions of his role there. Since the phrase, with its mirroring repetition, remains a purely verbal achievement, one that conveys an act of abstraction and moralizing interpretation on Chamberlain's part, as opposed to some detail in the factual record of events, we can return profitably at this point to Grant's statement about wars, stories, and belief: "Wars produce many stories of fiction, some of which are told until they are believed to be true." With this statement in mind, let us move toward closure by considering three recent invocations of Chamberlain's salute and their very different contexts.

The first invocation appeared in a 1996 book by Gordon R. Sullivan and Michael R. Harper entitled *Hope Is Not a Method: What Business Leaders Can Learn from America's Army* and cataloged by the Library of Congress under the headings "industrial management" and "strategic planning." Here is how Sullivan and Harper made use of Chamberlain's story:

> When we think of what it means to value and respect
> people, our thoughts go to one of Grant's commanders,
> Joshua Chamberlain. . . . As a tribute to its heroism, Grant
> selected Chamberlain's division to formally accept the
> Confederate surrender at Appomattox, forming a line
> in front of which Gordon's II Corps surrendered their
> arms and battle flags as they marched off the field at
> Appomattox. . . . [Here the authors quote Gordon's account
> of the salute in his 1903 *Reminiscences of the Civil War*.]
>
> Chamberlain and Gordon, two of America's citizen
> soldiers, understood the most basic truth: leadership
> always comes back to people.[14]

The second invocation appeared in *To Forgive Is Human: How to Put Your Past in the Past*, published in 1997 by Michael E. McCullough, Steven J. Sandage, and Everett L. Worthington Jr., and classified by the Library of Congress under "forgiveness" and "interpersonal relations":

> The next act of healing in this story was initiated by Colonel
> Joshua L. Chamberlain, who had been a professor of
> theology and rhetoric at Bowdoin College in Maine prior to
> enlisting in the Union Army. . . .

Nearly one hundred thousand men passed by
Appomattox Court House. Chamberlain led his men
in a gesture of forgiveness toward those he tried to kill
the previous week. War seeks justice, but Chamberlain
understood that his enemies were human and deserved
more than justice. They deserved respect. In offering
a salute to the humiliated Confederates, Chamberlain
communicated that although justice would be served mercy
would also be extended. That is forgiveness.[15]

In the third and final example, Robert J. Wicks conjured up
Chamberlain in the second volume of his *Handbook of Spirituality for Ministers*, published in 2000 and classified by the Library
of Congress under "clergy," "religious life," and "pastoral theology":

At the end of the war, at Appomattox, Chamberlain is
chosen to be the officer in charge of the Union troops
receiving the surrender of the Confederate soldiers. As the
Confederates dejectedly march past the ranks of Union
soldiers, Chamberlain orders a salute of respect for these
gallant men. Confederate officers recognize the salute and
order a similar salute back—honor answering honor. And
Chamberlain writes, [here Wicks quotes the sentence from
version six that ends with "the passing of the dead!"].
    Is God in all this? Can God be apart from it all?
Our theology today tells us that the world and God
are inseparable. God is the depth level of all human
experience.[16]

Industrial management, strategic planning, forgiveness, interpersonal relations, clergy, religious life, pastoral theology: this
list covers the spectrum from the commercial and pragmatic, on
one end, through the social and emotional, in the middle, and on
to the spiritual and religious, at the other end. The spectrum is
a distinctly American one, and Chamberlain's relevance to any
point on that spectrum—or more precisely, the widespread belief
in his relevance—testifies persuasively to the power of the story he

developed over fifty years. What is particularly remarkable, if not downright moving, about these varied uses of Chamberlain (and they are not the only uses, since he also shows up in writing about leadership and developing leadership skills[17]) is that they appear in the writing and work of people who do not necessarily know much about the Civil War (consider the wildly exaggerated figure of "nearly one hundred thousand men" passing by Appomattox Court House, cited by McCullough et al.) but who recognize in a story from the Civil War a paradigm or a parable for complicated and difficult moments in contemporary civilian life.

To make this claim is not to pretend for a moment that skeptics about the details of Chamberlain's salute will be persuaded, or should be persuaded, to accept everything he has written as credulously as the nonspecialist writers making use of his story now. But it is to make the claim that the gesture he made toward Gordon and the Confederate Second Corps on the raw morning of April 12, 1865, whatever that gesture may have been, amounts to only one aspect of his achievement and legacy, a legacy subsequently developed during the late nineteenth and early twentieth centuries, against the backdrops of Reconstruction and its end, war with Spain, and varying degrees of reconciliation between the white populations of the antagonistic sections. As we see now, a second aspect of his legacy continues today in widely diverging contexts of American economic, social, and spiritual life, each with its own set of attitudes and concerns, which show little or no awareness of, or need for, the uncertainties of that raw April morning.

Last Words

The abundant diversity of Civil War narratives soundly refutes the easy sophism "victors write the histories." This cliché has harsh relevance to totalitarian governments founded on propaganda and censorship, imagined most chillingly in George Orwell's *Nineteen Eighty-Four* (1949), in which the Ministry of Truth employs the protagonist, Winston Smith, to rewrite newspaper articles and align the historical record with the ideology of Big Brother. But in the United States of the last 150 years, the fierce idealizing of individual opinion, informed or not, and the protective hallowing of the First Amendment, with which citizens maintain a range of relationships, occasionally dysfunctional, have rendered impossible the homogenizing of a single narrative account of the American Civil War. In the case of this war, anyone arguing that victory granted a narrative monopoly to the victors, or to those who subsequently have advanced the victor's version of events, must scramble hard to explain away the influential narrative achievements of, among many others, Jubal Early, Mary Chesnut, Edward Porter Alexander, Douglas Southall Freeman, Edmund Wilson, William Faulkner, Margaret Mitchell, Robert Penn Warren, and Shelby Foote, as well as those of organizations such as the Southern Historical Society and the United Daughters of the Confederacy, which oversaw the publication of history textbooks used in schools throughout the South.

With a large share of popular imagination still orbiting these achievements, or the books, films, and visual art they have begotten, it is difficult to avoid the conclusion that, at least in the imaginations of many white people uninfluenced by academic trends in Civil War historiography, it is the vanquished whose histories have prevailed.[1] In many of the imaginations where southern narratives have not prevailed, those narratives have contested to something like a draw. But to say so is not to say that there are no differences between the most popular southern narratives of the war and the most popular northern ones. Considering the Spanish Civil War, in April 1937, from the perspective of an Englishman devoted to the losing cause, W. H. Auden closed his poem "Spain" with the aphoristic lines, "History to the defeated / May say Alas but cannot help or pardon."[2] One can argue against Auden that in the case of southern versions of the Civil War, history has not only said alas, as it did at many moments in Mary Chesnut's hands; it has striven mightily, beginning in April 1865 with Robert E. Lee's General Orders Number 9 at Appomattox and the Lost Cause narratives that quickly followed, to help and pardon.

One cannot reduce all southern narratives to alas, help, or pardon, but one can argue that many of the most famous—both explicitly pro-Confederate ones and more balanced examples—adopted the rhetoric of revision. Although it is facile to assert that victors' histories always eclipse the histories of the vanquished, at least with respect to the Civil War, it does make sense to claim that narratives advanced by the eventual victors to justify themselves before, during, and after the war inevitably prompted the vanquished to respond by challenging, supplementing, and correcting them. In a society in which anyone willing to pay can publish almost anything, it is not that only the victors write histories in wide circulation; it is that, fairly or unfairly, defeat places the burden of correction on the vanquished. Or at least all but the most detached, reconciled, or indifferent among the defeated feel that it does.

Victors tend not to feel burdened in the same way, although there are large exceptions to this rule, as in the case of northern narrators, such as Grant, who felt deeply uncomfortable about the prosecution of the Mexican War by the United States: "For myself, I was bitterly opposed to the measure [the annexation of Texas], and to this day regard the war which resulted as one of the most unjust ever waged by a stronger against a weaker nation." Grant's opposition to the Mexican War tinged his view of the later war caused by "Southern rebellion," which he understood as "largely the outgrowth of the Mexican war": "Nations, like individuals, are punished for their transgressions. We got our punishment in the most sanguinary and expensive war of modern times." The leading soldier of the victorious side, he thought both wars "unholy."[3] In the case of Grant, one has a northern narrator who did not assume that victory necessarily conferred on his side what Robert Penn Warren later referred to in *The Legacy of the Civil War* (1961) as "The Treasury of Virtue."

Ostensibly freed from the burdens of revision and correction, northern narrators have exercised great freedom in adopting and reflecting various attitudes toward the war. In his Second Inaugural Address, Lincoln, like Grant, represented the war as punishment, but whereas Grant left divinity out of his account, Lincoln's narrative, deftly compressed into one of his deliberately segmented, momentum-gathering sentences, imagined the punishment as divine: "If we shall suppose that American Slavery is one of those offences which, in the providence of God, must needs come, but which, having continued through His appointed time, He now wills to remove, and that He gives to both North and South, this terrible war, as the woe due to those by whom the offence came, shall we discern therein any departure from those divine attributes which the believers in a Living God always ascribe to Him?"

Partly theological and appropriate to the pulpit, partly forensic and appropriate to the courtroom, perhaps in a closing statement before a jury, this sublimely orchestrated sentence, immediately followed by the rhyming, hymnlike one discussed in the first chapter, was, after all, a question, not a statement. Not only did Lincoln choose to couch his implied narrative of belligerent cause-and-effect as an interrogative; he framed the question, in a way reminiscent of many moments in his debates with Douglas six and a half years earlier, as an if-then proposition, with the dependent "if" clause occupying about three-quarters of its length and functioning covertly, and not at all dependently, as an implied assertion of the causal role of slavery and the shared culpability of North and South. Many have heard in this address, particularly in this moment, evidence of Lincoln's increasingly religious or philosophical vision of human history, and their hearing may be accurate. But the experienced lawyer left himself a sizable loophole by not identifying himself explicitly with the group of "believers in a Living God."

Although his vision of human history could not have helped changing between October 1858 and March 1865, Lincoln said nothing in the latter month that directly and necessarily obviated or retracted a cause-and-effect narrative of national agitation he had sketched in his debates with Douglas. Three times in those debates—at Jonesboro, at Quincy, and at Alton—Lincoln referred to a statement by South Carolina's Preston Brooks that the framers of the Constitution never expected slavery to last as long as it did but that the invention of the cotton gin had made it a perpetual necessity.[4] In recurring to Brooks's claim, Lincoln took care to state his agreement with the congressman's understanding of the framers' intention and to identify Douglas with the economic interests benefiting from the necessity of the cotton gin.

Cotton gin or Living God? Leave it to Lincoln, master of an elusive, protean slipperiness Douglas worked hard to pin down on many occasions, to define the endpoints of a narrative spectrum. At one end a narrator could, and can, tell the story of the American Civil War from a material, utilitarian perspective, and at the other, from an ideal, transcendent one. Legalistic narratives that focus on the constitutionality of slavery or of secession tend to fall toward the middle of the spectrum, depending on a particular narrator's attitude toward the concept of law, its origin, and its implications. Lincoln himself could work this middle ground as productively as anyone. Other narratives have arranged themselves along the full range of the spectrum. In "The Bear," for example, one of seven stories William Faulkner collected in *Go Down, Moses and Other Stories* (1942), Ike McCaslin's vision of the South as cursed by slavery fell toward the transcendent, nonutilitarian end of

Lincoln's spectrum: "'Don't you see?' he cried, 'Don't you see? This whole land, the whole South, is cursed, and all of us who derive from it, whom it ever suckled, white and black both, lie under the curse?'"[5] Although the Civil War punished the offence of slavery, expiation of the offence continued well into the twentieth century in Faulkner's Yoknapatawpha County.

Among the northern narrators considered here, Whitman came closest to viewing the war from an abstract, philosophical perspective. His homespun brand of self-taught and imperfectly understood Hegelianism pointed him toward something like a dialectical vision of a national psyche. Writing one of the concluding notes to his *Memoranda* during the summer of 1875, he united "the whole conflict, both sides, the South and North, really into One" and viewed it "as a struggle going on within One Identity," concluding with this question: "What is any Nation, after all—and what is a human being—but a struggle between conflicting, paradoxical, opposing elements—and they themselves and their most violent contests, important parts of that One Identity and of its developments?"

Leading the way among American poets as explorer of inner conflict that Freud would soon describe with the new coinage *Ambivalenz*, Whitman projected an image of human beings as microcosmic nation-states and nation-states as macrocosmic human beings. Whitman was nothing if not expansive, and his narrative of the Civil War proved no exception, as he worked to behold it "from a point of view sufficiently comprehensive," one that included a role for divinity: "Rather, is there not, behind all, some vast average, sufficiently definite, uniform and unswervable Purpose, in the development of America, (may I not say divine purpose? only all is divine purpose,) which pursues its own will, maybe unconscious of itself—of which the puerilities often called history, are merely crude and temporary emanations, rather than influences or causes?"[6] Although Robert Penn Warren's version of a narrative point of view "sufficiently comprehensive" did not include a role for divinity comparable to that imagined by Whitman, whom he did not mention once in *The Legacy of the Civil War*,

Warren did share Whitman's expansively aerial view of the war as microcosm mirroring macrocosm: "In a civil war . . . all the self-divisions within individuals become a series of mirrors in which the plight of the country is reflected, and the self-division of the country a great mirror in which the individual may see imaged his own deep conflicts, not only the conflicts of political loyalties, but those more profoundly personal."[7] For both the northerner and the southerner, what the latter called the "inwardness" of many Americans' experience of the Civil War accounts for much of its continuing hold on them.

Despite Sherman's lifelong affiliations with art and literature, little could be further from Whitman's abstract, eclectic, would-be comprehensiveness than his undistracted narrative pragmatism, when it came to plotting the causes of the war. In the chapter that concluded the first edition of the *Memoirs*, penultimate in the second, Sherman had lessons to teach and morals to draw, but he stoutly set aside larger moralizing of the kind that Lincoln, Whitman, Faulkner, and Warren embraced. Having, in the second paragraph of the chapter, attributed the statement that no government could exist half slave and half free to William Seward rather than to Lincoln's House Divided speech, he opened the fourth paragraph this way: "The slave population in 1860 was near four millions, and the money value thereof not far from twenty-five hundred million dollars. Now, ignoring the moral side of the question, a cause that endangered so vast a moneyed interest was an adequate cause of anxiety and preparation, and the Northern leaders surely ought to have foreseen the danger and prepared for it." For a much briefer period than Lincoln, Sherman, too, was a lawyer, but in equating 4 million slaves to 2.5 billion dollars, he read this cause of the war through the eyes of a banker, "ignoring the moral side of the question." Sherman's economic narrative differed from the one Marx and Engels advanced in *Die Presse* in November 1861. For the founding fathers of communism the narrative of the American Civil War pitted competing economic systems against one another; for Sherman, gold-rush banker and canny capitalist, the narrative led through the blundering of northern leaders whose vigilance over the consequences of endangering "so vast a moneyed interest" lapsed reprehensibly.

Although Sherman chose to comb out an economic strand for his narrative at this concluding moment in his *Memoirs*, that strand could make way for others elsewhere in his writings. Like Grant, he assigned the Mexican War a leading role in constructing the beginning of his plot. But unlike Grant's, his *Memoirs* did not fret over the rightness or wrongness of that war, which he avoided reading as a punishable transgression. Instead, he focused on the heated debate over whether newly acquired California should be slave or free, mentioned the Wilmot Proviso, and summarized, "This matter of California being a free State, afterward, in the national Congress, gave rise to angry debates, which at one time threatened civil war." Meanwhile, however, Sherman also represented himself as "startled" by Winfield Scott's assertion in 1850 that "'our country was on the eve of a terrible civil war,'" as well as deeply disappointed by having missed action in Mexico, which he thought would be his only chance to hear "a hostile shot."

Sherman was decisively utilitarian and hardheaded when it came to the narrative thread of secession and its legality: "I think my general opinions were well known and understood, viz., that 'secession was treason, was *war*.'" Many others held the same general opinion, but Sherman was not as interested in a theory of constitutional contract as he was in another firmly practical reality, the physical geography of the United States. In a letter to David F. Boyd, one of the instructors at the Louisiana State Seminary during his tenure as superintendent, written May 13, 1861, he indulged in what he called "Generalisms" about the coming war: "No one now talks of the negro. The integrity of the Union and the relative power of state and General Government are the issues in this war; were it not for the physical geography of the country it might be that People could consent to divide and separate in peace. But the Mississippi is too grand an element to be divided, and all its extent must of necessity be under one government." In decrying "this terrible anarchy" of secession, Sherman showed that, once again, economic factors played a part in his narrative. Having set aside slavery, he focused on the Union and secession, but for him the Union was not a pure abstraction to which he blindly pledged allegiance. From these generalizations it appears that secession might not have been wholly unacceptable to him, were it not for the vast moneyed interests involved in trade and transportation along the Mississippi. Preserving the Union meant preserving control of the river, "too grand an element to be divided."

Sherman knew himself and knew that "as a Red headed person"—as he referred to himself in a letter of January 20, 1861, to George Mason Graham—he was neither patient nor given to overly subtle nuance in some of his thinking and self-expression. His impatience extended to a refusal to braid the different narrative strands he followed at various times into a single neat rope of coherent cause-and-effect storytelling. In his mind southerners were "manifestly the aggressors," and the war they brought on, as he wrote in a long letter of September 17, 1863, to Henry Halleck, not quite seventeen years after their voyage together on the *Lexington*, was "a salutary schooling" of "all the people of our country," one that was teaching them "lessons which might have been acquired from the experience of other people." Ever didactic, he continued by claiming that "were this war to cease now, the experience gained, though dear, would be worth the expense." In this image of war-as-instruction, Sherman's narrative impulse imagined narrative closure positively: the tuition was high, but the lessons were worth it.[8]

The two remaining narrators, Ambrose Bierce and Joshua Lawrence Chamberlain, both volunteer soldiers, would appear to have divided in their responses to Sherman's narrative judgment that the American Civil War was "worth the expense," a judgment not all could share, whether victors or vanquished. If we accept Bierce's carefully cultivated pose as cynic-in-chief, we might expect the author of *The Devil's Dictionary* (1911) to scoff at Sherman's bottom line. Defining "war" in that infernal lexicon as "a by-product of the arts of peace" and "cynic" as "a blackguard whose faulty vision sees things as they are, not as they ought to be," Bierce squarely opposed the cynic to the author of "romance," "fiction that owes no allegiance to the God of Things as They Are."[9] Although a reader of Sir Walter Scott, Sherman was hardly a romancer when it came to narrating his version of the war, and yet the trajectory of his narrative tended toward optimism, whereas Bierce's, in nonfictional pieces such as "What I Saw of Shiloh" or "The Crime at Pickett's Mill" or fictional ones such as "An Occurrence at Owl Creek Bridge" or "Chickamauga," most certainly did not. But it is not at all clear that Bierce's self-styled cynicism or anti-romanticism necessarily excluded all redeeming value from his war narratives of things as they are. Many moments in his war stories and nonfictional pieces, particularly when focused on officers he admired or on individual acts of bravery, reflected Sherman's definition of "true courage," which appeared halfway through the original concluding chapter of his *Memoirs*: "All men naturally shrink from pain and danger, and only incur their risk from some higher motive, or from habit; so that I would define true courage to be a perfect sensibility of the measure of danger, and a mental willingness to incur it, rather than that insensibility to danger, of which I have heard far more than I have seen."[10]

Bierce defined neither "courage" nor "bravery" in *The Devil's Dictionary*, but he could not have expected a definition to be any truer to things as they are than Sherman's. In writing about the war, Bierce did not spend his time on large, comprehensive visions of transcendent causes, nor did he focus much on the utilitarian, cotton gin end of the spectrum, although he enjoyed deflating self-aggrandizing humbuggery with reductively pragmatic assertions such as "Chickamauga was a fight for possession of a road."[11] Instead, Bierce focused his narratives on individuals, on their behavior in the face of pain and danger. In the process he demonstrated repeatedly his devotion to an ethical code of conduct that no doubt owed much to the habits developed by soldiers in wartime, but at the same time was not wholly without higher motives many a cynic would be too embarrassed to acknowledge.

Joshua Lawrence Chamberlain would seem at first to be Ambrose Bierce's exact opposite, the former given to pronouncements from which even his more sympathetic readers at times have felt it necessary to distance themselves. In the final chapter of *The Passing of the Armies* (1915), for example, Chamberlain confronted head-on Sherman's familiar description of war as hell:

> Then as to the reactionary effect of warfare on the
> participants,—in the first place we cannot accept General
> Sherman's synonym as a complete connotation or definition
> of war. Fighting and destruction are terrible; but are
> sometimes agencies of heavenly rather than hellish powers.
> In the privations and sufferings endured as well as in the
> strenuous action of battle, some of the highest qualities
> of manhood are called forth,—courage, self-command,
> sacrifice of self for the sake of something held higher,—
> wherein we take it chivalry finds value; and on another
> side fortitude, patience, warmth of comradeship, and in
> the darkest hours tenderness of caring for the wounded
> and stricken—exhaustless and unceasing as that of gentlest
> womanhood which allies us to highest personality.[12]

Whether or not chivalry is dead in the United States of the present moment, the word "chivalry," with its etymological connection to knightly cavaliers, is likely to make some readers wince. A much younger narrator, Stephen Crane, was already submitting notions of chivalry and heroism to critical inspection during Chamberlain's lifetime, and that critical inspection had many severe opportunities to intensify during the following century. Even Chamberlain's admiring biographer William M. Wallace followed his quotation of the passage above with the summary judgment, "In the last analysis Chamberlain was a romantic who could cheerfully defy war's terrors."[13]

But does this statement necessarily constitute the last analysis? In his response to Sherman, Chamberlain concluded his narrative by turning to what he called "the reactionary effect of warfare on the participants." In other words, Chamberlain attempted to incorporate into his narrative of large, public, historical events the private implications of those events for the interior worlds of individual people involved in them. Although some readers might find Chamberlain's attempt cloying, he did not do anything the other narrators did not do at some point as well. In his definition of true courage, Sherman anticipated Chamberlain's "something held higher" with the phrase "higher motive." In his *Memoranda During the War*, Whitman turned many times to the interior worlds of the soldiers he visited, as well as to his own. In his two most famous addresses, Lincoln focused on the interior worlds of his listeners when he called on them, highly resolved, to dedicate themselves in new ways and to foster in themselves charity without malice. In "What I Saw of Shiloh," even Bierce projected his battle narrative against an interiorized backdrop of human emotion: "Lead had scored its old-time victory over steel; the heroic had broken its great heart against the commonplace."[14]

Narrators of the American Civil War have placed their narratives along a spectrum running from heroic to commonplace, as well as on one running from Living God to cotton gin. The language of the heroic, of "something higher" or "higher motive" or the highly resolved, provokes mixed and ambivalent responses in many readers of the early part of the twenty-first century, as does the language of human interiority, about which a certain inarticulateness remains inescapable. But before various citizens of the twenty-first century, in their turn, settle on narratives that cast a perspective such as Chamberlain's in the role of old-fashioned, obsolete, misty-eyed quaintness, they would do well to consider the stories many people still tell others, or still try to get others to tell themselves, in the face of military service, which always includes the prospect of war. The official Internet homepage of the United States Army directs those who wish to join up to another website. Those who continue to this site will find the heading "For Parents." Under this rubric awaits a section called "Personal Growth," which describes, among other benefits of army life for young adults, living with the Seven Core Army Values: Loyalty, Duty, Respect, Selfless Service, Honor, Integrity, and Personal Courage.[15]

Here is another narrative, or potential narrative: a young adult who joins the army will grow under the influence of these values, none of which would be strange to Chamberlain or Lincoln

or Whitman or Sherman or even Bierce, who in later life continued to identify himself with the army, even though each had his
own stories of how events threatened to break, or succeeded in
breaking, the heart of these values at particular moments. To be
sure, between the outbreak of the American Civil War and the
present, many counter-narratives that deny or reject this story of
growth have emerged, too; yet the persistence of the story, which
in many cases the vanquished have told as eloquently as the victors, has much to say to us about the war, about the people who
lived through it, and about people who still read and think about
the people who lived through the war.

Few have read and thought about them as probingly, and written about them as eloquently, as Warren, whose meditations fifty
years ago on the legacy of the war—what professional historians
and many others would now call Civil War memory—provide a
useful landmark for locating where we stand fifty years later in
relation to those who lived through the war and have left us their
stories. Here is the closing paragraph of his book:

> Looking back on the years 1861–65, we see how the
> individual men, despite failings, blindness, and vice, may
> affirm for us the possibility of the dignity of life. It is a
> tragic dignity that their story affirms, but it may evoke
> strength. And in contemplation of the story, some of that
> grandeur, even in the midst of the confused issues, shadowy
> chances, and brutal ambivalences of our life and historical
> moment, may rub off on us. And that may be what we yearn
> for after all.[16]

A yearning for dignity, strength, and grandeur amid the confusing, brutal shadows of our lives at this moment. It is a powerful and unembarrassed testimony of Warren's own relation to the
legacy of the Civil War, which at this remove cannot be separated
from the legacy of Civil War narratives that constitute much, if not
most, of our experience of the war now. And Warren's personal
testimony cannot help but resonate still with the feelings of others,
among them, perhaps, those of young warriors-in-training, who

have joined the army or one of the other branches of the armed forces. It may also resonate with many, perhaps most, of those who attend meetings of a local Civil War roundtable or who reenact battles or who sit in armchairs and, for various reasons and in various ways, give themselves over to wartime narrators.

But fifty years after his meditations on the centennial of the war, does Warren's testimony resonate with other citizens of the United States, the great majority of whom do not serve in the armed forces, do not belong to roundtables or reenact battles, do not spend large amounts of time reading the stories of those who lived through the war? Some will argue that Warren's own whiteness and maleness, and his preoccupation with white males in his discussion, necessarily limits the dimensions of his "we." Perhaps they are right, although one can read numerous stories left by black narrators and female narrators that also affirm dignity, strength, and grandeur in the midst of wartime confusions, shadows, and brutal ambivalences. White male narrators of the Civil War do not have a monopoly on these things. Instead, what may mute or distort the resonances of Warren's testimony for many people now are not so much his race and gender, which are the easiest, most obvious markers and targets, as the distance of his historical moment from our own.

Allusions he makes to contemporary events show that Warren was yearning for dignity, strength, and grandeur in the domestic aftermath of the 1954 Supreme Court ruling in *Brown v. Board of Education of Topeka* and in the midst of "naked geo-political confrontation with Russia."[17] It would be inaccurate to say that our own historical moment involves the ongoing effects and consequences of neither, but even a brief and selective inventory of events and developments since the publication of Warren's book in 1961 suggests that recent history may well have complicated any yearning toward the dignity, strength, and grandeur of the nineteenth century: the Cuban missile crisis; the publication of Rachel Carson's *Silent Spring* and the beginning of the environmental movement; the assassination of President Kennedy; the escalation and subsequent course of the Vietnam War; *Roe v. Wade*; the

Arab oil embargo; Watergate; the assassinations of Martin Luther King Jr. and Robert Kennedy; the embassy hostages in Tehran; the Iran-Contra scandal; the development of the World Wide Web; the attacks of September 2001; war in Afghanistan; war in Iraq; and the Great Recession that began in December 2007.

The point of making such a list is not to claim that the confused issues, shadowy chances, and brutal ambivalences of our moment are any more confused, shadowy, and brutal to us than those of Warren and, one hundred years earlier, Lincoln, Whitman, Sherman, Bierce, and Chamberlain were to them. But it is to acknowledge the estranging effects of time and history, to acknowledge that one day the Civil War will be as distant from students of history as the Middle Ages and a medieval European worldview are from us, and to acknowledge that we are fifty years closer to that point in time than Warren was. In light of these estranging effects, can we say that more than 150 years after the beginning of the Civil War, we value narratives of the war because we yearn for their dignity, strength, and grandeur to rub off on us?

To some extent, even if that extent has diminished since 1961 and will continue to diminish as we move toward the bicentennial in 2061, the answer must be yes. What Warren called "the corrosive of historical realism" may cause some to balk at his word "grandeur," but dignity and strength have not disappeared from any widely shared list of values, although there may be great variations in notions of what constitutes each. In his meditations Warren sketched a troubled world characterized by "communication without communion," one that fuels "our secret yearning for the old-fashioned concept of the person" and its corollary, "the notion of community." If anything, his vision of a world without communion between people sounds even truer of the United States fifty years after he wrote this appraisal: "In our world of restless mobility, where every Main Street looks like the one before and the throughway is always the same, of communication without communion, of the ad-man's nauseating surrogate for family sense and community in the word *togetherness*, we look back nostalgically on the romantic image of some right and natural relation of man to place and man to man, fulfilled in worthy action."[18] Narratives of the Civil War will continue to offer many nostalgic readers examples of these relations "fulfilled in worthy action," and there is no reason to assume such nostalgia will wane rather than wax. Bad as Warren's jeremiad makes 1961 sound, his invocations of Main Street and the ad-man can stir their own nostalgia among people whose Main Streets have been superseded by vast malls and online consumerism, whose images of individual ad-men have been effaced by the digital anonymity of global corporations.

Nostalgia is at least as old as the painful homesickness of Odysseus for Ithaka. It is a forceful human motivation, and it is a constant in the stories people have told throughout the world and throughout time. In the West one can feel nostalgia when reading of worthy actions during the American Civil War or in medieval Europe or in ancient Rome and Greece. The yearning for something apparently more abundant in the past than in the present may be enough to sustain interest in the American Civil War through the bicentennial and far beyond, no matter how corrosive the historical realities of the future.

But it may also be that with the passage of enough time narratives produced by the Civil War will have to be ranked with the historical classics of antiquity, such as Xenophon's *Anabasis* or Julius Caesar's *Commentarii de Bello Gallico*, if they are to be valuable to the future. While some may read these ancient works in the hope that the dignity, strength, and grandeur of their chief actors may rub off, others read them out of sheer curiosity and interest in events and conditions so unlike theirs that yearning for likeness is no longer primary. If Civil War narratives one day become ancient classics, reading them may have to do more with fascination and illumination by differences than with yearning for likeness. If future readers value them, they will do so, in part, because the narratives offer vivid encounters with something remote, unfamiliar, strange, perhaps even exotic. At that point, whenever it comes, if it comes at all—for any number of reasons the reading of Civil War narratives may cease altogether well beforehand—it may be that one reads the writing of, say, Grant or Sherman primarily for the same reason that students of Greek have read the writing of Xenophon or students of Latin that of Caesar. Though works of military history, they are also distinguished models of well-managed prose. Though works of military history, the aesthetic qualities of their narratives have outlasted most readers' working knowledge of the circumstances and events they narrate. In narrating the history they present, these ancient works did it so effectively that they themselves have become the objects of histories, which future readers, though increasingly removed from the events that forged the stories, will join and continue. Whatever Civil War narratives the distant future will read, the distant future will have to judge to have done likewise. At that point the historical and the aesthetic will have become so fused that their separation will become even more difficult than it is today.

Notes

1. Douglas L. Wilson, *Lincoln's Sword: The Presidency and the Power of Words* (New York: Alfred A. Knopf, 2006). As will become clear, my discussion owes a great deal to Wilson's work, and I am grateful to him for his generous correspondence and conversation. Selective examples of other studies of Lincoln's artfulness could include John G. Nicolay, "Lincoln's Literary Experiments," *Century Magazine* 47, no. 6 (April 1894): 823–32; Daniel Kilham Dodge, *Abraham Lincoln: Master of Words* (New York: D. Appleton and Company, 1924); Gilbert Highet, *The Classical Tradition: Greek and Roman Influences on Western Literature* (New York: Oxford University Press, 1949), 112–13, 334 (on Lincoln's use of the tricolon, or three-part syntactic unit); Edmund Wilson, *Patriotic Gore: Studies in the Literature of the American Civil War* (New York: Oxford University Press, 1962), chap. 3; Don E. Fehrenbacher, "The Words of Lincoln," *Lincoln in Text and Context: Collected Essays* (Stanford: Stanford University Press, 1987); Ronald C. White, *Lincoln's Greatest Speech: The Second Inaugural* (New York: Simon and Schuster, 2002); John Channing Briggs, *Lincoln's Speeches Reconsidered* (Baltimore: Johns Hopkins University Press, 2005); and Fred Kaplan, *Lincoln: The Biography of a Writer* (New York: HarperCollins, 2008).

2. "American Civilization," *Miscellanies*, vol. 11 of *The Complete Works of Ralph Waldo Emerson*, ed. Edward W. Emerson (Boston: Houghton Mifflin, 1911), 302, 309. For brief accounts of the meetings between Lincoln and Emerson, see Ralph L. Rusk, *The Life of Ralph Waldo Emerson* (New York: Charles Scribner's Sons, 1949), 414–15; Gay Wilson Allen, *Waldo Emerson* (New York: Viking, 1981), 613–14; Len Gougeon, *Virtue's Hero: Emerson, Antislavery, and Reform* (Athens: University of Georgia Press, 1990), 276–77; Robert D. Richardson Jr., *Emerson: The Mind on Fire* (Berkeley: University of California Press, 1995), 547–48. Richardson commented, "Lincoln may have heard the lectures; he was certainly aware of them" (548), but Allen concluded, "The President and members of his Cabinet were so busy that, most witnesses agree, they did not attend the lecture on 'American Civilization'" (613). Allen's conclusion echoed Edward

Emerson's headnote to "Washington in Wartime," his excerpt from his father's journal, *Atlantic Monthly* 94 (July 1904): 1. For more on Emerson's speech in the context of emancipation, see Gougeon, *Virtue's Hero*, 279–81; for Emerson on emancipation in general, see Gougeon, passim, and Michael Magee, "Emerson's Emancipation Proclamations," *Raritan* 20, no. 4 (2001): 96–116.

3. Two exceptions are Carl Sandburg, *Abraham Lincoln: The War Years*, 4 vols. (New York: Harcourt Brace, 1939), 2:325, which quoted the description of Lincoln from Emerson's journal in the text below, and David Herbert Donald, *Lincoln* (New York: Simon and Schuster, 1995), 328, which included one sentence about the meeting, based on the very short account in Rusk's biography of Emerson. There was nothing, for example, in John G. Nicolay and John Hay, *Abraham Lincoln: A History* (New York: Century Co., 1904), 10 vols., and as of April 4, 2013, the entry for January 31, 1862, in *The Lincoln Log*, http://www.thelincolnlog.org/view, says nothing about Lincoln's attending Emerson's speech. Such omissions, though understandable given all Lincoln was facing in February 1862, both politically and personally, are especially interesting in the case of Doris Kearns Goodwin's *Team of Rivals: The Political Genius of Abraham Lincoln* (New York: Simon and Schuster, 2005), since Goodwin quoted Emerson several times. (I have based my statement about the location of wartime hospitals on Goodwin's map, pp. 2–3.) Meanwhile, in *Lincoln: The Biography of a Writer*, Fred Kaplan did allude, in a single sentence, to the 1862 meeting in the midst of remarks (235) about Lincoln hearing Emerson lecture in Springfield, Illinois, in January 1853. As will become clear below, there are reasons to question the apparent assurance behind Kaplan's remarks.

4. See, for example, the report filed in Washington by J. M. H. on February 1, 1862, and printed in *The Liberator* on Friday, February 14, under the title "Ralph W. Emerson at Washington": "Last evening, the largest audience ever convened in the lecture-room of the Smithsonian Institute came together to hear Ralph Waldo Emerson. Considering the state of the weather, and the muddy condition of the streets, the large turnout was a most flattering compliment to the lecturer; but when the audience heartily applauded his most radical sayings, and hardest hits against slavery, it was equally a compliment to the speaker and the good sense of his hearers" (27). If Lincoln had appeared at the Smithsonian among those applauding Emerson's most radical sayings, it is hard to believe a correspondent for *The Liberator* would have let such a significant fact go unremarked. I am grateful to Jon Grinspan for bringing this report to my attention.

5. *The Journals and Miscellaneous Notebooks of Ralph Waldo Emerson*, ed. Linda Allardt and David W. Hill (Cambridge: Belknap Press of Harvard University Press, 1982), 15:169 (hereafter, *Journals*). Quotations from this edition do not attempt to reproduce its editorial symbols and abbreviations, which annotate Emerson's changes and insertions. Emerson mistook the date of his first meeting with Lincoln, noting that Senator Charles Sumner took him to see Lincoln,

among others, on February 2 (*Journals*, 186), but February 2 was a Sunday, and on the same day Emerson met Lincoln for the first time he also met Secretary of State William Seward, who asked Emerson, "'will you come & go to church with me tomorrow'" (*Journals*, 189). Emerson agreed, went to church with Seward on Sunday, February 2, and then paid a call on Lincoln, meeting him for the second time. As of April 4, 2013, *The Lincoln Log* follows Emerson's mistaken dating.

6. Emerson, "Visit to Washington," *Journals*, 187, 194–95.

7. In the first published version of Emerson's journal account, "Washington in Wartime," 2, Edward Emerson omitted the reference to the smutty story with a discreet ellipsis, as he did in *Journals of Ralph Waldo Emerson* (Boston: Houghton Mifflin, 1913), 9:377.

8. Emerson, "Visit to Washington," *Journals*, 188, 194–95.

9. Ibid., 187.

10. Emerson, "Abraham Lincoln," *Miscellanies*, 331–32. See 330–31 for Emerson's support of Seward for the 1860 Republican presidential nomination.

11. Walt Whitman, "The Inauguration, March 4," *Memoranda During the War*, ed. Peter Coviello (New York: Oxford University Press, 2004), 77.

12. Emerson, "Abraham Lincoln," *Miscellanies*, 335.

13. Emerson, "Visit to Washington," *Journals*, 187; italics and quotation marks as in original.

14. Harold Holzer, *Lincoln President-Elect: Abraham Lincoln and the Great Secession Winter, 1860-1861* (New York: Simon and Schuster, 2008), 314–15.

15. Wilson's ten-page acceptance speech, delivered April 30, 2007, has not been published. I am grateful to him for sharing it.

16. Sources for this paragraph are *The Letters of Ralph Waldo Emerson*, ed. Ralph L. Rusk, 10 vols. (New York: Columbia University Press, 1939), 4:342; Allen, *Waldo Emerson*, 568; and entries for January 10, 11, and 12, 1853, *Diary of Orville Hickman Browning*, ed. Theodore Calvin Pease and James G. Randall, vol. 1, *1850-1864* (Springfield: Illinois State Historical Library, 1925), 90–91. See also the notices and reviews of Emerson's lectures in the *Illinois Daily Journal*, a four-page newspaper consisting mostly of notices and advertisements. The first notice appeared on the third page of the edition for Thursday, January 6, 1853, and was followed by items in the editions of Friday, January 7 (3); Saturday, January 8 (2, 3); Monday, January 10 (2); Tuesday, January 11 (3), Wednesday, January 12 (2, 3); Thursday, January 13 (2, 3); and Friday, January 14 (3). Of particular interest are the longer items on p. 2 of the January 8 edition and p. 2 of the January 13 edition. A noteworthy contrast to the extensive coverage of Emerson's visit in the *Daily Journal* was the silence about that visit in the *Illinois State Register*, which on p. 3 of its January 11 edition mentioned the banquet to be given "by the ladies of the Bell Society of the First Presbyterian Church" in the Senate Chamber that night but made no mention of Emerson's lecture preceding it. Kaplan (*Lincoln*, 235) stated that Lincoln attended the second of Emerson's lectures, but

he neither gave nor cited any evidence for this statement, perhaps assuming that because Mary Lincoln was one of the ladies of the First Presbyterian Church, her husband had to have been there.

17. For brief remarks on Lincoln's attending lyceums, see Kenneth J. Winkle, *The Young Eagle: The Rise of Abraham Lincoln* (Dallas: Taylor Trade Publishing, 2001), 181–82. Winkle did not make any claims about whether or not Lincoln heard Emerson in Springfield.

18. Headnote to "The Anglo-American," *The Later Lectures of Ralph Waldo Emerson, 1843–1871*, vol. 1 of 2, *1843–1854*, ed. Ronald A. Bosco and Joel Myerson (Athens: University of Georgia Press, 2001), 277. This headnote explains that the original title of the lecture was "The Anglo-Saxon," and Emerson first used the title "The Anglo-American" in Philadelphia, two months after his appearance in Springfield. For the sake of consistency with the Springfield lecture, subsequent references to this text of "The Anglo-American" will appear as "Anglo-Saxon."

19. "Anglo-Saxon," 291.

20. Ibid., 288.

21. Ibid., 285.

22. Ibid., 283.

23. Ibid., 294.

24. "Power," *The Conduct of Life*, vol. 6 of *The Complete Works of Ralph Waldo Emerson*, ed. Edward W. Emerson (Boston: Houghton Mifflin, 1904), 63.

25. Ibid., 53, 53, 54, 58, 62, 65, 65.

26. Ibid., 54.

27. "Culture," *The Conduct of Life*, vol. 6 of *The Complete Works of Ralph Waldo Emerson*, ed. Edward W. Emerson (Boston: Houghton Mifflin, 1904), 131, 132, 139.

28. Ibid., 142.

29. Ward H. Lamon, *The Life of Abraham Lincoln; from his birth to his inauguration as president* (Boston: J. R. Osgood, 1872), 494–95.

30. Sandburg, *Abraham Lincoln*, 2:309–10. See Kaplan, *Lincoln*, 30–36, for a portrait of Lincoln as a young reader. For other recent treatments of Lincoln's reading, see the chapter "Abe" in Daniel Wolff, *How Lincoln Learned to Read: Twelve Great Americans and the Educations That Made Them* (New York: Bloomsbury, 2009), and Robert Bray, *Reading with Lincoln* (Carbondale: Southern Illinois University Press, 2010). Bray's appendix, which reprinted his "What Abraham Lincoln Read: An Annotated and Evaluative Bibliography" from the *Journal of the Abraham Lincoln Association* 28, no. 2 (Summer 2007): 28–81, listed both Emerson's *Essays, First Series* (1841) and *Representative Men* (1850) among the books that Lincoln read; however, returning to Bray's original essay, we find that he judged Lincoln's reading of these books to be "somewhat likely" (41), as opposed to "very likely."

31. "Culture," 162.

32. "Fate," *The Conduct of Life*, vol. 6 of *The Complete Works of Ralph Waldo Emerson*, ed. Edward W. Emerson (Boston: Houghton Mifflin, 1904), 15.

33. Robert Chambers, *Vestiges of the Natural History of Creation* (London: John Churchill, 1844); reprinted in facsimile in *Vestiges of the Natural History of Creation and Other Evolutionary Writings*, ed. James A. Secord (Chicago: University of Chicago Press, 1994). I am grateful to Douglas Wilson for directing me to Chambers's work, which Ronald C. White also included in a list of books read by Lincoln (see *Lincoln's Greatest Speech*, 135). For Bray's remarks on Lincoln's reading of *Vestiges*, see *Reading with Lincoln*, 158–62.

34. William H. Herndon and Jesse W. Weik, *Herndon's Lincoln*, ed. Douglas L. Wilson and Rodney O. Davis (Urbana: Knox College Studies Center and University of Illinois Press, 2006), 264–65.

35. Chambers, *Vestiges*, 365–66.

36. Ibid., 390.

37. Rusk, *Life of Ralph Waldo Emerson*, 338–39; Richardson, *Emerson*, 444.

38. Not all commentators accept that comparisons of Lincoln and Emerson benefit each man. For a bracingly contrarian view, consider Edgar Lee Masters's assertion in his biography *Lincoln: The Man* (New York: Dodd, Mead and Co., 1931), 444: "Our greatest Americans are Jefferson, Whitman and Emerson; and the praise that has been bestowed on Lincoln is a robbery of these, his superiors."

39. Bosco and Myerson, eds. "Historical and Textual Introduction," *Later Lectures*, xxviii.

40. Richardson, *Emerson*, 418.

41. Bosco and Myerson, eds., *Later Lectures*, 55.

42. "Washington in Wartime," 1. In Bosco and Myerson, eds., *Later Lectures*, Emerson's lecture is titled "New England: Genius, Manners, and Customs." See pp. 39–40 for dates and names of places Emerson gave this lecture.

43. See *The Lincoln Log*, as of April 4, 2013.

44. William Charvat, *Emerson's American Lecture Engagements: A Chronological List* (New York: New York Public Library, 1961). For other dates in this paragraph, see *The Lincoln Log* and Allen, *Waldo Emerson*, 495, 518, 522.

45. For Emerson's account of his trip to Kentucky and eventually to St. Louis, see his long letter to his wife, "To Lidian Emerson, St. Louis, June 16 and 17, 1850," *Letters*, 4:209–14.

46. "Self-Reliance," *Essays, First Series* (Boston: Houghton, Mifflin and Co., 1883), 54–55; first published in 1841.

47. Roy P. Blaser, comp. and intro., *Lincoln's Gettysburg Address in Translation* (Washington, D.C.: Library of Congress, 1972), unpaginated.

48. One early appreciation of the Gettysburg Address, although it followed Lincoln's death, came from Ralph Waldo Emerson: "His brief speech at Gettysburg will not easily be surpassed by words on any recorded occasion." See "Abraham Lincoln," *Miscellanies*, 311.

49. Gabor Boritt, *The Gettysburg Gospel: The Lincoln Speech that Nobody Knows* (New York: Simon and Schuster, 2006), 272–75.

50. See O. B. Hardison Jr., and Roger M. A. Allen, "Rhyme-Prose," in *Princeton Encyclopedia of Poetry and Poetics*, ed. Roland Greene, Stephen Cushman, et al., 4th ed. (Princeton, N.J.: Princeton University Press, 2012).

51. *The American Political Tradition and the Men Who Made It* (New York: Alfred A. Knopf, 1948), 131.

52. John Bartlett, *Familiar Quotations*, 14th ed., ed. Emily Morrison Beck (Boston: Little, Brown and Co., 1969), 639n.

53. *The Collected Works of Abraham Lincoln*, ed. Roy P. Basler, 9 vols. (New Brunswick, N.J.: Rutgers University Press, 1953–55), 1:115.

54. See, for example, Reuven Tsur, *What Makes Sound Patterns Expressive: The Poetic Mode of Speech Perception* (Durham, N.C.: Duke University Press, 1992), 63–66.

55. Boritt, *Gettysburg Gospel*, 264.

56. He himself does not equate Lincoln with Hitler, but the work of Thomas DiLorenzo has encouraged others to make the connection, though some also make the connection with no reference to DiLorenzo, as browsing the Internet confirms. See DiLorenzo, *The Real Lincoln: A New Look at Abraham Lincoln, His Agenda, and an Unnecessary War* (New York: Three Rivers Press, 2003), esp. the Afterword, 282–85.

57. Kenneth Burke, *The Philosophy of Literary Form: Studies in Symbolic Action*, 3rd ed. (Berkeley: University of California Press, 1973), 203.

58. Boritt, *Gettysburg Gospel*, 272.

59. Karl Marx and Frederick Engels, *The Civil War in the United States*, ed. Richard Enmale, vol. 30 of the Marxist Library, 2nd ed. (New York: International Publishers, 1940), 81.

60. "The Sixth Joint Debate at Quincy," *The Lincoln-Douglas Debates: The First Complete, Unexpurgated Text*, ed. Harold Holzer (New York: HarperCollins, 1993), 311. The version of this debate printed by the *Chicago Daily Times* included the audience response to Douglas's admonitory quotation of Matthew, "Good, and applause." For a recent treatment of the Lincoln-Douglas Debates, see John Burt, *Lincoln's Tragic Pragmatism: Lincoln, Douglas, and Moral Conflict* (Cambridge: Harvard University Press, 2013).

61. Albert Christ-Janer, Charles W. Hughes, Carleton Sprague Smith, eds., *American Hymns Old and New* (New York: Columbia University Press, 1980), 557.

CHAPTER TWO

1. See David S. Reynolds, *Walt Whitman's America: A Cultural Biography* (New York: Alfred A. Knopf, 1995), 531.

2. University of Virginia Special Collections, to the staff of which I am most grateful, has two copies of Whitman's *Memoranda During the War* (Camden, N.J.: author's publication, 1875–76), in which this passage appears on p. 5. The copy with gold letters on its cover is inscribed "Lou Whitman / from Walt." (Louisa Whitman was the wife of Whitman's brother George, a veteran of the Fifty-first New York.) A facsimile of this book was published by Applewood Books, Boston, in 1990, and the pagination is the same as the original. A more recent edition is *Memoranda During the War*, ed. Peter Coviello (New York: Oxford University Press, 2004), in which this passage appears on p. 6. Subsequent references to *Memoranda* will appear parenthetically in the text and give the page number in the original edition, followed by that in Coviello's.

3. For a persuasive recent discussion of nationalism in *Memoranda*, see Coviello's introduction, esp. pp. xl–xlvii. For my own discussion of Whitman's complicated brand of patriotism, see Stephen Cushman, "Whitman and Patriotism," *Virginia Quarterly Review* 81, no. 2 (Spring 2005): 163–77.

4. Walt Whitman, *Prose Works 1892*, vol. 1 (New York: New York University Press, 1963), 116. Subsequent references to this edition appear parenthetically in the text as *PW*. *Specimen Days & Collect* was originally published by Reese Welsh and Co. (later David McKay) in Philadelphia in 1882.

5. David Blight, *Race and Reunion: The Civil War in American Memory* (Cambridge: Belknap Press of Harvard University Press, 2001), 19.

6. *Leaves of Grass: A Textual Variorum of the Printed Poems*, vol. 2, ed. Sculley Bradley, Harold W. Blodgett, Arthur Golden, and William White (New York: New York University Press, 1980), 382.

7. A transcription of the manuscript draft of this sentence, originally headed "May 2—'63," appears in *Notebooks and Unpublished Prose Manuscripts*, vol. 2, ed. Edward F. Grier (New York: New York University Press, 1984), 921: "We talk of the Histories of our Union War, (which have already begun to accumulate, many volumes, both sides and a few partially good ones.)"

8. That here Whitman himself italicized "real" obviously supports readings of "the real war will never get in the books" that implicitly do the same, but it does not preclude the insights we generate from shifting the emphasis, for the sake of this discussion, to "books."

9. Rochelle Gurstein, "On Weather," *The New Republic Online* (post date July 20, 2005), http://www.tnr.com/doc.mhtml?i=w050718&s=gurstein072005.

10. Among significant works that include material on or discussion of Whitman and the war are Daniel Aaron, *The Unwritten War: American Writers and the Civil War* (New York: Alfred A. Knopf, 1973); Robert Leigh Davis, *Whitman and the Romance of Medicine* (Berkeley: University of California Press, 1997); Daniel Mark Epstein, *Lincoln and Whitman: Parallel Lives in Civil War Washington* (New York: Ballantine Books, 2004); Betsy Erkkila, *Whitman the Political Poet* (New York: Oxford University Press, 1989); Ted Genoways, *Walt Whitman*

and the Civil War: America's Poet during the Lost Years of 1860–1862 (Berkeley: University of California Press, 2009); Charles I. Glicksberg, ed., *Walt Whitman and the Civil War* (Philadelphia: University of Pennsylvania Press, 1933); Justin Kaplan, *Walt Whitman: A Life* (New York: Simon and Schuster, 1980); Kerry C. Larson, *Whitman's Drama of Consensus* (Chicago: University of Chicago Press, 1988); Walter Lowenfels, ed., *Walt Whitman's Civil War* (New York: Alfred A. Knopf, 1961); John Harmon McElroy, *The Sacrificial Years: A Chronicle of Walt Whitman's Experiences in the Civil War* (Boston: David R. Godine, 1999); Roy Morris Jr., *The Better Angel* (New York: Oxford University Press, 2000); Reynolds, *Walt Whitman's America*; Timothy Sweet, *Traces of War: Poetry, Photography, and the Crisis of the Union* (Baltimore: Johns Hopkins University Press, 1990); and M. Wynn Thomas, *The Lunar Light of Whitman's Poetry* (Cambridge: Harvard University Press, 1987), which contains insightful remarks about the theatricality of the Chancellorsville "set piece" (213–15).

11. For details about the battle I have relied on Stephen W. Sears, *Chancellorsville* (Boston: Houghton Mifflin, 1996), 300–302.

12. Gary W. Gallagher, ed., *Fighting for the Confederacy: The Personal Recollections of General Edward Porter Alexander* (Chapel Hill: University of North Carolina Press, 1989), 206.

13. See *Notebooks and Unpublished Prose Manuscripts*, 2:533, for Whitman's entry for May 3, 1863: "Hooker's advance still fighting   glorious nights—soft fine full moon" (extra space in original).

14. Excerpted in Lee Steinmetz, ed., *The Poetry of the American Civil War* (East Lansing: Michigan State University Press, 1991), 228. Originally published in 1960.

15. The manuscript, in University of Virginia Special Collections, shows that Whitman canceled and revised words and phrases on his way to producing the iambic pattern. See "Fragment from the manuscript of 'Memoranda During the War,'" Call #3829-ac, Special Collections, University of Virginia, Charlottesville.

16. See Alexander Gardner, *Gardner's Sketch Book of the Civil War* (New York: Dover, 1959), plate 41 (unpaginated), and William A. Frassanito, *Gettysburg: A Journey in Time* (New York: Charles Scribner's Sons, 1975), 186–92.

17. *Notebooks and Unpublished Prose Manuscripts*, 2:615.

18. Sam R. Watkins, *"Co. Aytch": A Side Show of the Big Show* (New York: Macmillan, 1962), 19.

19. See, for example, Sweet, *Traces of War*, 48, and Coviello, introduction to *Memoranda*, xliv.

20. See Cushman, "Whitman and Patriotism," 170.

21. For help with these percentages, I am grateful to Gary Gallagher, who directed me to James M. McPherson's *Battle Cry of Freedom: The Civil War Era* (New York: Oxford, 1987), 606, n. 31, and *Ordeal by Fire: The Civil War and Reconstruction*, 2nd ed. (New York: McGraw-Hill, 1992), 357. McPherson cites

Ella Lonn's *Foreigners in the Confederacy* (Chapel Hill: University of North Carolina Press, 1940), 200–240, esp. 200 and 218–20. These sources give figures of 24 percent for foreign soldiers in the Union army and 9 or 10 percent in the Confederate. In correspondence Gallagher explained that he differs slightly from McPherson, preferring a figure of 25 percent for foreign soldiers in the Union army.

22. In connection with this and the following sentences, see Glicksberg, *Walt Whitman and the Civil War*, 148–54.

23. One example is Charles Royster's *The Destructive War: William Tecumseh Sherman, Stonewall Jackson, and the Americans* (New York: Alfred A. Knopf, 1991). Although he chose to focus on two important generals rather than on ordinary soldiers, Royster explained in the opening paragraph of his short preface that his book, which focused primarily on "the scale of destruction to which the participants committed themselves," gave "particular attention" to Sherman and Jackson because for "large numbers of their contemporaries these men epitomized the waging of successful war by drastic measures justified with claims to righteousness." By rationalizing his samples as epitomes, while avoiding any language qualifying or questioning the representative value of his samples as epitomes (such as the qualification that the war in the East became much more destructive a full year after Jackson died), Royster adopted a method closer to Whitman's magnification of significant specimens than to Watkins's more qualified presentation.

CHAPTER THREE

1. Ernest Hemingway, *Selected Letters, 1917-1961*, ed. Carlos Baker (New York: Charles Scribner's Sons, 1981), 595.

2. William Tecumseh Sherman, *Memoirs of General William T. Sherman*, ed. Charles Royster (New York: Library of America, 1990), 1086. This text is based on the second, or 1886, edition of the *Memoirs*, published, like the first, in New York by D. Appleton and Company. Subsequent references to Royster's edition will appear parenthetically in the text as *Memoirs*. The source for this dating in Royster's chronology appears to be Lloyd Lewis, *Sherman: Fighting Prophet* (New York: Harcourt, Brace and Co., 1932), 51. Subsequent references to Lewis's biography will appear parenthetically in the text as *Fighting Prophet*.

3. Edmund Wilson, *Patriotic Gore: Studies in the Literature of the American Civil War* (New York: Oxford University Press, 1966), 205; originally published in 1962.

4. Ulysses S. Grant, *Personal Memoirs of U. S. Grant*, ed. James M. McPherson (New York: Penguin, 1999), 132; originally published in New York by C. L. Webster in two volumes, 1885 and 1886. Subsequent references to McPherson's edition will appear parenthetically in the text as *Personal Memoirs*.

5. The fullest treatment of this formative episode in Sherman's career is John F. Marszalek's in the chapter "'The Insane General,'" in *Sherman's Other War: The General and the Civil War Press* (Memphis: Memphis State University Press, 1981), 49–93.

6. *Home Letters of General Sherman*, ed. M. A. DeWolfe Howe (New York: Charles Scribner's Sons, 1909), 24. Subsequent references to this edition will appear parenthetically in the text as *Home Letters*.

7. *Sherman's Civil War: Selected Correspondence of William T. Sherman, 1860–1865*, ed. Brooks D. Simpson and Jean V. Berlin (Chapel Hill: University of North Carolina Press, 1999), 758. Subsequent references to this edition will appear parenthetically in the text as *Sherman's Civil War*.

8. *The Sherman Letters: Correspondence between General Sherman and Senator Sherman from 1837 to 1891*, ed. Rachel Sherman Thorndike (New York: Da Capo, 1969), 9; originally published in New York by Charles Scribner's Sons in 1894. Subsequent references to Thorndike's edition will appear parenthetically in the text as *Sherman Letters*.

9. See John F. Marszalek, *Sherman: A Soldier's Passion for Order* (New York: Free Press, 1993), 54–61. Subsequent references to this book will appear parenthetically in the text as *Passion for Order*.

10. *Register of the Officers and Cadets of the U. S. Military Academy, West Point, New-York. June, 1840* (New York: J. P. Wright, 1840), 8: "the names of the most distinguished cadets not exceeding five in each class."

11. I am grateful to Susan Lintelmann, Associate Director for Special Collections and Archives, United States Military Academy Library, West Point, N.Y., for providing these titles and dates.

12. Autobiography of William T. Sherman, 1820–1861, written in 1868, MSS 57, William T. Sherman Papers, Box 12, Ohio Historical Society, Columbus, Ohio.

13. At least one of Sherman's readers, Henry Boynton, Washington correspondent of the *Cincinnati Gazette*, attempted to discredit the general's representation of reality. In a book of nearly three hundred pages, provocatively titled *Sherman's Historical Raid: The Memoirs in the Light of the Record* (Cincinnati: Wilstach, Baldwin, and Co., 1875), Boynton claimed to be drawing on the official records "to show wherein the Memoirs of General Sherman fall far short of presenting the correct history of many great events of which they treat" (3). But subsequent historians and biographers, following Grant's vindication of Sherman in 1876, have tended to discredit Boynton in turn, if they notice him at all (see, for example, Marszalek, *Passion for Order*, 464–66).

14. William T. Sherman Papers, Library of Congress, Washington, D.C., Journal of the Mexican War, 1846–1847, box 102 or reel 49. Subsequent references to this item will appear parenthetically in the text as Journal.

15. Sherman made at least one earlier record of events. From November 1843 to March 1845, while stationed at Fort Moultrie, he kept a diary. William

T. Sherman Family Papers, University of Notre Dame Archive, South Bend, Ind., CSHR 6/01. The diary has been digitized and is available at http://archives .nd.edu/Sherman/png/12-0002.htm.

16. William T. Sherman to Samuel L. Clemens, September 15, 1885, Union Catalog of Letters to Clemens, 42676, Bancroft Library, University of California, Berkeley. I am grateful to Robert H. Hirst, General Editor, Mark Twain Project, for his generous assistance. In making this transcription from Sherman's hand-writing, I acknowledge that I was not always able to tell the difference between a true dash and a runny period or, in some cases, between lowercase and capital letters. I have not inserted *sic* after any punctuation or spelling in Sherman's letters (or in Twain's below). The only one of Sherman's biographers who seems to have examined this correspondence between Sherman and Clemens is Lloyd Lewis, who quoted the sentence about Sherman needing the money for his grand-children, soldier dependants, and beggars, as well as Sherman's request, "give me your honest opinion" (*Fighting Prophet*, 640). In the same paragraph Lewis quoted intermittently, and out of order, from the second and third paragraphs of Twain's response of October 5, 1885. Lewis did not examine the original letters, citing instead "Sherman Letter-book, mss. in Library of Congress, 44 vols," and some features of his quotation differ from the original. Lewis's quotation from this letter appears to be the source for the blurb from Twain on the back cover of the Da Capo printing of the first edition of the *Memoirs*, originally published in New York in 1984. I have not been able to locate the 294 pages of foolscap de-scribing Sherman's trip, nor have I seen citations of it in the published literature. Sherman's aide, Colonel Joseph C. Audenried, made notes of the trip. See MSS 57, William T. Sherman Papers, Box 11, Ohio Historical Society, Columbus, Ohio. See also Sherman's posthumously published article "General Sherman's Tour of Europe," *Century* 35 (1899): 729–40.

17. William T. Sherman to Samuel L. Clemens, October 9, 1885, Union Cata-log of Letters to Clemens, 42709, Bancroft Library, University of California, Berkeley.

18. Samuel L. Clemens to William T. Sherman, September 19, 1885, Union Catalog of Clemens Letters, 01606, Bancroft Library, University of California, Berkeley. Excerpts from Twain's letters are taken from typed transcripts.

19. Samuel L. Clemens to William T. Sherman, October 5 and 6, 1885, Union Catalog of Clemens Letters, 04126, Bancroft Library, University of California, Berkeley.

20. For background on Twain's humorous sketch and his two-week service in July 1861 with the pro-Confederate Marion Rangers, irregulars from Marion County, Missouri, see Tom Z. Parrish, "Civil War," *The Routledge Encyclopedia of Mark Twain*, ed. J. R. LeMaster and James D. Wilson (New York: Routledge, 2011), 146–48; first published as *The Mark Twain Encyclopedia* (New York: Gar-land, 1993).

21. Samuel L. Clemens to William T. Sherman, October 5 and 6, 1885, Union Catalog of Clemens Letters, 04126, Bancroft Library, University of California, Berkeley. Editorial material in brackets in transcription.

22. William T. Sherman to Samuel L. Clemens, September 22, 1885, Union Catalog of Letters to Clemens, 42684, Bancroft Library, University of California, Berkeley.

23. William S. McFeely, "Introduction to the Da Capo Edition," *Memoirs of General William T. Sherman* (New York: Da Capo, 1984), ix.

24. For more discussion of the overlapping meanings of, and distinctions among, autobiography, memoirs, and memoir, see Ben Yagoda, *Memoir: A History* (New York: Riverhead Books, 2009), 1–3. Yagoda gives some attention to Grant's memoirs (122–25), none to Sherman's.

25. In the *Memoirs*, Sherman's baldest statement of his Unionism appeared in a letter he included in the chapter "Savannah and Pocotaligo," one to Edwin M. Stanton, January 19, 1865, in which the general discussed policies to be adopted toward southerners and their cotton, whether they burned it or offered it to United States authorities for purchase: "We should assume a tone of perfect contempt for cotton and every thing else in comparison with the great object of the war—*the restoration of the Union, with all its rights and powers*" (*Memoirs*, 745; Sherman's italics). Both the sentiment behind this statement and the late date on which it was made confirm the arguments advanced by Gary Gallagher in *The Union War* (Cambridge: Harvard University Press, 2011).

26. Joan Waugh, *U. S. Grant: American Hero, American Myth* (Chapel Hill: University of North Carolina Press, 2009), passim, esp. 154–65.

27. Wilson, *Patriotic Gore*, 192.

28. William T. Sherman Papers, Library of Congress, Washington, D.C., box 105 or reel 49. Differences between this manuscript and a later one, copied out by someone with better handwriting than Sherman, tend to be minor. The later manuscript can be found in box 107 or reels 50–51.

29. William T. Sherman Papers, Library of Congress, Washington, D.C., box 105 or reel 49.

30. James M. Merrill, *William Tecumseh Sherman* (New York: Rand McNally, 1971), 356.

31. For Grant during the last stages of writing his memoirs, see Waugh, *U. S. Grant*, 193–201, and William S. McFeely, *Grant: A Biography* (New York: Norton, 1981), 509–16.

32. William T. Sherman Papers, Library of Congress, Washington, D.C., box 106 or reel 50.

33. Ibid.

34. Ernest Hemingway, *Death in the Afternoon* (New York: Charles Scribner's Sons, 1932), 192.

35. For a statement by James on the craft of narrative omission, see his preface to *The Spoils of Poynton* (1897; first published serially in the *Atlantic Monthly*, 1896) in Henry James, *Literary Criticism*, Vol. 2: *European Writers and Prefaces to the New York Edition*, ed. Leon Edel and Mark Wilson (New York: Library of America, 1984), 1138. I am grateful to my colleague Stephen Arata for bringing this passage to my attention.

36. Ambrose Bierce, *The Collected Works of Ambrose Bierce*, 12 vols. (New York: Neale Publishing Company, 1909–12), 1:279.

CHAPTER FOUR

1. S. T. Joshi and David E. Schultz, eds., *A Much Misunderstood Man: Selected Letters of Ambrose Bierce* (Columbus: Ohio State University Press, 2003), 27; cited hereafter parenthetically in the text as *Selected Letters*.

2. National Park Service, http://www.nps.gov/hps/abpp/battles/ga004.htm (October 30, 2013).

3. H. W. Fowler and F. G. Fowler, *The Works of Lucian of Samosata*, vol. 2 (Oxford: Clarendon Press, 1905), 126; cited hereafter parenthetically in the text as *Lucian*. Although Bierce could have seen this translation late in his life, its publication date shows that it is not the one he would have had in mind for Blanche Partington.

4. Archibald Gracie, *The Truth about Chickamauga* (Boston and New York: Houghton Mifflin, 1911), ix; cited hereafter parenthetically in the text as *Truth*.

5. See Peter Cozzens, *This Terrible Sound: The Battle of Chickamauga* (Urbana: University of Illinois Press, 1992), 418; cited hereafter parenthetically in the text as *Terrible Sound*. Cozzens does include Gracie's book in his bibliography of secondary works.

6. For an account of Boynton's role with the Thirty-fifth Ohio on Horseshoe Ridge that suggests he did have good reason to be proud of that role, see Cozzens, *Terrible Sound*, 505–9.

7. For a more recent perspective on the credit deserved by the Ninth Indiana, see Laurence D. Conley, "The Truth about Chickamauga: A Ninth Indiana Regiment's Perspective," *Indiana Magazine of History* 98 (June 2002): 114–43. I am grateful to Lee White, Chickamauga and Chattanooga National Battlefield Park, for directing me to this essay.

8. Of Albert's letter Carey McWilliams has written, "'Old Sloots,' as Ambrose called his brother, was rather shy about relating his feats of gallantry, but he finally wrote an account of what he saw of Chickamauga for Mr. Gracie, who was his brother's friend. Ambrose was rather shocked at the document and forwarded it to Mr. Gracie with a world of apology for the style!" (*Ambrose Bierce: A Biography* [New York: Albert and Charles Boni, 1929], 50). McWilliams has cited no

source for the claim that Bierce was shocked by his brother's style. Meanwhile, Albert must have written at least two accounts of what he saw of Chickamauga, or either Bierce or Gracie must have rewritten his original account, since the one quoted by Gracie is not the same as the one, dated March 29, 1911, housed in the Ambrose Bierce Collection, Albert and Shirley Small Special Collections Library, University of Virginia, Charlottesville (MSS 5992-a, Box 1, Item 41; see Appendix). Bierce's letter to Gracie appeared first, without salutation or signature, in Ambrose Bierce, *A Sole Survivor: Bits of Autobiography*, ed. S. T. Joshi and David E. Schultz (Knoxville: University of Tennessee Press, 1998), 34–35, and was subsequently reprinted the same way in *Phantoms of a Blood-Stained Period: The Complete Civil War Writings of Ambrose Bierce*, ed. Russell Duncan and David J. Klooster (Amherst: University of Massachusetts Press, 2002), 202–4 (cited parenthetically in the text hereafter as *Sole Survivor* and *Phantoms*, respectively). It then appeared with salutation and signature in *Selected Letters*, which is my text here.

9. See Cozzens, *Terrible Sound*, 450; Glenn Tucker, *Chickamauga: Bloody Battle in the West* (Dayton, Ohio: Morningside Bookshop, 1984), 368, originally published by Bobbs-Merrill, 1961, and cited hereafter parenthetically in the text as *Bloody Battle*; and William Glenn Robertson, "The Chickamauga Campaign: The Battle of Chickamauga, Day 2, September 20, 1863," *Blue and Gray* 25, no. 2 (Summer 2008): 46.

10. *Collected Works of Ambrose Bierce*, 12 vols. (New York: Neale Publishing Co., 1909–12), 1:275–76; cited hereafter parenthetically as *CW*.

11. *The War of the Rebellion: A Compilation of the Official Records of the Union and Confederate Armies*, ser. 1, vol. 30, pt. 1 (Washington, D.C.: U.S. Government Printing Office, 1890), 855.

12. Henry V. Boynton, *The National Military Park, Chickamauga-Chattanooga, An Historical Guide, With Maps and Illustrations* (Cincinnati: Robert Clarke, 1895); see pp. xvi, 53, 55, e.g.

13. Daniel H. Hill, "Chickamauga—The Great Battle of the West," *Battles and Leaders of the Civil War*, ed. Robert Underwood Johnson and Clarence Clough Buel, vol. 3 (New York: Century Co., 1888), 641; cited hereafter parenthetically in the text as "Great Battle."

14. For Boynton's narrative of the creation of the park at Chickamauga, see his *National Military Park*, 219–50.

15. Donald T. Blume, *Ambrose Bierce's Civilians and Soldiers in Context* (Kent, Ohio: Kent State University Press, 2004), chap. 7, passim. Although suggestive, Blume's argument becomes heavy-handed, as it reduces the story "Chickamauga" to an allegory of the situation in Samoa. It is also marred by mistakes, such as the confusing of Archibald Gracie, author of *The Truth about Chickamauga*, with his father, the general (370 n23), and the shortening of the battle to only September 20, 1863 (142).

16. See Carey McWilliams, *Ambrose Bierce*, 189–90, for this version of Bierce's separation from his wife. For a very different version, which puts Bierce in the wrong ("when he rashly unbosomed himself to the wife of his bosom and sang of another's charms"), see Walter Neale, *Life of Ambrose Bierce* (New York: Walter Neale, 1929), 132–36.

17. See Neale, *Life of Ambrose Bierce*, 73.

18. Wotherspoon's letters to Bierce are in the Ambrose Bierce Collection, Albert and Shirley Small Special Collections Library, University of Virginia, Charlottesville, MSS 5992-a, Box 1, Items 35, 36, 37. Bierce's commission to Brevet Major is Item 12 in the same box. Item 14 is his commission to second lieutenant, Fifth United States Infantry, April 3, 1867.

19. Neale, *Life of Ambrose Bierce*, 73.

20. Roy Morris Jr., *Ambrose Bierce: Alone in Bad Company* (New York: Crown, 1995), 16.

21. For example, Morris endorses another reader's assessment of Bierce's Civil War stories as "enduring peace tracts" (*Ambrose Bierce*, 63). Although Bierce's war experiences certainly disabused him of any romantic illusions about warmaking, saying so is not at all the same thing as projecting an oversimplified and undifferentiated pacifism onto those stories. In *On Killing: The Psychological Cost of Learning to Kill in War and Society* (Boston: Little, Brown and Co., 1995), Dave Gossman quotes this telling statement from Douglas MacArthur: "The soldier above all other people prays for peace, for they [*sic*] must suffer and bear the deepest wounds and scars of war" (xxiv). A soldier's prayer for peace differs from that of a Quaker or a conscientious objector. The latter believes war-making to be morally wrong and refuses to participate in it; the former, if he is a professional, recognizes that war is an inevitable component of human affairs; that it must not be undertaken rashly; and that it must be anticipated with thorough training and preparation, since when it does come, as it always has, he or she will have to participate in it. Bierce's life and work show that his inclinations toward peacefulness belong to the soldier's category, not the Quaker's. See also H. L. Mencken, "Ambrose Bierce," in *Critical Essays on Ambrose Bierce*, ed. Cathy N. Davidson (Boston: G. K. Hall, 1982), 61–62; originally published in 1927.

22. Gracie's letters to Bierce are Items 43 and 44 in Box 1, MSS 5992-a, Ambrose Bierce Collection, Albert and Shirley Small Special Collections Library, University of Virginia, Charlottesville; Bierce's reply is Item 45; Suman's letter to Bierce is Item 28.

23. See letter of Paul O. Hardt to "Superintendent, Chickamauga National Battlefield," July 18, 1975, in Ambrose Bierce file, Chickamauga and Chattanooga National Military Park, Fort Oglethorpe, Ga. I am grateful to Lee White for providing me with copies of this letter and the one from Robert L. Deskins responding to it. For recent examples of those who draw parallels between the facts of Chickamauga and Bierce's story, see David M. Owens, *The Devil's Topographer:*

Ambrose Bierce and the American War Story (Knoxville: University of Tennessee Press, 2006), 93–99, and Sharon Talley, *Ambrose Bierce and the Dance of Death* (Knoxville: University of Tennessee Press, 2009), 94–95; see Morris, *Ambrose Bierce*, 56–64, for discussion of both the battle and the story, though Morris does not insist on specific parallels between fact and Bierce's fiction, beyond pointing out that "the child's experiences ironically mirror those of the Union army during the battle" (62).

24. Letter of Robert L. Deskins to Paul O. Hardt, July 24, 1975, Ambrose Bierce file, Chickamauga and Chattanooga National Military Park, Fort Oglethorpe, Ga.

25. James Alfred Sartain, *History of Walker County, Georgia*, vol. 1 (Dalton, Ga.: A. J. Showalter Co., 1932), 100–101.

26. For biographical background on Bierce's interest in and care for Lily Walsh, see, for example, McWilliams, *Ambrose Bierce*, 250–51; M. E. Grenander, *Ambrose Bierce* (New York: Twayne, 1971), 64–65; Morris, *Ambrose Bierce*, 215. During 1895, until her death in October, Lily Walsh wrote Bierce approximately forty letters, which are in the Bancroft Library, University of California, Berkeley.

27. The best account of Bierce's complicated relationship to literary realism is Howard W. Bahr's "Ambrose Bierce and Realism," *Southern Quarterly* 1 (1963): 309–31, reprinted in Davidson, *Critical Essays*, 150–68.

28. See Christopher Krentz, *Writing Deafness: The Hearing Line in Nineteenth-Century American Literature* (Chapel Hill: University of North Carolina Press, 2007), 127. In light of Bierce's connection with Lily Walsh, Krentz's argument that Bierce subscribed to negative stereotypes of his fictional character's deafness may need reconsideration.

29. Mencken, "Ambrose Bierce," 61: "Bierce, I believe, was the first writer of fiction ever to treat war realistically."

30. Cathy N. Davidson refers to "the mangled body of his probably raped ('the clothing deranged') and definitely murdered mother" in *The Experimental Fictions of Ambrose Bierce: Structuring the Ineffable* (Lincoln: University of Nebraska Press, 1984), 43. The story is quite clear that the mother has been hit by a shell or a shell fragment, the impact of which would certainly have been sufficient to derange her clothing as it knocked her to the ground. She was definitely not murdered, unless Davidson means that the accidental killing of a civilian caught on a battlefield is a form a murder, and the mother hardly could have been raped by any soldier in the midst of shelling, a soldier who somehow managed to derange her clothing, violate her, and continue unhurt at the very moment the shell fragment killed her before she could rearrange her clothing. Davidson frames her commentary on "Chickamauga" by labeling it "one of the most gruesome and arresting antiwar tales ever written" (36; see n. 21 above).

31. For an account of a bloody fantasy from Bierce's childhood, see Paul Fatout, *Ambrose Bierce: The Devil's Lexicographer* (Norman: University of Oklahoma Press, 1951), 22.

32. *Write It Right: A Little Blacklist of Literary Faults* (New York: Union Library Assoc., 1934), 46; originally published, New York: Neale Publishing Co., 1909.

33. Edmund Wilson, *Patriotic Gore: Studies in the Literature of the American Civil War* (New York: Oxford University Press, 1962), 632.

34. The technique of making the familiar strange, which twentieth-century Russian Formalist critics called *ostranenie*, usually translated "making strange" or "defamiliarization," was, according to them, the essence of the literary. Bierce's technique of defamiliarizing and then dispelling the unfamiliarity corresponds to what Ian Watt, in a discussion of Joseph Conrad, born fifteen years after Bierce, calls "delayed decoding." See Watt's *Conrad in the Nineteenth Century* (Berkeley: University of California Press, 1979), 175–79.

CHAPTER FIVE

1. Ulysses S. Grant, *Personal Memoirs of U. S. Grant*, ed. James M. McPherson (New York: Penguin, 1999), 601; originally published in New York by C. L. Webster in two volumes, 1885 and 1886. For examples of the apple-tree lore, see B. A. Botkin, ed., *A Civil War Treasury of Tales, Legends and Folklore* (Lincoln: University of Nebraska Press, 2000; originally published in 1960), 484, 489–90, 520, 534. Compare Chamberlain's statement to Ellis Spear in a letter of November 27, 1896: "The 'whole truth' is sometimes quite different in its bearing from what is called truth. But to make a part truth displace the whole is not in accordance with old-fashioned ethics" (Joshua Lawrence Chamberlain, *The Grand Old Man of Maine: Selected Letters of Joshua Lawrence Chamberlain, 1865–1914*, ed. Jeremiah E. Goulka [Chapel Hill: University of North Carolina Press, 2004], 155).

2. Alexander Brown, *The First Republic in America: An Account of the Origin of this Nation, Written from the Records then (1624) Concealed by the Council, rather than from the Histories Licensed by the Crown* (Boston and New York: Houghton, Mifflin, and Company, 1898), 194.

3. For details on the location of Chamberlain's line, see Alice Rains Trulock, *In the Hands of Providence: Joshua Lawrence Chamberlain and the American Civil War* (Chapel Hill: University of North Carolina Press, 1992), 502 n. 18. For Gibbon ordering Griffin to send a Fifth Corps division into Appomattox Court House, see William Marvel, *A Place Called Appomattox* (Chapel Hill: University of North Carolina Press, 2000), 258. For Chamberlain as the only soldier in the Fifth Corps to receive the Congressional Medal of Honor, see William H. Powell, *The Fifth Army Corps (Army of the Potomac): A Record of Operations during the Civil War in the United States of America, 1861–1865* (New York: G. P. Putnam's Sons, 1896), 873. For material relating to the belated awarding of Chamberlain's Medal of Honor, see Chamberlain, *The Grand Old Man of Maine*, xxii–xxiii, 145.

4. According to *The War of the Rebellion, A Compilation of the Official Records of the Union and Confederate Armies* (Washington, D.C.: Government Printing Office, 1880–1901), ser. 1, vol. 46, pt. 1, p. 569, the 9th, 18th, and 22nd Massachusetts; the 2nd Maine; and the 1st and 4th Michigan were not in the Third Brigade of the First Division of the Fifth Corps during the Appomattox Campaign. In naming these regiments to his sister, Chamberlain was including units that had been absorbed into others, as, for example, the 18th Massachusetts had been consolidated with the 32nd Massachusetts on October 21, 1864, and the three-year men of the 2nd Maine had been transferred to the 20th Maine after the former was mustered out on June 9, 1863. For brief regimental histories, see the National Park Service Civil War website, http://www.civilwar.nps.gov.

5. John J. Pullen, *Joshua Chamberlain: A Hero's Life and Legacy* (Mechanicsburg, Pa.: Stackpole Books, 1999), 7.

6. William Marvel, *A Place Called Appomattox*, 260, and *Lee's Last Retreat: The Flight to Appomattox* (Chapel Hill: University of North Carolina Press, 2002), 193. Marvel misread "Sae," the nickname of Chamberlain's sister, as "Sal"; he followed John B. Gordon's mistaken attribution of one of Chamberlain's accounts of the salute to the *New York Times* of May 4, 1901, which contains nothing on Chamberlain's role in the surrender at Appomattox; and he claimed that Gordon made no mention of the salute until nearly "four decades later," when he read Chamberlain's account of it, whereas in fact the *Harper's Weekly* of May 21, 1898 (p. 498), showed Gordon already telling his version of the salute (in which Chamberlain's troops "present" arms) closer to three decades later (by which time he could have read Chamberlain's 1894 version). Marvel also asserted that "Chamberlain was the only original source of the claim that he commanded the surrender ceremony; he offered no witnesses or documentation, and none has been found." Although regimental histories "published as early as 1880" named Chamberlain as commander, Marvel discounted these histories because they "came from regiments within his own brigade, and his private claim may have influenced those references." In making these assertions, Marvel had either missed or chosen to ignore Powell, *Fifth Army Corps*, 863: "General Joshua L. Chamberlain, commanding the 1st Brigade of Bartlett's division, had been designated to command the parade." According to his preface, William Henry Powell (1838–1901), identified as Lieutenant Colonel, Eleventh Infantry, was asked to assume the duty of writing the Fifth Corps history at the annual meeting of the Society of the Fifth Army Corps, held in Scranton, Pennsylvania, in June 1892 (iii). Presumably a veteran of the Fifth Corps, who obviously enjoyed the trust of the society, Powell turned twenty-seven in 1865. The National Park Service Civil War website lists under "Infantry" twenty William H. Powells and two William Henry Powells, neither of whom belonged to a unit of the Fifth Corps. Of the twenty William H. Powells, one belonged to a unit of the Fifth Corps, the Fourth Maryland. Since the Fourth Maryland belonged to the Second Brigade

of the Second Division, Marvel's assertion that support for Chamberlain's claim came only from regiments in his own brigade cannot be true. Even if this is not the same William H. Powell, there is no listing of a William H. Powell who belonged to any regiment in one of Chamberlain's brigades, either the First or the Third, nor is there any listing of a William Powell, of whom there are 115 under "Infantry," who belonged to such a regiment. See *A Place Called Appomattox*, 261, 278 n. 39; *Lee's Last Retreat*, 358 n. 38; and John B. Gordon, *Reminiscences of the Civil War* (Baton Rouge: Louisiana State University Press, 1993; originally published in 1903), 445.

7. Edward G. Longacre, *Joshua Chamberlain: The Soldier and Man* (Conshohocken, Pa.: Combined Publishing, 1999), 246–47. Two of Chamberlain's other biographers narrated the surrender ceremony, paraphrasing Chamberlain's accounts without acknowledging or discussing any doubts about those accounts. See William M. Wallace, *Soul of the Lion: A Biography of General Joshua L. Chamberlain* (New York: Thomas Nelson and Sons, 1960), 185–92, and Trulock, *In the Hands of Providence*, 301–11. Another account of the surrender ceremony that relied on Chamberlain's, but exceeded his in romantic flourishes, is that of Morris Schaff. See the final chapter of his *Sunset of the Confederacy* (Boston: J. W. Luce and Company, 1912), reprinted with introduction by Gary W. Gallagher (New York: Cooper Square Press, 2002). For Chamberlain's hedging assertion in a letter of January 23, 1906, "I do not like to say Grant honorably designated me," see Chamberlain, *The Grand Old Man of Maine*, 221.

8. (1) Joshua L. Chamberlain to "My dear Sae" [Sarah (Chamberlain) Farrington], Appomattox Court House, April 13, 1865, George J. Mitchell Department of Special Collections and Archives, Bowdoin College, Brunswick, Maine, Joshua L. Chamberlain Collection, M27; (2) "The Surrender of Gen. Lee," *Kennebec Journal* (Augusta, Maine; Friday, January 3, 1868): 1; (3) "The Third Brigade at Appomattox," *Proceedings of the Third Brigade Association, First Division, Fifth Army Corps, Army of the Potomac held at the time of the National Encampment, Grand Army of the Republic, Indianapolis, Indiana, 6 September 1893* (New York: Rider and Driver Pub. Co., 1894), 134–42; (4) "The Last Salute of the Army of Northern Virginia," *Southern Historical Society Papers*, vol. 32 (1904), 355–63, which mistakenly attributed the article to the *Boston Journal*, May 1901 (the correct date is Sunday, April 28, 1901, although other sources cited in these notes have followed the same mistake; this is the item that Gordon attributed to the *New York Times* of May 4, 1901); (5) "Appomattox: Paper Read before the New York Commandery, Loyal Legion of the United States, October Seventh, 1903" (a twenty-one-page pamphlet in the George J. Mitchell Department of Special Collections and Archives, Bowdoin College, Brunswick, Maine), reprinted and usually cited in *Personal Recollections of the War of the Rebellion: Addresses Delivered before the Commandery of the State of New York, Military Order of the Loyal Legion of the United States*, 3rd ser., ed. A. Noel Blakeman

[New York: G. P. Putnam's Sons, 1907], 260–80); (6) *The Passing of the Armies: An Account of the Final Campaign of the Army of the Potomac, Based Upon Personal Reminiscences of the Fifth Army Corps* (New York: Bantam, 1993; originally New York: G. P. Putnam's Sons, 1915). Subsequent page references to each of these items, this list of which does not constitute an exhaustive bibliography of Chamberlain's writings about Appomattox, will appear parenthetically in the text. For help in securing copies of materials owned by Bowdoin College, I am very grateful to Daniel Hope.

9. Douglas Southall Freeman, *Lee's Lieutenants: A Study in Command* (New York: Charles Scribner's Sons, 1944), 745 n. 77. Ralph Lowell Eckert spliced the same two versions in *John Brown Gordon: Soldier, Southerner, American* (Baton Rouge: Louisiana State University Press, 1989), 121–22. The image of Chamberlain that was circulating in the South in the early twentieth century also got a boost from John William Jones, *Life and Letters of Robert Edward Lee, Soldier and Man* (New York: Neale Publishing Company, 1906), 377: "A gallant colorbearer, as he delivered up the tattered remnant of his flag, burst into tears and said to the Federal soldiers who received it, 'Boys, this is not the first time you have seen that flag. I have borne it in the very forefront of the battle on many a victorious field, and I had rather die than surrender it now.' 'Brave fellow,' said General Chamberlain, of Maine, who heard the remark, 'I admire your noble spirit, and only regret that I have not the authority to bid you keep your flag and carry it home as a precious heirloom.'"

10. See Allan Nevins, *The War for the Union*, vol. 4, *The Organized War for Victory, 1864–1865* (New York: Scribner, 1971), 315–16, and James McPherson, *Battle Cry of Freedom: The Civil War Era* (New York: Oxford University Press, 1988), 850. Nevins drew on version six from *The Passing of the Armies*, McPherson on version four, "The Last Salute of the Army of Northern Virginia."

11. For General Orders No. 8, assigning Chamberlain to the Third Brigade and Pearson to the First on April 10, 1865, see *Official Records*, ser. 1, vol. 46, pt. 3, p. 691.

12. On Gordon's connection with the Klan, see Eckert, *John Brown Gordon*, 145–49.

13. *New York Times*, November 26, 1893, 5. See Chamberlain's letter to Frank A. Garnsey, January 18, 1899, for his discussion of a proposition that he and Gordon give their "lectures on the surrender in close connection in various places" (Chamberlain, *The Grand Old Man of Maine*, 166–67).

14. Gordon R. Sullivan and Michael V. Harper, *Hope Is Not a Method: What Business Leaders Can Learn from America's Army* (New York: Broadway Books, 1996), 240–41.

15. Michael E. McCullough, Steven J. Sandage, and Everett L. Worthington Jr., *To Forgive Is Human: How to Put Your Past in the Past* (Downers Grove, Ill.: InterVarsity Press, 1997), 36–37.

16. Robert J. Wicks, *Handbook of Spirituality for Ministers*, vol. 2 (New York: Paulist Press, 2000), 172–73.

17. See Stephen R. Covey, *The 8th Habit: From Effectiveness to Greatness* (New York: Free Press, 2004), 305–6.

LAST WORDS

1. See Gary W. Gallagher, *Causes Won, Lost, and Forgotten: How Hollywood and Popular Art Shape What We Know about the Civil War* (Chapel Hill: University of North Carolina Press, 2008).

2. W. H. Auden, *Selected Poems*, ed. Edward Mendelson (New York: Vintage Books, 1979), 55.

3. Ulysses S. Grant, *Personal Memoirs of U. S. Grant*, ed. James M. McPherson (New York: Penguin, 1999), 25, 26, 23; originally published in New York by C. L. Webster in two volumes, 1885 and 1886.

4. *The Lincoln-Douglas Debates: The First Complete, Unexpurgated Text*, ed. Harold Holzer (New York: HarperCollins, 1993), 157, 314, 360.

5. William Faulkner, *Go Down, Moses and Other Stories* (New York: Random House, 1942), 278.

6. Walt Whitman, *Memoranda During the War*, 65–67 in original edition, 125–31 in Coviello edition (see chap. 2, n. 2, on the different editions).

7. Robert Penn Warren, *The Legacy of the Civil War: Meditations on the Centennial* (New York: Vintage, 1964), 83–84; originally published in New York by Random House, 1961.

8. Sources for these paragraphs on Sherman are *Memoirs of General William T. Sherman*, ed. Charles Royster (New York: Library of America, 1990), 873–74, 100–101, 104, 171, 180, 364, and *Sherman's Civil War: Selected Correspondence of William T. Sherman, 1860–1865*, ed. Brooks D. Simpson and Jean V. Berlin (Chapel Hill: University of North Carolina Press, 1999), 84, 44.

9. *The Collected Works of Ambrose Bierce*, 12 vols. (New York: Neale Publishing Co., 1909–12), 3:61, 298, 361.

10. Sherman, *Memoirs*, 886.

11. *The Collected Works of Ambrose Bierce*, 1:271.

12. Joshua Lawrence Chamberlain, *The Passing of the Armies: An Account of the Final Campaign of the Army of the Potomac, Based upon Personal Reminiscences of the Fifth Army Corps* (New York: Bantam, 1993), 295; originally published New York: G. P. Putnam's Sons, 1915. For the provenance of Sherman's statement that war is hell, see Lloyd Lewis, *Sherman: Fighting Prophet* (New York: Harcourt, Brace and Co., 1932), 635–37.

13. William M. Wallace, *Soul of the Lion: A Biography of General Joshua L. Chamberlain* (New York: Thomas Nelson and Sons, 1960), 201.

14. *The Collected Works of Ambrose Bierce*, 1:265.

15. The addresses for these sites, consulted November 1, 2013, are www.army.mil and www.goarmy.com.

16. Warren, *Legacy of the Civil War*, 108–9.

17. For Warren's references to Arkansas governor Orval Faubus's 1957 attempt to block integration of a high school in Little Rock and to relations between the United States and the former Soviet Union, see *Legacy of the Civil War*, 57, 101–2.

18. Warren, *Legacy of the Civil War*, 91–92.

Index